QUESTIONS & ANSWERS:
BANKRUPTCY

QUESTIONS & ANSWERS: BANKRUPTCY

Multiple Choice and Short-Answer Questions and Answers

Bruce A. Markell
U.S. Bankruptcy Judge, District of Nevada
Senior Fellow in Bankruptcy and Commercial Law
University of Nevada, Las Vegas
William S. Boyd School of Law

Mary Jo Wiggins
Associate Dean and Professor of Law
University of San Diego School of Law

ISBN: 978–0–8205–5673–4

> **NOTE TO USERS**
>
> To ensure that you are using the latest materials available in this area, please be sure to periodically check the LexisNexis Law School web site for downloadable updates and supplements at www.lexisnexis.com/lawschool.

Editorial Offices
121 Chanlon Rd., New Providence, NJ 07974 (908) 464-6800
201 Mission St., San Francisco, CA 94105-1831 (415) 908-3200
www.lexisnexis.com

MATTHEW◆BENDER

DEDICATIONS

To all my students who taught me how to teach them. Thanks.—B.A.M.

To D.C.W., N.C.W., M.M.W., J.R.N., and E.J.N., Sr., in gratitude for your constant support and love. Thanks.—M.J.W.

ABOUT THE AUTHORS

Bruce A. Markell has been a Bankruptcy judge since 2004, and a member of the Ninth Circuit's Bankruptcy Appellate Panel since 2007. He came to the bench from the academy; since 1999, he had been the Doris S. and Theodore B. Lee Professor of Law at the William S. Boyd School of Law at the University of Nevada, Las Vegas, where he taught Contracts, Commercial Law, Securitization and Bankruptcy. He maintains a position at the Boyd School of Law as their Senior Fellow in Bankruptcy and Commercial Law.

Judge Markell is a 1977 graduate of Pitzer College, and a 1980 graduate of the King Hall School of Law, University of California at Davis, where he was first in his class and editor-in-chief of the law review. Following graduation, he clerked for then-judge Anthony M. Kennedy when Justice Kennedy was a member of the Ninth Circuit Court of Appeals. Before becoming an academic in 1990, he was a partner in the Los Angeles office of Sidley & Austin, specializing in workouts and bankruptcy matters. From 1990 to 1999, he taught at the Indiana University School of Law — Bloomington. During 1999, he was the Bruce W. Nichols Visiting Professor of Law at Harvard Law School. He has also visited at Emory University School of Law and King Hall School of Law at the University of California at Davis. While an academic, he served in an "Of Counsel" capacity to Ancel & Dunlap (Indianapolis, 1996-2000) and Stutman, Treister & Glatt, Professional Corporation (Los Angeles, 2001-2004).

Judge Markell is the author of numerous articles on bankruptcy and commercial Law. He is a member of the editorial board of *Collier on Bankruptcy*, and contributes several chapters to that publication. In early 2005, he published a bankruptcy casebook, *Bankruptcy: 21st Century Debtor-Creditor Law*, with David Epstein, Steve Nickles and Elizabeth Perris; due to the enactment of BAPCPA, a second edition was published in late 2005, and a third edition is scheduled for 2010. In 1999 he was elected a conferee of the National Bankruptcy Conference, in 1997 he was selected as a member of the American Law Institute, and in 2000 he was selected as a member of the International Insolvency Institute and as a fellow of the American College of Bankruptcy.

Mary Jo Wiggins is Professor of Law & Associate Dean for Academic Affairs at the University of San Diego School of Law. She has been a member of the USD law faculty for 20 years, and has been recognized as a Herzog Endowed Scholar and as the Class of 1975 Endowed Professor of Law by the University. Professor Wiggins teaches and writes in the areas of Corporate and Consumer Bankruptcy, Debtor-Creditor Law, and Property. Professor Wiggins is "Of Counsel" with the San Diego law firm of Procopio, Cory, Hargreaves & Savitch and has been named one of "San Diego's Top Attorneys."

Professor Wiggins received her undergraduate degree with highest departmental honors from Smith College in Northampton, Massachusetts. She received her law degree from the University of Michigan Law School where she was Notes Editor of the *Michigan Law Review*. Before becoming an academic, she practiced bankruptcy law and commercial litigation at the law firm of Ice, Miller, Donadio & Ryan in Indianapolis, Indiana.

Professor Wiggins is the author of numerous articles and book chapters on the topics of bankruptcy and debtor-creditor law. She is an elected member of the American Law Institute, and is a contributing author to *Collier on Bankruptcy*. In 1988, she was selected to serve on the United States Judicial Conference Advisory Committee on the Federal Rules of Bankruptcy Procedure. She was appointed to the Advisory Committee by then United States Supreme Court Justice William H. Rehnquist and she served two consecutive terms on the Advisory Committee. Professor Wiggins has also served as: Chair of the American Association of Law Schools' Section on Debtor's and Creditor's Rights; Reporter for the Ninth Circuit Judicial Council's Committee for Review of Local Bankruptcy Rules of Procedure; Chair of the California State Bar Insolvency Law Committee's Bankruptcy Rules Review Project; Member of the Advisory Board of the American Bankruptcy Institute Law Review; Consultant for two recent RAND Corporation Research Studies on the consumer bankruptcy system; Faculty Advisor and Coach of the University of San Diego School of Law's Duberstein Moot Court Bankruptcy Team.

PREFACE

The primary source for Bankruptcy is Title 11 of the United States Code, often just referred to as the Bankruptcy Code. This study guide uses multiple-choice and short-answer questions to test your knowledge of the Bankruptcy Code and its occasional intersection with other sources of law (such as Article 9 of the Uniform Commercial Code and various parts of state law including property law and family law). These materials are based upon the Bankruptcy Code as in effect on May 1, 2010, which can be found in many softbound statutory supplements used in most law schools.

Throughout the book, we try to keep our explanations as concise as possible. In particular, we do not provide lengthy recitations of bankruptcy doctrine in each answer since you can get that from your bankruptcy course, or from other sources. We provide only as much doctrine as is necessary to assist you in understanding our answers. Moreover, in the interest of keeping the book readable and "user-friendly," we do not use footnotes or laborious citations. Finally, the book emphasizes frequently used Code sections over those you will be less likely to encounter in the "real world."

Most of the short-answer questions should be answered in no more than ten sentences and you should not spend more than fifteen minutes a question. Our answers are sometimes longer than that, but only when we think it will help enhance your understanding. We believe that you'll better understand the materials if you prepare your own answer before peeking in the back to see what we think.

We both enjoy teaching bankruptcy in its many forms, and wish you the best in using our study guide to supplement your understanding of this interesting, relevant and challenging subject.

Bruce A. Markell
United States Bankruptcy Judge
Senior Fellow in Bankruptcy and Commercial Law,
William S. Boyd School of Law,
University of Nevada, Las Vegas
Las Vegas, Nevada

Mary Jo Wiggins
Professor of Law & Associate Dean for Academic Affairs,
The University of San Diego School of Law
San Diego, California
May 2010

TABLE OF CONTENTS

TABLE OF CONTENTS

QUESTIONS

TOPIC 1
BANKRUPTCY PRELIMINARIES

Subtopic A. Structure of the Code

Alf is a debtor and debtor in possession under chapter 11 of the Bankruptcy Code. He wants to dismiss his case. He notes that Section 1307(b) allows a debtor to dismiss his or her case at any time, and further states that any waiver of that right is unenforceable.

1. May Alf use Section 1307(b) to dismiss his case?

   (A) Yes, because Alf is an individual and Section 1307(b) applies to individuals;

   (B) No, because Alf is a chapter 11 debtor, not a chapter 13 debtor;

   (C) Yes, because the policy expressed in Section 1307(b) ought to apply to all individual debtors;

   (D) No, because he hasn't executed a waiver that Section 1307(b) can override.

Alf again from the last problem. Now he wants to bring an avoiding powers action — he wishes to recover a preference — under Section 547.

2. May he?

   (A) No, because Alf is a debtor under chapter 11, and the avoiding powers, including preferences, are in chapter 5;

   (B) Yes, but only if he gets permission from the court;

   (C) No, only a trustee may bring such an action;

   (D) Yes.

Garry is a chapter 13 debtor. Sam is a creditor, and knows of several fraudulent transfers that Garry made just before Garry filed his chapter 13 case. Sam reads Section 727(a)(2) to provide for the denial of the discharge if a debtor commits fraudulent transfers during the year before filing.

3. May Sam file and prosecute a denial of discharge action against Garry?

ANSWER:

Subtopic B. Players in a Bankruptcy Case and Their Roles

Debbie is a chapter 7 debtor. She made a payment before her filing that is clearly recoverable as a preference.

4.   As between the following, who may be the plaintiff in the action to recover the preference?

(A) Debbie;

(B) The Office of the United States Trustee;

(C) Debbie's chapter 7 trustee;

(D) Any of Debbie's legitimate creditors.

Frederated, Inc. is a large retail chain that has filed for chapter 11 bankruptcy. Its prepetition management resigned just after the filing, and is under indictment for embezzlement and fraud against Frederated. The current acting Chief Executive Officer was the prepetition Chief Financial Officer, and is untainted by the fraud.

You represent a large creditor who wants change, or at least knowledge about what went on prepetition.

5.   Outline the possible changes, and what each type of change would yield in terms of information.
ANSWER:

Subtopic C. Bankruptcy Procedure, Notice and Hearings

Reggie, Inc., is a debtor in possession under chapter 11 of the Code. It has brought a motion to avoid the lien of Hardcore Bank, claiming (correctly) that Hardcore failed to file a financing statement to perfect its security interest in Reggie's inventory, and thus Hardcore's lien is avoidable under Section 544(a) of the Code. As a matter of substantive law, Reggie is correct. Nevertheless, Hardcore brings a motion to dismiss the motion and prevails.

6.   The most likely reason that Hardcore won is because:

(A) Reggie has no standing to bring avoidance actions under Section 544; the terms of that Section apply only to "trustees";

(B) The creditors' committee is an indispensible party to any avoidance powers action;

(C) Avoidance of a lien under Section 544 can only be accomplished by an adversary proceeding, not a motion;

(D) Reggie had not yet filed or confirmed its proposed plan of reorganization under chapter 11.

Al is the chapter 7 trustee of Cannery, Inc. He is in the process of liquidating one of Cannery's factories, and learns that the personal property located at the plant is worth less than the lien on it in favor of the secured creditor, Botbank. Al therefore sends out a notice to all creditors that he intends to abandon and surrender all the property at the plant to Botbank unless someone objects within 21 days of the notice. No hearing date is specified in the notice, although the process by which a hearing date may be obtained is specified.

Section 554(a) of the Bankruptcy Code, which governs abandonment, requires "a notice and a hearing" before abandonment can occur.

7.   If challenged after the fact by a creditor with standing to object, the abandonment will:

   (A)   Be set aside, since the required hearing was not held;

   (B)   Be allowed to stand only if the abandonment was caused by exigent circumstances and was time sensitive;

   (C)   Be set aside, because the trustee was required to obtain a hearing date even if no hearing was held due to the lack of an objection;

   (D)   Be allowed to stand.

Subtopic A. Eligibility for Bankruptcy under Section 109: Credit Counseling

Hal farms a 40-acre tract in Jefferson County, located in northern New York. He resides, however, in Kingston, Ontario in Canada. He owes his bank $100,000, and thirty other creditors an aggregate amount of $150,000. No creditor holds security. Hal has stopped paying all his debts.

8.   If the bank and ten other creditors join together and file an involuntary proceeding against Hal, which is the most likely outcome?

    (A)   The court will grant the petition;

    (B)   The court will deny the petition because Hal is a Canadian citizen;

    (C)   The court will deny the petition because Hal is a farmer;

    (D)   The court will deny the petition unless the creditors can first show that their nonbankruptcy remedies are inadequate.

Redfern is behind on her house payments. She has gotten a lot of official-looking mail from her bank, but she doesn't understand most of it. Finally, she gets and accepts a letter by certified mail that says she will lose her house on February 2, 2006. She takes this letter and all the other correspondence to you, and tells you that you are the only person to whom she has talked about this problem. After examining it, you discover that Redfern has missed her last three house payments and that her bank will indeed foreclose on February 2 at 9:00 a.m. It is now February 1, 2006 at 3:00 p.m.

9.   Which of the following best describes the options available to Redfern?

    (A)   She may not file bankruptcy because she has not had credit counseling within the last 180-day period;

    (B)   She may file bankruptcy because, after checking, there are no approved credit counselors who will see her on such short notice, and you can document this situation;

    (C)   She may not file bankruptcy because even though you can find an approved credit counselor that will see her, she does not have handy the documentation necessary for that counselor to perform a detailed and comprehensive credit and budget analysis for her;

    (D)   She may file bankruptcy without credit counseling, because a court will find that there are exigent circumstances that excuse her from mandatory counseling.

Subtopic B. Commencing a Voluntary Case under Section 301

James is a single man, age 27. He has not done much with his life. One day, bothered by one particular collection agent, he files a bankruptcy case under chapter 11. He dutifully files schedules and statements that indicate he is solvent; specifically, they show assets of about $50,000 and consumer debts of about $45,000. One of his principal creditors, Charge-a-Lot Credit Card. Co., moves to dismiss his case, or in the alternate for the court to abstain.

10.   The most likely result of the motion is:

(A)   The court will dismiss the case because chapter 11 is not to be used for the reorganization of consumer debts;

(B)   The court will dismiss the case because James is solvent;

(C)   The court will abstain from the case if it is convinced that Charge-a-Lot is the only creditor whom James is not paying, and that state law remedies are adequate to resolve the dispute;

(D)   The court will not dismiss the case or abstain.

Subtopic C. Commencing an Involuntary Case under Section 303

Edward has fifteen creditors, but only four to whom he owes $5,000 or more. They are: Alice, to whom he owes $5,000 for a loan she made to him last year; Ben, to whom he owes $6,000 for a car Edward purchased from Ben two years ago; Cathy, for whom Edward has guaranteed $25,000 because Edward's son has borrowed from Cathy; and Debbie, with whom Edward is embroiled in a contentious lawsuit over whether Edward negligently drove his car into Debbie's house, causing Debbie an alleged $50,000 in damages. Edward stopped paying all bills a month ago.

11.   If all of these creditors join in an involuntary petition against Edward, the most likely result will be:

(A)   An order for relief will be entered against Edward because he stopped paying his bills;

(B)   An order for relief will be entered against Edward because he owes his creditors more than $14,425;

(C)   An order for relief will not be entered against Edward unless Alice and Ben accelerate the maturity dates of their loans and make demand on Edward for the accelerated sum;

(D)   An order for relief will not be entered against Edward because neither Cathy nor Debbie qualify as petitioning creditors.

Same facts as the previous question, but more time has passed and Debbie has obtained a $50,000 judgment against Edward. Edward did not move to stay enforcement of the judgment, and has not appealed from it.

12.   If all of these creditors again join in an involuntary petition against Edward, the most likely result will be:

(A)   An order for relief will be entered against Edward because he stopped paying his bills;

(B) An order for relief will be entered against Edward because he owes his creditors more than $14,425;

(C) An order for relief will not be entered against Edward unless Alice and Ben accelerate the maturity dates of their loans and make demand on Edward for the accelerated sum;

(D) An order for relief will not be entered against Edward because neither Cathy nor Debbie qualify as petitioning creditors.

Same facts as above, except now assume that Debbie's claim, instead of being represented by a judgment, is now a $50,000 loan secured by all of Edward's assets.

13. If all of these creditors again join in an involuntary petition against Edward, the most likely result will be:

(A) An order for relief will be entered against Edward because he stopped paying his bills;

(B) An order for relief will be entered against Edward because he owes his creditors more than $14,425;

(C) An order for relief will not be entered against Edward unless Debbie agrees to waive a portion of her secured claim;

(D) An order for relief will not be entered against Edward because Cathy's claim does not qualify her as a petitioning creditor, and without her there is not $14,425 in unsecured claims.

Same facts as before, except that Debbie now refuses to join the involuntary petition. It is filed nonetheless by Alice, Ben, and Cathy. One day before the trial on the involuntary petition, Frank joins the petition. Frank claims Edward owes him $4,000, but Edward disputes this in good faith. At the opening of the trial on the involuntary petition, Edward's attorney moves to dismiss the case for lack of the necessary number of creditors holding the requisite claims.

14. The most likely outcome of this motion will be:

(A) The court will grant the motion and dismiss the petition because creditors may not join an involuntary petition just before trial;

(B) The court will grant the motion and dismiss the petition because Frank's claim is subject to a bona fide dispute;

(C) The court will deny the motion only after it determines the validity of Frank's claim;

(D) The court will deny the motion.

Subtopic D. Filings Required When Case Is Commenced, or Shortly Thereafter

Harriette was being harassed by one creditor. To stop his constant calls, she files a two-page chapter 7 bankruptcy petition that has a list of her creditors attached. She files nothing else in the case.

15. On the 46th day after the petition is filed, may the creditor resume collection against Harriette? Why or why not?

ANSWER:

Same facts as before, except now Harriette files all documents required by Section 521(a). Approximately ten days before the attendance at the required meeting of creditors under Section 341(a) of the Bankruptcy Code, however, she receives a letter from her trustee demanding the last five years of tax returns. She is shocked by this invasion of privacy and refuses to comply.

16.　　The trustee then moves to dismiss Harriette's case. Which of the following best describes the outcome of the motion?

(A)　The trustee will win, because a debtor must turn over to the trustee all information the trustee requests;

(B)　Harriette will win, because tax information is always private;

(C)　The trustee will win, because individual debtors are required to deliver a copy of their most recent tax return (or a transcript thereof) to the trustee;

(D)　Harriette will win because the trustee demanded more than she is entitled to receive under the Bankruptcy Code.

Janice files her chapter 7 case and all her required schedules. She doesn't do anything else and sits at home waiting for the court to mail her a discharge. Instead, she gets a notice that her case will be dismissed for lack of cooperation for not attending a meeting.

17.　　Janice asks you what meeting she missed. Give an answer and tell her what to expect.

ANSWER:

Subtopic E. Abstention under Section 305

Megacorp manufactures rocking chairs. It fell upon hard times, due to decreased demand. Its president, Fred, calls a meeting of all creditors, and most present agree to a moratorium on Megacorp's payment of its debt obligations; that is, they agreed that Megacorp could defer payments on its debt obligations. The moratorium was scheduled to last 120 days, and was conditioned upon Megacorp giving all creditors a security interest in all its assets to secure the amounts its creditors are deferring. (This is often called a "workout" or an "out-of-court workout.")

One group of creditors, holding collectively $16,000 in debt (all of which is uncontested and presently payable), doesn't like the deal and 89 days after it closes, files an involuntary petition against Megacorp. The $16,000 represents less than 1% of Megacorp's outstanding debt; all of Megacorp's other creditors make their wishes known that they are quite happy with the out-of-court moratorium.

18.　　If properly litigated, which of the following represents the most likely result at the hearing on the creditors' involuntary petition?

(A)　An order for relief will not be entered against Megacorp;

(B) An order for relief will be entered against Megacorp, but all activity in the case will be stayed until further order of the court;

(C) An order for relief will be entered against Megacorp, but only as to the three petitioning creditors (the creditors who agreed to the workout will not be affected by the case);

(D) An order for relief will be entered against Megacorp, and the case will thereafter proceed as if the workout had never occurred.

Subtopic A. Sources and Types of Property of the Estate

Jeb wrote and owns a copyright to the song "Be Still My Beating Heart," a classic country and western tune. He has licensed the use of the song in the United States to BeatBack Records, Inc., until 2015; BeatBack agreed to pay Jeb 20% of the gross royalties it receives from its marketing and sales efforts. Raylene believes that Jeb stole the song from her; she has filed suit in United States District Court seeking to invalidate the copyright and for an accounting of profits. Jeb has counterclaimed for trade libel, and seeks damages arising from Raylene's false (as Jeb believes) statements about his authorship of the song.

The litigation with Raylene causes Jeb to file for protection under chapter 7.

19. With respect to the assets listed above, Jeb's bankruptcy estate will include:

  (A) The copyright only;

  (B) The copyright and the royalty agreement with BeatBack only;

  (C) The copyright and 20% of the royalty agreement;

  (D) The copyright, the royalty agreement, and Jeb's contingent rights against Raylene.

Fran runs Flowers & More, a boutique that sells flowers and flower vases. She is a sole proprietor. The store has fallen on hard times, and Fran files for bankruptcy under chapter 7. At the time of filing, Fran listed $25,000 in property on her schedules.

It is now four months after filing. In that four-month period, the trustee authorized Fran to keep Flowers & More open, and Fran has managed to make a profit of $5,000 after Fran took a salary of $2,000 (a reasonable salary under the circumstances). The trustee has also identified and collected a $2,000 prepetition payment as a preference, and still holds the other $25,000 in property.

20. Which of the following are property of Fran's bankruptcy estate?

  (A) The $5,000 profit, the $2,000 preference recovery, and the $25,000 in other property;

  (B) The $5,000 profit, the $2,000 salary paid to Fran, the $2,000 preference recovery, and the $25,000 in other property;

  (C) Only the $5,000 profit and the $25,000 in other property;

  (D) Only the $25,000 in other property.

Same facts as the last question, but now Fran is a debtor under chapter 11, and has possession of all of the property as a debtor in possession under that chapter.

21. Which of the following are property of Fran's bankruptcy estate?

   (A) The $5,000 profit, the $2,000 preference recovery, and the $25,000 in other property;

   (B) The $5,000 profit, the $2,000 salary paid to Fran, the $2,000 preference recovery, and the $25,000 in other property;

   (C) Only the $5,000 profit and the $25,000 in other property;

   (D) Only the $25,000 in other property.

Subtopic B. Exclusions from Property of the Estate

Sally files a chapter 7 bankruptcy case. She does not list in her schedules of assets her interest in her 401(k) plan, which is a retirement plan subject to ERISA. She also does not list her house (that she lives in and manages, and which is subject to a joint mortgage with her husband), because it is held as community property with her husband. One month after she files, she receives a $10,000 inheritance from a long-lost aunt's estate.

22. Which of the following will Sally have to turn over to her chapter 7 trustee because they are property of her bankruptcy estate?

   (A) The 401(k) plan, the house and the inheritance;

   (B) Only the house and the inheritance;

   (C) Only the house;

   (D) None of these assets.

Subtopic A. Scope of the Automatic Stay under Section 362(a)

Jake is being sued by Francis for fraud in the sale of a car by Jake to Francis. The case is in state court. Jury selection is underway when a lawyer enters the courtroom and hands to Francis' attorney a copy of the bankruptcy petition she had filed for Jake that morning. "Too late, bub," says Francis's attorney, who continues with jury selection.

23. Which of the following best describes Jake's position?

   (A) Francis has violated the automatic stay;

   (B) Francis has not violated the automatic stay because jury selection had started without notice of Jake's filing;

   (C) Francis has not violated the automatic stay because Jake's bankruptcy lawyer did not show the copy of the petition to the state court judge;

   (D) Francis has not violated the automatic stay since there is no order from the bankruptcy court that binds Francis in any way.

Bart has a mortgage on Dee's real property. Dee is in default, and Bart has scheduled a non-judicial foreclosure sale (permitted by local state law) for April 30. Bart has scheduled the foreclosure for 10:00 a.m. At the appointed date and time, Bart conducts the foreclosure. The only people appearing are Bart, his lawyer and Chris, a purchaser who buys the property at the sale for an amount equal to Bart's debt (which is about 40% of the fair market value of the property).

The next day, May 1, Dee faxes to Bart a copy of her bankruptcy petition, which shows that Dee filed on April 30 at 9:59 a.m. This is first that Bart has ever heard of Dee's filing.

24. If properly litigated before a fair-minded judge, which of the following best describes the most likely outcome?

   (A) Chris will keep the property, and Bart will have to pay Dee's trustee the amount he received at the sale;

   (B) Chris will have to give up the property since the sale was a fraudulent transfer;

   (C) Chris will have to give up the property to Dee's trustee;

   (D) Chris will have to give up the property, but only if Dee or Dee's trustee tenders to Chris an amount equal to what Chris paid at the foreclosure sale.

Driving his car back from filing his chapter 7 bankruptcy petition, Leonard negligently runs over Macie, a pedestrian, causing Macie thousands of dollars of damages. Macie sues Leonard in state court, and because of the bankruptcy Leonard does not defend, and Macie obtains a default judgment. She thereafter obtains an order garnishing Leonard's wages to the fullest extent permissible by local law.

25. Leonard files a motion in his bankruptcy case seeking to recover damages for violation of the automatic stay. If properly litigated before a fair-minded judge, which of the following is the most likely result?

   (A) Leonard will win;

   (B) Leonard will win, but only if he can show that Macie knew of his bankruptcy before obtaining the garnishment;

   (C) Macie will win;

   (D) Macie will win, but only if she can show that she did not willfully violate the automatic stay.

Same facts as the last question, except that Leonard filed a chapter 13 case, not a chapter 7 case, and his confirmed chapter 13 plan does not address the status of his postpetition wages.

26. Under these revised facts, Leonard files a motion in his bankruptcy case seeking to recover damages for violation of the automatic stay. If properly litigated before a fair-minded judge, which of the following is the most likely result?

   (A) Leonard will win;

   (B) Leonard will win, but only if he can show that Macie knew of his bankruptcy before obtaining the garnishment;

   (C) Macie will win;

   (D) Macie will win, but only if she can show that she did not willfully violate the automatic stay.

Harrison bought a lawnmower from JP Lawnmower Co. for $500. JP Lawnmower agreed to allow Harrison to pay off the debt at $100 per month. Harrison makes the first month's payment, and then files a bankruptcy case under chapter 7.

You represent JP Lawnmower. The collection manager writes you for advice — it seems that Harrison is entitled to $75 rebate. The collection manager asks if she can just net out the rebate against the $400 that Harrison owes.

27. What is your answer to the collection manager's question?

ANSWER:

Subtopic B. Exemptions from the Automatic Stay under Section 362(a)

PuffCo is an old-line manufacturer of ball-bearings. Its manufacturing process creates many toxic by-products. Indeed, it is currently under an administrative order from the state environmental agency to clean up one of its "toxic pits" located at the rear of its current manufacturing facility. This cleanup will cost in excess of $1,000,000, and PuffCo does not believe it can afford that cost and still stay in business. PuffCo files for bankruptcy under chapter 11.

28. If, in accordance with its normal operating procedures, the state environmental agency seeks to exercise its power to shut down PuffCo for failure to comply with its cleanup order, the most likely result is:

  (A) The state environmental agency will be found to have violated the automatic stay because it is enforcing an administrative order, as opposed to enforcing the criminal laws of the state;

  (B) The state environmental agency will be found to have violated the automatic stay because it is only a state agency, and bankruptcy law is federal law and thus supreme;

  (C) The state environmental agency will be found to have violated the automatic stay because shutting down PuffCo first requires the permission of the bankruptcy court as the order is more than a simple monetary judgment;

  (D) The state environmental agency will not be found to have violated the automatic stay.

Dr. John is in the middle of a messy divorce with his soon to be ex-wife, Cathy. After a depressing session with his accountant, Dr. John decides the only way that he can survive economically is to file for chapter 11 bankruptcy. He files the next day.

29. One week after he files, he receives papers from Cathy's attorney. They purport to require him to do the following (all of which were requested post-filing and all of which would otherwise be appropriate under relevant state and federal law). Which of these are violations of the automatic stay?

  (A) An order, sought post-filing, to increase temporary support payments by $1,000 per month;

  (B) An order requiring Dr. John to submit to a paternity test to establish his liability for the support of Denise, an infant that Dr. John steadfastly has maintained is not his child;

  (C) An order requiring Dr. John to surrender his medical license and to cease the practice of medicine until he becomes current on his delinquent support payments;

  (D) None of these.

Harry is a tenant of Joan. Harry is not a very good tenant; he is six months behind in his rent, and constantly smokes pot in the house he rents from Joan (it is located on the rear of the property where Joan has her principal residence). Fed up, Joan commences eviction procedures in state court and gets an order of eviction, which entitled Joan to exclusive possession of the rented property. She takes the order to Harry, and tries to show it to him in a haze of marijuana smoke. Harry looks at the order and says "I just need another week to get my stuff together." Joan says no, and leaves to get a constable to physically evict Harry, which is the appropriate procedure under state law.

Before Joan can return with the constable, Harry has run out in a paranoid fit and filed a chapter 7 petition, a copy of which he has taped upon the front door of the rented house. Harry has checked the box on page 2 of the petition indicating that Joan has obtained a judgment of possession for the rented house. He has not checked the box indicating that he can cure under state law, nor did he provide the bankruptcy clerk with any rent money. He did not file any certifications regarding his ability or intent to pay any rent, past or present.

30. Joan calls you on her mobile phone with constable at her side from the front of the rented house. Which of the following is the best advice under the circumstances if Joan tells you that she really needs to immediately evict Harry?

(A) Joan should instruct the constable to enter the dwelling and remove all of Harry's possessions in accordance with state law procedures;

(B) Joan should halt the eviction and attempt to resume it in 15 days;

(C) Joan should halt the eviction and attempt to resume it in 30 days;

(D) Joan should tell the constable that the eviction has been stayed indefinitely by the bankruptcy court, and that she will have to start a new state court action.

Subtopic C. Duration of Automatic Stay under Section 362(c); Repeat Filers

Henry filed bankruptcy in 2001, and received a chapter 7 discharge in 2002. He filed a chapter 13 bankruptcy in March of 2007 but quickly dismissed it in April of 2007, on his own motion when he realized it was not necessary. It is now March of 2008. Henry files another chapter 7 bankruptcy to stop the foreclosure of his house by CityWide Bank.

31. You get a call from CityWide, telling you that they have just learned of Henry's chapter 7 filing. They want to know if they have to postpone their foreclosure. Which of the following represents the best advice under the circumstances if CityWide is willing to go to the limits (but not beyond the limits) of the law?

(A) CityWide can continue with the foreclosure because Henry will not be able to obtain a chapter 7 discharge;

(B) CityWide should continue with its foreclosure because Henry has two prior bankruptcy filings;

(C) CityWide should postpone the foreclosure indefinitely;

(D) CityWide should postpone its foreclosure for 30 days, and then check the bankruptcy court's docket to see if Henry has moved to extend the stay.

Subtopic D. Adequate Protection and Relief from Automatic Stay under Section 362(d)

Alan Industries filed for chapter 11 relief. AI is in the business of cement manufacturing. Its main and most profitable plant has a fair market value of $10,000,000 without consideration of any liens or encumbrances. The value of the property is stable. AI has granted a first lien on the property to secure a loan of $5,000,000 from First Bank, and a second lien on the property to secure a loan of $7,000,000 from Second Bank.

32. If First Bank moves for relief from stay, which of the following is the best summary of the result of its motion, assuming that the issue is adequately briefed before a fair-minded judge?

(A) First Bank will not receive relief from stay because its interest in the property is adequately protected;

(B) First Bank will receive relief from stay since there is no equity in the property for AI;

(C) First Bank will receive relief from stay but only if AI was in default under the loan when AI filed its chapter 11 case;

(D) First Bank will receive relief from stay unless AI provides assurances that First Bank's missed postpetition payments will receive administrative expense priority.

33. If Second Bank moves for relief from stay, which of the following is the best summary of the result of its motion, assuming that the issue is adequately briefed before a fair-minded judge?

(A) Second Bank will not receive relief from stay because its interest in the property is adequately protected;

(B) Second Bank will receive relief from stay since there is no equity in the property for AI;

(C) Second Bank will receive relief from stay because it cannot provide adequate protection of Second Bank's interest in the property;

(D) Second Bank will receive relief from stay unless AI provides assurances that Second Bank's missed postpetition payments will receive administrative expense priority.

34. Same facts as the prior problem, except now assume that AI filed a chapter 7 case. If Second Bank moves for relief from stay under these revised facts, which of the following is the best summary of the result of its motion, assuming that the issue is adequately briefed before a fair-minded judge?

(A) Second Bank will not receive relief from stay because its interest in the property is adequately protected;

(B) Second Bank will receive relief from stay since there is no equity in the property for AI;

(C) Second Bank will receive relief from stay because it cannot provide adequate protection of Second Bank's interest in the property;

(D) Second Bank will receive relief from stay unless AI provides assurances that Second Bank's missed postpetition payments will receive administrative expense priority.

35. Does the result change in the prior problem if the movant is First Bank instead of Second Bank? Why or why not?

ANSWER:

Subtopic A. Claims under Section 101(5)

Acme Corporation has filed for chapter 7 bankruptcy. Prior to the filing, Acme polluted a river located in a state park and state officials were aware of the situation. After the filing, the state obtained a court judgment against Acme in connection with the pollution. The state now seeks your advice on whether or not it has a claim in the bankruptcy under Section 101(5) of the Code.

36.   What do you need to know about the court judgment in order to properly advise the state?

    (A)   Whether the judgment arose from a violation of state or federal law;

    (B)   Whether the judgment was rendered by a judge or a jury;

    (C)   Whether the judgment gave the state a monetary or a non-monetary right;

    (D)   Whether Acme's pollution was the result of negligent or reckless conduct.

Assume all of the same facts in the last problem. Now further assume that a bankruptcy court rules that the state has a claim in the bankruptcy.

37.   Which of the following statements is true?

    (A)   The state's judgment is dischargeable in the bankruptcy and will become part of the liquidation process in chapter 7;

    (B)   The state's judgment is not dischargeable in the bankruptcy and will not become part of the liquidation process in chapter 7;

    (C)   The state's judgment will not become part of the liquidation process because only consensual claims are included in that process;

    (D)   The state's judgment is not dischargeable in the bankruptcy because claims based on court judgments are not subject to discharge.

Subtopic B. Unmatured, Contingent and Unliquidated Claims

Acme Corporation issued bonds to its investors. The bonds had a ten-year term. One year after the issue date, Acme filed for chapter 11 bankruptcy.

38.   On the date of the bankruptcy filing, do the bondholders have a claim under Section 101(5) of the Code?

ANSWER:

Harry Jones bought a condominium. The purchase contract required the purchaser to pay monthly maintenance assessments for upkeep and repairs to common areas. Three years after the purchase, Jones filed for chapter 7 bankruptcy. The condominium board wants to know if it has a claim under Section 101(5) of the Code for future maintenance fees.

39.   What is the correct answer?

(A)   No, because Jones filed a chapter 7 bankruptcy and Section 101(5) does not apply to chapter 7;

(B)   No, because the board is seeking future fees, not past ones;

(C)   The answer depends on whether the board has a final judgment against Jones;

(D)   Yes.

Tacos Forever is the best taco restaurant in town. Sarah Smith visited the restaurant and slipped on a wet spot in the restaurant lobby. Sarah sued the restaurant and three days later, Tacos Forever filed for chapter 11 bankruptcy.

40.   Does Sarah have a claim under Section 101(5) of the Code?

(A)   Yes, because she actually filed her lawsuit three days before the restaurant filed for chapter 11;

(B)   Yes, because unliquidated claims are covered under Section 101(5);

(C)   No, because the bankruptcy court cannot, on the date of the filing, determine exactly how much she might win in her lawsuit;

(D)   No, because tort actions are not "claims" under Section 101(5).

Subtopic C. Priority Claims under Section 507

Sally Mae owns a smoothie and sandwich shop near the local high school. The shop was very successful until one of her employees was hospitalized with a serious food-borne illness. Sally disclosed the illness to the public, and most of the shop's customers, even the most loyal ones, stopped eating there. One of the students at the local high school wrote about the entire incident on a blog that was popular with Sally's younger customers. Sally was forced to close her store and file for chapter 7 bankruptcy. A trustee was appointed.

The trustee sold the estate property and the proceeds of the sale will soon be paid to creditors. Four claims were timely filed and allowed in the case: (1) The store manager's portion of social security taxes which the debtor was required to withhold; (2) Salary due to the store manager for three weeks prior to the filing of the petition; (3) Salary due to the store manager for two weeks after the filing of the petition; (4) Fees due to Sally's attorney whom she consulted in order to determine whether she might be able to sue the student blogger for defamation.

41.   Which of these claims will be paid first?

(A)   The salary due to the store manager for two weeks after the filing of the petition;

    (B)   The store manager's portion of social security taxes which the debtor was required to withhold;

    (C)   The salary due to the store manager for three weeks prior to the filing of the petition;

    (D)   The fees due to the attorney.

Jane and Tom Smith got divorced. They had two kids, ages 11 and 13. Shortly after the divorce, Tom filed for chapter 7 bankruptcy. Pursuant to the divorce settlement agreement, Tom was obligated to pay alimony and child support. The chapter 7 bankruptcy trustee sold the couple's home and other property. In order to get the home sold, the trustee incurred fees to a real estate appraiser and a broker. The proceeds from the sale of the home will go toward paying Jane's alimony and the child support obligations.

42.   When it comes time to pay all of the creditor's claims in Tom's bankruptcy, will the alimony and child support claims have a higher priority than the claim of the trustee for the fees incurred in connection with the sale of the home?

ANSWER:

Joe Schmoe is an individual who ended up filing for chapter 7 bankruptcy. Joe filed his petition on February 1, 2008. At the time of the filing, the I.R.S. had income tax claims against Joe for the following taxable years: 2003, 2004, 2005, 2006, 2007, and 2008.

43.   Assuming that Joe is a calendar year taxpayer, which of these claims will be entitled to priority payment under the Code?

ANSWER:

Subtopic D. Secured Claims (Including Setoff) under Sections 506 and 552

Myra bought a townhouse in a nice neighborhood for $300,000. Myra designed jewelry and handbags which she supplied to local merchants. She worked on her designs in a rented loft near her townhouse. In order to finance the rental and business expenses, Myra took out several unsecured lines of credit and came close to using most of the credit available to her under the credit lines.

Unfortunately, Myra became very ill last year and the medical bills and business loans became too much for her to handle. She ended up filing for chapter 7 bankruptcy. At the time of the filing, the townhouse market hit a severe market slump and her townhouse was valued at only $175,000. The First Bank had a mortgage on the townhouse of $200,000.

44.   Under Section 506(a)(1) of the Code, what will happen to First Bank's mortgage claim?

    (A)   The mortgage claim will be secured to the extent of $200,000 because that is the amount of the total debt;

    (B)   The mortgage claim will be split into a secured claim for $175,000 and an unsecured claim for $25,000;

    (C)   The mortgage claim will be completely unsecured due to the depreciation in the value of the townhouse;

    (D)   The mortgage claim will be secured to the extent of $300,000 because that was the original purchase price.

Assume all of the same facts in the last problem. Now further assume that before the filing, Myra purchased a small van that she used solely for the purpose of transporting her products to various retailers. She owes $10,000 on the van, but the value of the van is uncertain. The company that financed her purchase of the van has a security interest in the vehicle and is pressing its claim in Myra's bankruptcy. They want to know how the bankruptcy court will proceed with respect to the valuation of the van.

    45.   What will you tell them?

       (A)   Since Myra is an individual in a case under chapter 7 and since the van is a consumer good, the valuation standard the bankruptcy court will use is the price a retail merchant would charge for a van like the one Myra has;

       (B)   Since Myra is an individual in a case under chapter 7 and since she is using the van solely for her business, the valuation standard the bankruptcy court will use is the replacement value of the property at the date of filing without any deduction for the costs of sale or marketing;

       (C)   Since this is a chapter 7 liquidation case, the bankruptcy court will use liquidation value as the valuation standard;

       (D)   The bankruptcy court would value the van in light of the purpose of the valuation and the proposed use of the van.

GoGo Trucking, Inc. is a trucking company. The company transports commercial goods all over the state. Tiptop, Inc. is a uniform supplier that makes and sells employee uniforms to various businesses, including GoGo. GoGo transports uniforms for Tiptop on an unsecured basis and Tiptop fails to pay the trucking costs of $20,000. TipTop sells employee uniforms to GoGo also on an unsecured basis and GoGo fails to pay for them. GoGo owes $10,000 for the uniforms. Tiptop files for chapter 11 bankruptcy.

    46.   Can GoGo successfully demand that it be treated as the holder of a secured claim in TipTop's bankruptcy case?

ANSWER:

Assume the same facts as in the last problem. Assume further that the CEO of GoGo was also a prepetition creditor of TipTop to the tune of $10,000 on a completely separate unsecured transaction and that he is also trying to assert a setoff right against TipTop. Assume further that the CEO of GoGo does not owe a debt or obligation of any kind to Tiptop.

    47.   Can GoGo's CEO successfully demand that he be treated as the holder of a secured claim in Tiptop's bankruptcy case?

ANSWER:

Dealer, Inc. sells new cars. In order to obtain financing for expansion of the dealership, Dealer gave First Bank a security interest in its inventory, including all after-acquired inventory. First Bank took all steps necessary to create and perfect its security interest in inventory. Dealer sold 200 cars and put the proceeds from the sale into a bank account at First Bank. The Dealer filed for chapter 7 bankruptcy. The Dealer acquired more cars using funds from a separate account at another bank.

48. Will First Bank's security interest continue in the cars acquired after the Dealer filed chapter 7?

   (A) No, because after-acquired property clauses are per se unenforceable;

   (B) Yes, because First Bank took all steps necessary to create and perfect its security interest in the inventory;

   (C) Yes, because the security interest specifically covers after-acquired inventory;

   (D) No, because the Code invalidates First Bank's security interest in the after-acquired inventory.

Assume all of the same facts as in the last problem. Assume that after the chapter 7 filing, the Dealer sold some of its prepetition inventory and immediately deposited the cash generated from those sales into a bank account at Second Bank.

49. Will First Bank's security interest continue in the cash generated from those sales?

   (A) Yes, because the Dealer immediately deposited the cash in a bank account;

   (B) It would depend on whether First Bank specifically mentioned that it intended to maintain its security interest in the cash;

   (C) No, because the Dealer deposited the cash in a bank account at another bank instead of at First Bank;

   (D) Yes, because the Code allows for First Bank's security interest to continue in the cash generated from the sale.

Subtopic E. Allowance and Disallowance of Claims under Section 502

Widgets, Inc. files for chapter 7 bankruptcy. Acme, Inc. is a creditor of Widgets. Acme properly files a proof of claim under Section 501 of the Code in the amount of $25,000 for an unpaid shipment. No party in interest objects to the claim.

50. Will the claim be valid and enforceable in Widget's bankruptcy?

   (A) No, because Acme has not filed a separate motion with the bankruptcy court asking the court to adjudicate both the validity and the amount of the claim;

   (B) No, because the proof of claim filed in accordance with Section 501 is not prima facie evidence of the validity and amount of the claim;

(C) Yes, because a claim, proof of which is filed under Section 501 of the Code, is deemed allowed unless a party in interest objects;

(D) Yes, because Acme is a trade creditor.

ThinkTank is a chemicals manufacturing company in chapter 11. On its property are various deposits of toxic waste. The Environmental Protection Agency knows of the waste, but has not yet taken any action. ThinkTank's immediate predecessor in title to its real property was Spillwill, who originally deposited the toxic waste on the site. Under nonbankruptcy federal law, both ThinkTank and Spillwell are jointly and severally liable to the EPA for all cleanup costs, but such law also provides that the EPA may not collect anything from either until after the cleanup is completed, which is when such nonbankruptcy federal law states that the EPA will have a "claim."

Assume that the EPA's right to receive payment is an existing claim against ThinkTank within the meaning of Section 101(5) of the Code. After passage of the claims filing bar date, ThinkTank files a proof of claim for the EPA, and moves to disallow under Section 502(e) any claim by Spillwell related to such proof of claim.

51.   Will ThinkTank prevail on its motion?

ANSWER:

Sam's Fine Chocolates ("SFC") has ten stores in the city. After some unhappiness with its sugar supplier, SFC decides to switch to a different one. SFC decides to enter into a long-term contract with MetroConfectioners ("MC"). Under the contract, SFC decides to pay the wholesale market rate for sugar upon each delivery which, under the contract, will occur every 30 days. The parties begin to perform and one month later, the price of sugar on the wholesale market falls. After an overly aggressive expansion, SFC ends up in chapter 7 bankruptcy and the trustee decides to reject the contract with MC. MC argues that since the trustee rejected the contract postpetition, its claim for breach of contract is not governed by the bankruptcy process.

52.   Does MC have a valid argument?

(A) No, because MC's claim would be treated as if it arose prepetition;

(B) No, because MC's claim arises under a private contract;

(C) Yes, because MC's claim would be treated as a postpetition claim;

(D) Yes, because the fall in the wholesale market price of sugar was not MC's fault.

Marvin is a chapter 13 debtor. One of her creditors (not a governmental unit) fails to file its proof of claim on a timely basis.

53.   Will the creditor's claim be allowed in Marvin's bankruptcy case?

ANSWER:

Subtopic F. Subordination of Claims under Section 510

American Hardware Supply ("AHS") is in chapter 11 bankruptcy. Emily Major ("Major") was president and the sole stockholder of AHS until ten years ago, when she transferred fifty (50) percent of the stock to the sales manager. Six years after that sale, she withdrew from the business and sold her remaining fifty (50) percent to the corporation, taking back a promissory note secured by assets of the company. She was to be paid in installments over ten years with interest. The sale provided no benefit to AHS. Four years after the transaction, AHS defaulted on the note and became insolvent. Upon a motion by AHS, the bankruptcy court ruled that Major's claim was to be subordinated under Section 510(c) of the Code.

54. What is the correct legal theory that supports subordination of Major's claim?

  (A) That Major's claim has no basis in law and is thus not enforceable against AHS;

  (B) That enforcement of Major's claim would prejudice the interests of AHS's other creditors or confer an unfair advantage on Major;

  (C) That Major's claim was obtained under duress;

  (D) That Major's actions violated federal antitrust laws.

Assume all of the same facts as in the last problem.

55. If Major's claim is subordinated under Section 510(c), what will happen to it?

  (A) Major's otherwise valid claim will be disallowed;

  (B) AHS will receive damages for Major's conduct;

  (C) Major's claim will be postponed in rank until the claims of the other creditors are paid;

  (D) Major will no longer be a creditor of AHS.

Subtopic G. Distribution to Allowed Claims under Section 726

In a chapter 7 corporate liquidation case, the trustee is ready to distribute assets of the liquidated estate to creditors. The trustee is confronted with the following claims: (1) an allowed unsecured prepetition tax penalty that is not compensation for actual pecuniary loss; (2) an allowed unsecured claim tardily filed by a creditor where the creditor had notice of the case in time for a timely filing; (3) an allowed unsecured claim tardily filed by a creditor where the creditor did not have notice of the case in time for a timely filing; (4) a priority claim under Section 507.

56. What is the order of payment of these claims?

  (A) 4, 3, 2, 1;

  (B) 3, 2, 4, 1;

  (C) 1, 2, 3, 4;

  (D) 2, 4, 3, 1.

Don Baumer ("Baumer"), president and CEO of Smith Industries ("Smith"), guaranteed an unsecured corporate loan to the company. The loan was from United Bank ("the Bank"). Smith ended up in chapter 7 bankruptcy. At the time of the filing, the remaining amount due on the loan was $50,000. The Bank was undergoing problems of its own and Baumer became concerned that the Bank was not going to file, on a timely basis, a proof of claim in Smith's bankruptcy. Baumer filed a proof of claim on behalf of the Bank to which Baumer was also liable under the terms of the guaranty agreement. As it turns out, Baumer's prediction proved correct. The Bank did not file a proof of claim in the Smith bankruptcy.

57.   Will the Bank be able to receive payment under Section 726 even though it did not file its own proof of claim?

ANSWER:

The victim of over-expansion and a sour economy, Widgets, Inc. ended up in chapter 11 bankruptcy and attorneys were hired by the trustee and approved by the court to work on the reorganization. The chapter 11 case continued for well over a year when it became apparent that Widgets could not survive at all as an ongoing concern. The case was converted to a chapter 7 case. New attorneys were hired by the trustee and approved by the court to work on the liquidation. When it came time for the assets of Widgets to be distributed to creditors, the new attorneys submitted a claim for payment of their fees.

58.   Who will get paid first, the chapter 11 attorneys or the chapter 7 attorneys?

(A)   The chapter 11 attorneys because they were hired first;

(B)   The chapter 11 attorneys because the case began as a chapter 11 case;

(C)   The chapter 7 attorneys because they need an incentive to work on the liquidation;

(D)   The chapter 7 attorneys because chapter 7 is a preferred method of insolvency under the Code.

BioMed willfully infringed on the patent of one its closest competitors, AmCon. BioMed later ended up filing for chapter 7 bankruptcy. Prior to the chapter 7 filing, AmCon was awarded basic damages under the federal patent statute and treble damages for the willful infringement under the same statute. AmCon filed a timely proof of claim in BioMed's bankruptcy for the entire damage claim.

59.   What treatment will AmCon's damage claim receive under Section 726 of the Code?

(A)   Only the basic damage claim will be entitled to repayment;

(B)   AmCon's damage claim will not be entitled to payment out of the bankruptcy estate because the claim arises from the violation of another federal statute;

(C)   Only the treble damage claim will be entitled to repayment;

(D)   The basic damage claim is payable under Section 726(a)(2) while the treble damage claim is payable under Section 726(a)(4).

Subtopic H. Substantive Consolidation

Wilson Goods is a wholly-owned subsidiary of Wilson, Inc. Wilson Goods has, over the years, guaranteed some of Wilson, Inc's debts. Wilson Goods is insolvent and Wilson, Inc. is not doing much better. Both Wilson Goods and Wilson, Inc. have commingled some of their cash and neither company has been careful about observing corporate formalities. Wilson Goods and Wilson, Inc. file for chapter 11 bankruptcy. Wilson Goods and Wilson, Inc. have filed a motion seeking substantive consolidation of their separate bankruptcy proceedings.

60. What is the source of the bankruptcy court's authority to order substantive consolidation?

   (A) Specific statutory authority in the Bankruptcy Code;

   (B) General authority in the Bankruptcy Rules;

   (C) Specific authority in the Federal Rules of Civil Procedure;

   (D) General discretionary equity powers in the Bankruptcy Code.

Assume all of the same facts as in the previous problem.

61. What is the most important issue that the bankruptcy court will have to decide in the hearing on the motion for substantive consolidation?

   (A) Whether the creditors dealt with Wilson Goods and Wilson, Inc. as a single economic unit;

   (B) Whether the substantive consolidation would save time and money;

   (C) Whether assets of the entities were commingled;

   (D) Whether consolidation would make it easier for the debtors to confirm a chapter 11 plan.

Assume the same facts as in the previous problem. Also assume that the bankruptcy court orders substantive consolidation of Wilson, Inc. and Wilson Goods.

62. What would be the legal effect of such a move?

   (A) The debtors' respective chapter 11 plans would be automatically confirmed;

   (B) A trustee would be appointed for the consolidated cases;

   (C) The assets and liabilities of both debtors would be combined into a single pool;

   (D) All valid liens against both debtors would be voided.

Subtopic A. Estate's Ability to Use or Lease Property of the Estate under Section 363

Mariners Way, Inc. ("Mariners") sells boats for recreational use. Mariners ends up in chapter 11 bankruptcy. Mariners' management team proposes to use its existing inventory of boats to launch a complete boating travel service in which Mariners would rent boats instead of sell them and coordinate travel excursions for boat renters. Mariners would book the trips, hire tour guides, and arrange the itineraries.

63. Will Mariners be able to use the boats in the travel service without notice and hearing?

    (A) Yes, because this is a chapter 11 case and not a chapter 7 case;

    (B) No, because the proposed use of the boats is not in the ordinary course of business of Mariners;

    (C) No, because Mariners sells boats for recreational and not commercial use;

    (D) Yes, because the proposed use of the boats is in the ordinary course of business of Mariners.

A large gambling casino files for chapter 11 bankruptcy. The company wants to continue to use 250 of its video poker machines and lease 250 other machines to a small casino that the large casino is thinking about acquiring. The large casino routinely leases its inventory to other businesses in the casino gambling industry.

64. Can the large casino lease the machines to the small casino?

    (A) Yes, because the lease is in the ordinary course of business;

    (B) No, because the lease is not in the ordinary course of business;

    (C) Yes, but only if the large casino provides for notice and a hearing;

    (D) No, because the bankruptcy filing prevents such a transaction.

Assume all of the same facts in the last problem. Now further assume that the casino has in its possession 500 checks that have been written to it in the past month from wealthy gamblers who incurred gambling debts. The checks are subject to a security interest held by First Bank. The casino has immediate cash needs, so it wants to cash the checks and use the proceeds to meet its payroll.

65. Can the casino do that without creditor consent or court approval?

ANSWER:

Subtopic B. Estate's Ability to Sell Property Free and Clear of Claims and Interests under Section 363

Miller's Auto is a car dealership. Miller's inventory is encumbered by a first-position security interest held by First Bank and a second-position security interest held by Second Bank. First Bank's lien is valued at $250,000 and Second Bank's lien is valued at $150,000. Miller files for chapter 7 bankruptcy. The bankruptcy trustee proposes to sell all of Miller's inventory to another car dealership in town and state law authorizes such sales. The sale price will be approximately $650,000.

66.   Can the trustee sell the inventory?

   (A) No;

   (B) It depends on whether First Bank and Second Bank consent to the sale;

   (C) No, because the inventory is encumbered by liens;

   (D) Yes.

Assume all of the same facts as in the last problem. Assume further that you are First Bank's lawyer and that you have just received a call from First Bank. A loan officer at First Bank has just discovered the following clause in its loan documents with Miller's: "If Miller's files a bankruptcy petition, its property rights in the inventory subject to this security interest are immediately null and void and all such property rights are not assignable to any trustee in bankruptcy." The loan officer asks you, "Now that we have found this clause, they can't sell the inventory, can they?"

67.   How would you respond?

   (A) The loan officer is correct because the clause in the loan documents is clear;

   (B) It would depend on whether Miller's corporate officers really understood the clause when they signed the documents;

   (C) The clause in the loan document is unenforceable in bankruptcy;

   (D) It would depend on the relevant state law.

Books-R-Us.Com ("Books-R-Us") is an internet business that specializes in obtaining and selling out-of-print editions of thousands of book titles. Books-R-Us filed for chapter 7 bankruptcy. Books-R-Us has a customer list that contains thousands of names, addresses, and other personally identifiable information from customers who have ordered books over the years. Books-R-Us has a written policy posted on its website which states: "Books-R-Us will not sell its customer list to any entity that is not affiliated with us unless such sale is authorized by the customer and permitted by state and federal law." The chapter 7 trustee wants to sell the customer list to GargantuanBooks.Com ("Gargantuan"), the leading web-based bookseller. Gargantuan is not affiliated with Books-R-Us.

68.   Can the trustee sell the customer list?

   (A) No, because the policy on the website trumps bankruptcy law;

   (B) No, unless the individual customers are given the right to intervene in the bankruptcy;

    (C) Yes, as long as the sale fulfills certain conditions;

    (D) Yes.

Subtopic C. Estate's Ability to Incur Unsecured and Secured Credit under Section 364

A company that makes and sells golf carts ends up in chapter 11 bankruptcy. It has a long-standing relationship with a local supplier of small tires for golf carts. The supplier is concerned and you are their lawyer. The supplier calls you and says, "I want to keep selling these guys my tires, but now that they are in chapter 11, I'm concerned. If I keep going with this, am I going to be left high and dry?"

69.   What will you say?

ANSWER:

Assume that a debtor in possession in a chapter 11 case seeks to obtain unsecured credit outside the ordinary course of business under Section 364(b) of the Code.

70.   Will notice and a hearing be required?

    (A) Yes;

    (B) Yes, but only if there is an objection by a creditor;

    (C) It depends on whether a creditors' committee has been appointed;

    (D) No.

Assume the debtor in possession in a chapter 11 bankruptcy seeks to obtain credit by granting a junior security interest on assets that are already encumbered by senior liens. A senior lienholder objects to the debtor in possession's move by arguing that its loan documents with the debtor contain restrictions that prevent the debtor from granting such a junior lien on already encumbered property.

71.   Will the senior lienholder prevail?

    (A) No;

    (B) Yes;

    (C) It would depend on whether the loan documents were signed within 90 days of the filing of the bankruptcy petition;

    (D) It would depend on whether the debtor in possession had first sought and failed to obtain credit by granting the creditor a superpriority over all administrative expenses.

Subtopic D. Utility Deposits under Section 366

Assume you are the general counsel for a local utility company. The chief of the company's collection division calls you and says, "I've got a great idea that I think will really help improve our collection rates. Thanks to improved technology and the Internet, we now have real-time access to the bankruptcy filings in our town. Let's monitor those filings and, if we find out that an individual consumer files a chapter 7 or 13 bankruptcy, immediately send them a letter demanding a cash deposit for utility services provided after the filing. I think we should demand that such a deposit be sent within 10 days of the filing." The chief asks you to comment on this proposal.

72.   What should you say?

   (A)   This proposal is illegal under Section 366(a).

   (B)   This proposal is legal under Section 366(b), but we must give the customers twenty (20) days from the date of the filing to provide a deposit;

   (C)   This proposal is illegal under Section 366(b);

   (D)   This proposal is legal under Section 366(b), but the deposit must not exceed 10% of the customer's outstanding bill.

Assume you are general counsel for the same utility described in the previous problem. A corporate customer goes into chapter 11. The customer insists that instead of a cash deposit, the utility company will be given an administrative expense priority in the customer's bankruptcy plan.

73.   Must the utility accept the administrative priority instead of a cash deposit?

   (A)   No, because an administrative expense priority would not provide enough security for the utility;

   (B)   Yes, because it would be commercially unreasonable for the utility to reject an administrative expense priority;

   (C)   It would depend on the extent of the administrative expense priority;

   (D)   No.

A utility has a claim against a chapter 11 debtor. After the debtor files its bankruptcy case, the utility tries to setoff that claim against a security deposit that the debtor provided to the utility. After the setoff, neither party will have a claim against the other. Assume that two months before the debtor filed for bankruptcy, the state passed a statute outlawing such utility setoffs.

74.   Can the utility still do the setoff?

ANSWER:

Subtopic E. Abandonment under Section 554(b)

Assume a party other than the trustee seeks to abandon property of the estate under Section 554(b) of the Code. The party files a motion seeking such abandonment.

75.   Is a court order granting the motion required?

   (A)   Yes;

   (B)   No;

(C)   Yes, but only if the dollar value of the property exceeds $100,000, adjusted yearly for inflation;

(D)   No, because the legal standard for abandonment under Section 554(b) is not complex.

A creditor in a chapter 7 bankruptcy case is contemplating filing a motion under Section 554(b) to seek abandonment of property of the estate. The debtor filed its bankruptcy petition two months ago.

76.   How much time does the creditor have to file its motion?

(A)   Since two months have passed, the creditor has thirty (30) days left to file its motion;

(B)   Since this is a chapter 7 case, the creditor has sixty (60) days left to file its motion;

(C)   It is not clear. A lot depends on the circumstances of the case;

(D)   The creditor has 180 days from the date of the petition to file its motion.

The debtor in a chapter 7 case has rights to property and the property is subject to a lien. After an appropriate motion and hearing, a court orders abandonment of the property under Section 554(b).

77.   What happens to the property?

(A)   It is sold to the highest bidder;

(B)   It goes to the state;

(C)   It goes back to the debtor;

(D)   It goes into a pool of assets for unsecured creditors.

Assume a debtor files chapter 7. Assume the debtor owns an item of property that is worth $10,000 and it is subject to a security interest of $8,000. Assume the debtor has an exemption of $4,000 in the property and claims the exemption.

78.   Will this property likely be abandoned under Section 554?

(A)   Yes, because the estate has no interest in the property;

(B)   It depends on whether the property is a car or not;

(C)   No;

(D)   No, because the estate has an interest in the property.

Subtopic A. Defining Executory Contracts

A movie studio and an insurance company enter into an insurance policy contract. The policy provides liability protection to the movie studio in the event of any damage or injury to the studio's real or personal property that results from any accidents or mishaps that occur during the filming of the studio's movies. The movie studio files for bankruptcy and three days after the filing, the policy expires due to non-payment of premiums.

79. Was the insurance policy contract an executory contract at the time of the filing?

 (A) Yes, because on the date of the petition both parties had mutual obligations to perform;

 (B) No, because insurance policy contracts cannot be executory;

 (C) No, because only three days elapsed between the time of the filing and the expiration of the policy;

 (D) It would depend on whether the case was filed in chapter 7 or chapter 11.

Assume that an insurance policy contract has a clause that states as follows, "A bankruptcy filing will not relieve the insurer of its obligations even if the insured stops paying premiums." Assume further that the insured files for bankruptcy and then stops paying premiums.

80. Is the insurance policy contract an executory contract?

 (A) Yes, because both parties must still perform;

 (B) No, because the Code says that a bankruptcy filing automatically voids an insurance policy;

 (C) No, because under the terms of the contract the debtor's non-performance of its obligations is not a breach that would excuse the insurer of its obligation to perform;

 (D) Yes, because under the terms of the contract the debtor's non-performance of its obligations is a breach that would excuse the insurer of its obligation to perform.

Subtopic B. Assumption and Its Effects

Freshfruit Juice Company ("Freshfruit") has a contract with a cranberry grower under which the grower delivers, on unsecured credit, cranberries each week. The cranberry grower files chapter 7 bankruptcy. The trustee elects to maintain the contract with Freshfruit.

81. Which of the following entities is now liable under the contract?

    (A) The bankruptcy estate;

    (B) Freshfruit;

    (C) The trustee;

    (D) The debtor in possession.

Assume all of the same facts as in the previous problem. Following the assumption of the contract between Freshfruit and the grower, Freshfruit has a claim in the grower's bankruptcy.

  82.   What type of claim does Freshfruit have?

    (A) A secured claim;

    (B) An administrative claim;

    (C) A voided claim;

    (D) An undersecured claim.

Corsine, Inc. files a chapter 11 case in April of 2009. Corsine's main office is leased from Snidely, Inc. The lease requires that Corsine keep the premises insured at all times; failure to do so is a breach of the lease entitling Snidely to terminate the lease.

Due to financial difficulties, Corsine let its insurance lapse during a two-month period in late 2008. There were no losses during that period, and ever since then Corsine has maintained insurance that satisfies the lease provisions. It cannot obtain insurance to cover the two-month gap.

Corsine moves to assume the lease in its chapter 11, offering evidence that it has purchased insurance for the remainder of the lease term. Snidely opposes.

  83.   Which of the following best describes the most likely outcome of the motion to assume?

    (A) Corsine will lose, since the breach of the lease cannot be cured;

    (B) Corsine will lose because there is no way to compensate Snidely for the breach of the lease at this time;

    (C) Corsine will win since the breach of the lease was a non-monetary breach which is impossible to cure at this time;

    (D) Corsine will win only if it posts a letter of credit in the amount of Snidely's maximum possible loss.

Subtopic C. Rejection and Its Effects

Stan's carpet cleaners (Stan's) is the largest carpet cleaning company in a major metropolitan city and has a staff of two hundred (200) employees. Stan's has a contract with a uniform company called "Spiffy Duds" to supply uniforms to its carpet cleaning staff. Stan's files chapter 7 bankruptcy and the bankruptcy trustee determines that it can get uniforms from another company in town for a lot cheaper than the price in the contract with Spiffy. The trustee elects to reject the Spiffy Duds contract.

84. What happens to Spiffy?

    (A) It has a claim for damages for breach of contract;

    (B) It has no claim;

    (C) It has a secured claim;

    (D) It has a claim for treble damages under the Code.

Assume all of the same facts as in the previous problem.

85. When did the breach of contract occur under the Code?

    (A) Under the Code, the breach occurred prepetition;

    (B) Under the Code, the breach occurred postpetition;

    (C) Under the Code, the breach does not occur until the bankruptcy case has concluded;

    (D) Under the Code, the breach is retroactive to the date of the contract.

Subtopic D. Assignment and Its Effects

An auto parts manufacturer has a contract with a steelmaker. The steelmaker supplies steel used in the manufacturing process in exchange for payment. The steelmaker goes into chapter 7 bankruptcy. The steelmaker cannot perform the contract even though it is economically favorable. The bankruptcy trustee wants to assign the contract to another steelmaker. There have been no defaults under the contract or any prohibitions on assignment, contractual or otherwise.

86. What will the trustee have to do in order to assign the contract?

    (A) Assume the contract and make sure the assignee can provide adequate assurance of future performance;

    (B) Assume the contract;

    (C) Assume the contract and go into state court to force the assignee to accept the assignment;

    (D) Reject the contract and then make sure the assignee can provide adequate assurance of future performance.

Assume all of the same facts as in the previous problem. Assume further that the assignment is approved by the bankruptcy court and the assignee begins to perform under the contract. Shortly thereafter, however, the assignee breaches.

87. Can the auto parts manufacturer sue the bankruptcy estate for breach of contract?

    (A) Yes;

    (B) No;

(C) It would depend on whether the auto parts manufacturer sued in federal or state court;

(D) It would depend on whether the auto parts manufacturer could get relief from the automatic stay.

Assume all of the facts in the previous problem, except now assume that there is a provision in the contract between the auto parts manufacturer and the assignor that says the following, "Under no circumstances will this contract be assigned unless the steelmaker has given express consent and certain financial conditions are met."

88. Can the contract still be assigned?

(A) No, because the contractual provision will override bankruptcy law;

(B) No, because a bankruptcy judge would never allow it;

(C) Yes, because a bankruptcy judge could use his or her equity powers under Section 105 to override the contract;

(D) Yes, because Section 365(f)(1) invalidates contractual anti-assignment clauses such as the one in the problem.

Subtopic E. Special Rules for Nonresidential Real Estate

A chapter 7 debtor is a lessee of nonresidential real property and the rent under the unexpired lease is due in ten (10) days. The lease has not yet been assumed or rejected and the bankruptcy petition was filed two weeks ago. The bankruptcy trustee seeks advice from you about whether or not she has to pay the rent in a timely fashion in light of the bankruptcy filing. She asserts that she should not have to pay the rent because the debtor/lessee is in bankruptcy and the lease has not yet been assumed or rejected.

89. What would you advise?

(A) The trustee is correct because the bankruptcy filing invalidates the lease;

(B) The trustee is correct because the lease has not yet been assumed or rejected;

(C) The trustee is incorrect because of Section 365(d)(3);

(D) The trustee is incorrect because of Section 365(d)(2).

A chapter 7 debtor is a lessee of nonresidential real property and five months have passed since the bankruptcy petition was filed. The bankruptcy case has had three different trustees appointed since the filing because the debtor is unusually difficult. The latest trustee to be appointed in the case discovers that none of the previous trustees assumed or rejected the unexpired lease even though it would benefit the estate greatly for the lease to be assumed.

90. Can the newly appointed trustee assume the lease?

(A) Yes, because the trustee can ask for an extension of time to assume the lease;

(B) Yes, because the current trustee has only recently discovered the problem;

(C) No, because the lease is deemed rejected;

(D) Yes, because the lease is deemed assumed.

Subtopic F. Special Rules for Intellectual Property

A chapter 11 debtor in possession/licensor rejects a licensing agreement with a licensee pursuant to Section 365(a). The debtor in possession/licensor invented a weight-loss drink called "DrinkYourselfSkinny" and the licensee runs a spa/weight-loss facility. The agreement between the two parties called for the debtor in possession/licensor to license its invention to the spa/weight-loss facility so that the facility would have exclusive rights to offer the drink to its customers.

91. Now that the debtor in possession/licensor has rejected the agreement under Section 365(a), what are the licensee's options?

    (A) The licensee can sue the licensor in state court for punitive damages;

    (B) The licensee may choose to either treat the license as terminated or retain its rights;

    (C) The licensee can block the rejection altogether and return the parties to the status quo;

    (D) The licensee may choose to treat the license as a quasi-contract.

Assume all of the same facts as in the previous problem. Assume further that the licensee chooses to retain its rights.

92. Will the licensee be able to enforce the exclusivity provision of the licensing agreement?

    (A) Yes, because Section 365(n)(1)(B) says so;

    (B) No, because Section 365(n)(1)(B) allows for enforcement of any right of specific performance, but does not allow for enforcement of exclusivity provisions;

    (C) No, because state law controls and state law would not allow for such enforcement;

    (D) No, because an invention is not "intellectual property" under the Code.

Stayinplace® Hairspray, Inc. has a licensing agreement with a company that runs beauty pageants. Pursuant to this agreement, the pageant company can use the Stayinplace® logo on all of its advertising and promotional materials. The Stayinplace® logo consists of a small figure of a woman's head with a tall, beehive hairdo. Stayinplace files a chapter 11 bankruptcy petition and seeks to reject its contract with the pageant company.

93. Would Section 365(n) apply?

    (A) Yes, because a trademark is considered intellectual property under the Code;

    (B) No, because a trademark is not considered intellectual property under the Code;

    (C) No, because this is a chapter 11 case;

(D)   Yes, because the policy of protecting the legitimate expectations of the licensee remains the same.

AVOIDING POWERS: TRUSTEE'S STRONG ARM POWERS UNDER SECTION 544(a)

Subtopic A. Status of a Judicial Lien Creditor under Section 544(a)(1)

XYZ Logging Co, Inc. (XYZ) borrowed $300,000 from the First National Bank (The Bank) and entered into a security agreement with the Bank. The security agreement gave the bank a security interest in XYZ's equipment. The equipment has a value of $175,000. The president of XYZ signed a personal guarantee for any amount due under the loan. Due to a computer glitch, a financing statement is never filed on the equipment as required by Article 9 of the Uniform Commercial Code (U.C.C.). Several months after the security agreement is signed by the parties, XYZ files a chapter 11 bankruptcy petition.

94. Can the debtor in possession avoid the Bank's security interest in the equipment?

    (A) No, because the failure to file the financing statement was not based on a willful act;

    (B) No, because the Bank obtained a personal guarantee from the company president;

    (C) Yes, because the transfer would be considered a fraudulent transfer under Section 548;

    (D) Yes, because Section 544(a)(1) allows the debtor in possession to avoid the security interest.

Legal Eagles, Inc (LEI) provides office space for lease to attorneys and furnishes certain services to them, including use of a law library owned by LEI. Anderson Publishing (AP), a legal publisher, sold books to LEI for the purchase price of $85,000. The purchase order, signed by both parties, constituted an installment sales contract under applicable law and it was the intention of the parties that the law books currently in the law library would be the collateral securing the deal. Thereafter, AP filed a financing statement as required by Article 9 of the U.C.C. The financing statement contained all of the required information, except for a description of the collateral. Legal Eagles, Inc. then files a chapter 7 bankruptcy petition.

95. Can the trustee avoid AP's security interest in the law books?

    (A) Yes, because AP's failure to provide a description of the collateral in the financing statement renders the financing statement ineffective to perfect AP's security interest;

    (B) Yes, because there was never an actual security agreement in this case. Without a security agreement, no security interest was ever created, let alone perfected;

    (C) No, because AP's failure to provide a description of the collateral was not a material omission;

    (D) Yes, but only if the security interest was created within 90 days of the bankruptcy filing.

Jane Smith runs a struggling catering company with a staff of three employees and several impatient creditors. She really needs to cut back on staff and let at least one of the employees go, but she is very loyal.

In an effort to be more efficient, Jane decides to computerize billing, payroll, and order operations. She visits the local computer store. Despite its shaky credit, the catering company purchases three desktop computers, business software, and other accessories. The entire purchase price is $35,000. The computer store extends credit for the purchase and takes a note and security interest in the computer system.

Fifteen days after the company takes delivery of the items and with creditors descending, Jane decides that the company has no choice but to file a chapter 7 petition. Two days after the bankruptcy petition is filed, the computer store files an appropriate financing statement in the correct location.

96. Can the bankruptcy trustee use Section 544(a)(1) to avoid the computer store's security interest?

    (A) Yes, because the security interest was unperfected on the date of bankruptcy;

    (B) No, because the security interest is a purchase money security interest;

    (C) No, because the trustee had constructive knowledge of the financing statement;

    (D) It would depend on whether the trustee had actual knowledge of the financing statement.

Subtopic B. Status of a Bona Fide Purchaser of Real Estate under Section 544(a)(3)

Greentree Horse Farms ("Greentree") mortgaged 2.5 acres of its land to the Second National Bank ("the Bank"). The Bank does not record the mortgage. Shortly thereafter, Greentree files a chapter 7 bankruptcy petition.

97. Can the trustee avoid the Bank's mortgage?

    (A) Yes, because Section 544(a)(3) applies;

    (B) Yes, because Section 544(a)(2) applies;

    (C) No, because this case involves personal property;

    (D) It depends on whether there was an actual bona fide purchaser (BFP) involved.

Assume all of the same facts as in the previous problem, except now the Bank can prove that the trustee had constructive knowledge of the unrecorded mortgage.

98. How would that affect the outcome?

    (A) It would not matter because the trustee's constructive knowledge is irrelevant under Section 544(a)(3);

    (B) It would not matter because the Bank still should have recorded promptly;

    (C) It would matter because the trustee's constructive knowledge is relevant under Section 544(a)(3);

    (D) None of the above.

Acme Corporation owns real property consisting of 6 acres in the town of Greenwood. In 2003, Acme borrowed $1,000,000 from the local bank. Acme executed a promissory note in the amount of $1,000,000 secured by two mortgages, one of which covered the 6 acres. The other mortgage covered a 10-acre parcel in another city. The bank recorded a mortgage on the 6-acre property, but neglected to record a mortgage on the 10-acre parcel. Shortly thereafter, Acme filed a chapter 11 bankruptcy petition. Acme, as debtor in possession, seeks to avoid the unrecorded mortgage on the 10-acre parcel.

99.   Can the debtor in possession avoid the bank's mortgage on the 10-acre parcel?

   (A)   Yes;

   (B)   No;

   (C)   It would depend on whether the debtor in possession had actual knowledge;

   (D)   It would depend on whether the debtor in possession actually paid value for the property.

Subtopic A. Definition of a Preference under Section 547(b)

Jack owes Geezer $100,000. Jack owns a Lamborghini worth $100,000. Tired of excuses, Geezer sues Jack and obtains a default judgment. Geezer then obtains a writ of execution, and has the local sheriff levy upon the car. The next week, in accordance with local law, the sheriff sells the car at auction for $50,000 to Brad. Jack immediately files for chapter 11 bankruptcy, and sues to avoid the seizure and sale. He is insolvent at all relevant times.

100. In the action, which of the following is the most likely outcome?

   (A) Jack will prevail because the transactions constituted a voidable preference, and only a voidable preference;

   (B) Jack will prevail because the transactions constituted a fraudulent transfer, and only a fraudulent transfer;

   (C) Jack will prevail because the transactions constituted both a voidable preference and a fraudulent transfer;

   (D) Jack will not prevail.

First National Bank ("FNB") makes a $500,000 unsecured loan to Acme Corporation ("Acme"). Acme's president guarantees payment of the loan. Acme pays FNB $100,000 on July 1, 2009. Acme files for chapter 7 bankruptcy on December 15, 2009.

101. Can the trustee recover $100, 000 from Acme's president?

ANSWER:

Subtopic B. Defenses to Preferences under Section 547(c)

Crunchtime provided ordinary services to Delay, Inc. in April of 2008. It is now July of 2008. The bill for Crunchtime's services was dated May 1, and indicated that it was due within 30 days. Crunchtime calls Delay and asks for payment. Delay responds by sending over an ordinary check for the bill, which is the usual way it pays its bills. What is unusual, however, is that Delay is usually very prompt with its payments; it averages about 25 days between presentation of a bill and payment.

At the time Delay sent Crunchtime's check, it was insolvent. Delay files for chapter 7 bankruptcy on August 1, 2008.

102. Which of the following best describes the most likely outcome of a preference action brought by Delay's trustee against Crunchtime?

(A) Crunchtime will prevail because it did not receive more by the payment than it would had it not received the payment, and received a bankruptcy dividend instead;

(B) The trustee will prevail because the payment to Crunchtime was not in Delay's ordinary course as shown by the variance between the time of payment and Delay's usual prompt practices;

(C) The trustee will prevail because the payment was not substantially contemporaneous with the provision of the services; or

(D) Crunchtime will prevail because the method of payment Delay used was the normal and ordinary way that all businesses such as Delay pay their bills.

A creditor receives a $10,000 preference on June 10, 2010 and makes an advance of new credit in the amount of $8,000 on July 10, 2010. The $10,000 payment was a preference under Section 547(b). The new credit was unsecured and it remained unpaid.

103. Can the trustee recover anything from the creditor?

(A) Yes, $2,000 is recoverable;

(B) Yes, $10,000 is recoverable;

(C) No, because the new credit was unsecured;

(D) No, because the new credit remained unpaid.

Assume the same facts as in the previous problem, except now assume that the $8,000 was fully secured and that the security interest itself was not avoidable.

104. Would that change the analysis?

ANSWER:

On January 1, 2010, a chapter 7 corporate debtor owes the local bank $110,000 and the bank has an Article 9 security interest in the debtor's accounts receivable. The accounts receivable have a value of $70,000 on January 1. The security agreement between the debtor and the bank contains an after-acquired property clause in the accounts receivable and thus will grant the bank a security interest in both the accounts receivable that the debtor owns and the accounts receivable that the debtor will acquire in the future.

The debtor files for bankruptcy on April 1, 2010. At the time of filing, the debtor owes $100,000 to the bank and the accounts receivable have a value of $80,000.

105. Can the trustee avoid the bank's security interest in the April 1 accounts receivable?

(A) Yes, but only to the extent of $20,000;

(B) Yes, to the full extent of $80,000;

(C) No, because there was no transfer on the date of the filing;

(D)   No, because accounts receivable cannot be subject to preference actions.

Douglas Debtor recently lost his job as a construction engineer. His unemployment and a few other personal setbacks have made it difficult to keep up with his debts on a number of credit cards and two personal, unsecured loans. At the suggestion of a friend, Douglas decides to go to a consumer credit counseling agency to get some help figuring out how to pay his debts. He is optimistic about getting back to work again because the state government is embarking on some new construction projects and he has a very good shot at getting a few lucrative contracts.

The folks at the consumer credit counseling agency are helpful. They work with Douglas and his creditors to assist in negotiating an alternative repayment schedule. Under the schedule approved by his four major unsecured creditors, the debtor is supposed to pay 53% of the unsecured creditors' debts to creditor 1, creditor 2, creditor 3, and creditor 4. In the meantime, the creditors agree not to report any negative information to credit scoring bureaus if Douglas makes the required payments. The credit counseling agency is on a list of approved agencies on file in the bankruptcy court clerk's office.

Douglas had good intentions, but four months have passed and Douglas has not paid any of the creditors. Through a stroke of good luck, creditor 4 finds out that Douglas is thinking about filing for bankruptcy. Creditor 4 then contacts Douglas and tells him that he'd better "pay up because if he doesn't, we'll report your nonpayment to a credit reporting bureau just like we do with all of the other deadbeats." Douglas hastily makes a $10,000 payment to creditor 4 and three days later, Douglas files for chapter 7 bankruptcy. None of the other creditors receive any payment from Douglas.

106.   Can the trustee recover the payment to creditor 4?

   (A)   Yes, because it is preference and no exceptions apply;

   (B)   No, because the ordinary course defense would protect creditor 4;

   (C)   Yes, because the promised payments under the alternative repayment schedule were unrealistic and allowing the trustee to recover the payment would deter creditors and debtors from putting together unrealistic plans;

   (D)   No, because Section 547(h) applies and allows a defense for creditor 4.

Subtopic C. Timing of Transfers under Section 547(e)

Widgets, Inc. makes widgets. The business is struggling under the weight of a sagging economy and slump in the demand for widgets. The company president decides to apply for a loan from the local bank. On April 1, Widgets borrows $200,000 from the bank and at the time of loan Widgets grants the bank a mortgage on Blackacre. On August 1, the bank records the mortgage. On October 1, Widgets files a chapter 11 bankruptcy petition.

107.   When did the transfer occur for purposes of Section 547(e) of the Code?

   (A)   The transfer occurred on August 1;

   (B)   The transfer occurred on April 1;

   (C)   The transfer occurred on October 1.

A contracts to sell Greenacre to X. Under nonbankruptcy law, either recording of the deed or open and notorious possession of the property by the purchaser will protect X against a subsequent purchaser from A. On July 1, X pays the agreed sales price of $75,000. On July 1, X establishes open and notorious possession. On September 15, X records the deed from A. On November 15, A files chapter 7 bankruptcy.

108. Is there a preferential transfer on September 15?

    (A) No, because the transfer occurred on July 1;

    (B) Yes, because the transfer occurred on September 15;

    (C) Yes, because the transfer occurred on November 15;

    (D) It would depend on X's state of mind on July 1.

On February 15, Creditor lends money to Debtor and takes a security interest in Debtor's existing inventory. On March 18, Creditor files the required notice and perfects its security interest under Article 9 of the U.C.C. On April 1, D files for bankruptcy.

109. When did the transfer occur under Section 547(e) of the Code?

    (A) On February 15;

    (B) On March 18;

    (C) There was no transfer because nothing was physically delivered to X;

    (D) There was no transfer because the security interest covered X's existing inventory.

Subtopic D. Insiders, Presumptions and Burdens in Pleading and Proving Preferences

Harry Evans is the President and sole shareholder of Corporation A. Corporation B seeks to buy Corporation A and the purchase price for Corporation A is $20 million, a fair valuation of the assets of Corporation A. According to the terms of the deal, Harry assumes the position of Vice President of Corporation B and Harry is required to use part of the proceeds of the sale to pay off the remaining debts of Corporation A. Pursuant to the deal, Harry is supposed to receive $5 million at the time of the closing and Corporation B executes a promissory note for the remaining $15 million payable in monthly installments of $250,000 for 60 months. The deal is executed and, as promised, Harry pays off the debts of Corporation A.

Corporation B makes three monthly payments to Harry and then, for reasons unrelated to the sale transaction, starts to experience financial distress. Two months later, Harry resigns his post as Vice President of Corporation B and begins to serve as an advisor to Corporation B. In this capacity, he provides management advice from time to time and solicits business for Corporation B. On April 1, Corporation B makes a monthly payment of $250,000 to Harry pursuant to the original agreement. On October 1, Corporation B files for bankruptcy and the trustee tries to avoid the April 1 payment under the Code.

110. Which of the following would be an important legal issue in the trustee's case?

    (A) Whether the officers of both companies used due diligence in the sale;

    (B) Whether the sales transaction was constructively fraudulent as to Corporation B;

    (C)   Whether Corporation B should have stopped making payments to Harry after Corporation B went into financial distress;

    (D)   Whether Harry was a person in control of Corporation B.

Assume all of the same facts as in the previous problem, but assume further that the trustee can prove that Harry had meaningful control over the debtor and that a bankruptcy judge so rules. The trustee thus decides to continue to pursue the April 1 payment and avoid it as a preference.

111. Will the presumption of insolvency in Section 547(f) apply to this case?

ANSWER:

Assume you are a new attorney in a small corporate law firm that has not handled many bankruptcy matters. Assume further that you are working for a senior partner who is an expert in real estate law. You and the senior partner are in the initial stages of handling a non-insider preference case for a chapter 7 trustee and after the senior partner reads Section 547(f), he says to you, "Great, we don't have the burden of proving insolvency, so we don't have to worry about that."

112. Is there anything you need to tell the senior partner?

ANSWER:

A trucking company routinely buys gasoline on credit from Big Oil Co, Inc. ("BOC"). Payments under the invoices are due within 10 days of the receipt of the gasoline. The trucking company files a chapter 7 bankruptcy petition. The trucking company makes two payments to BOC within the 90-day preference period. Each of these two payments was made by the trucking company between 15 and 35 days after the trucking company received the gasoline. The trustee can prove that the payments meet the requirements of Section 547(b).

113. Which of the following statements is true?

    (A)   The trustee has the burden of proving that the trucking company routinely paid its invoices between 15 and 35 days after presentation of the invoices;

    (B)   BOC has the burden of proving that it always demanded prompt payment and that these two late payments were the exception to the rule;

    (C)   The trustee has the burden of proving that the general industry practice was to accept late payments;

    (D)   BOC has the burden of proving that it has a habit of accepting late payments.

FRAUDULENT TRANSFERS UNDER SECTION 548 AND SECTION 544(b)

Subtopic A. Standing, Source of Law, and Recovery under Section 544(b)

On August 1, 2008, Debtor, while insolvent, gives Johnson, for less than a reasonably equivalent value, a security interest in personal property. Debtor files a chapter 7 bankruptcy petition on September 15, 2008.

114. If the trustee in Debtor's bankruptcy wants to obtain standing to challenge the August 1 transfer, what will she have to show?

    (A)   She will have to show that she is relying on federal law;

    (B)   She will have to show that she is asserting already existing rights belonging to an actual unsecured creditor;

    (C)   She will have to show that she is relying on state law;

    (D)   She will have to show that she has affirmatively claimed the right to challenge the August 1 transfer.

Debtor transfers property three years before bankruptcy. Assume the transfer was made with actual intent to defraud creditors. Assume that the statute of limitations under state fraudulent conveyance law is four years. Under Section 548 of the Code, the statute of limitations is two years.

115. Which of the following statements is true?

    (A)   Since the bankruptcy trustee cannot proceed under Section 548 due to the two-year limitation, then she also cannot use Section 544(b);

    (B)   The bankruptcy trustee can proceed under Section 544(b), but she will have to seek relief in state court since she is using state law;

    (C)   The fact that the trustee cannot proceed under Section 548 does not prevent her from using Section 544(b);

    (D)   Since actual fraud was involved, the bankruptcy trustee can use either Section 548 or Section 544(b).

A debtor makes a transfer of property. The property is worth $2,000,000. Under state law, only one type of unsecured creditor can avoid the transfer. There exists one creditor with a $1,000 allowable claim who has a right to avoid the transfer under state law. Moreover, under state law, that creditor is entitled to payment from the property transferred. Assume a bankruptcy trustee successfully avoids the transfer using Section 544(b).

116. What is the effect of successfully avoiding the transfer?

   (A) The transfer is avoided for the benefit of the creditor who would have been able to set aside the transfer under state law. The trustee can recover $1,000;

   (B) The transfer is avoided for the benefit of all creditors with unsecured claims in the bankruptcy. The trustee can recover $2,000,000;

   (C) The transfer is avoided for the benefit of the debtor but subject to a right of recovery by the creditor who would have been able to set aside the transfer under state law;

   (D) The transfer is avoided for the benefit of all creditors with unsecured claims, but the bankruptcy judge, after notice and a hearing, determines the amount of the recovery.

Subtopic B. Transfers Made with Actual Intent to Hinder, Delay, and Defraud

Ajax Corporation ("Ajax") is a defendant in a pending lawsuit involving allegations that Ajax unlawfully discharged toxic waste into ground water. Ajax sold a small parcel of real property to Buyer who paid the full market value of $700,000. Ajax took the proceeds of the sale and deposited them in an out-of-state bank account under the name of one of its subsidiaries. One year and six months after the sale, the plaintiffs in the environmental lawsuit won a judgment against Ajax. Ajax filed for bankruptcy two days later.

117. Can the bankruptcy trustee avoid the sale to the buyer under Section 548 of the Code?

ANSWER:

Assume the same facts as in the previous problem, except now assume that at the time the trustee avoided the sale to the Buyer, the property had a value of $720,000 and also assume that the Buyer did not know of Ajax's intentions at the time of the original sale.

118. Which of the following statements is correct?

   (A) Under Section 550(a)(1), the trustee can recover the property or its value from the Buyer;

   (B) The trustee cannot recover the property or its value because the property has appreciated in value;

   (C) The Buyer had a duty to investigate Ajax's situation and since it did not, answer (A) is incorrect;

   (D) This might be a case of constructive fraud under Section 548((a)(1)(B), but not actual fraud under Section 548 (a)(1)(A).

Assume all of the facts in the previous two problems, including the part about the property now having appreciated to $720,000 and the Buyer having no knowledge of the Debtor's intentions at the time of the sale.

119. What amount, if any, can the trustee recover from the Buyer?

(A) $700,000;

(B) $720,000;

(C) $20,000;

(D) Nothing, because the Buyer acted in good faith and paid full market value.

Subtopic C. Transfers Made and Obligations Incurred with Constructive Intent: Amount of Consideration

Donna Debtor is a property manager for a large condominium complex. She had embezzled significant sums of money from the condo company over a period of several years. Donna has a child with a lot of health problems and she is barely meeting his health and medical bills even with the embezzlement activity. The condo company hires an assistant property manager and Donna becomes nervous about being caught in the embezzlement scheme. She decides to transfer her house to her sister. The deed is recorded. The sister does not have knowledge of Donna's embezzlement activities. After the transfer, Donna's assets are worth less than the amount she owes the condo company. Within one year of the transfer, Donna files a chapter 7 bankruptcy petition.

120. Would the trustee be advised to investigate the transfer of the house to see if that transfer could be avoided?

    (A) Yes, because the transfer meets the requirements of Section 548(a)(1)(A);

    (B) Yes, because the transfer meets the requirements of Section 548(a)(1)(B);

    (C) No, because Donna's sister is not a creditor in Donna's bankruptcy case;

    (D) No, because Donna had a good reason to transfer the property.

A real estate developer purchased Greenacre on May 1, 2001 for $300,000. The developer bought Greenacre with the goal of building a residential subdivision on the site. On May 1, 2003, Greenacre was worth in the range of $320,000 to $340,000, largely due to the fact that another company announced plans to build a major shopping and entertainment center nearby. The real estate developer became over-extended on its debt. It needed to liquidate some of its holdings to pay creditors. It put the Greenacre property up for sale. The price was $310,000, payable in cash within 5 days. One buyer came forward and offered to pay $280,000 within 2 days. The developer balked, but no other buyers made offers. The developer sold Greenacre to the buyer for $280,000. The proceeds of the sale went to pay creditors of the developer. One year after the sale, the developer filed a chapter 7 bankruptcy petition.

121. Would the trustee be advised to investigate the transfer of Greenacre to see if the transfer could be avoided?

    (A) Yes, because the transfer could meet the requirements of Section 548(a)(1)(A);

    (B) No, because it is not the buyer's fault that the developer could not manage its business properly;

    (C) Yes, because the transfer could meet the requirement of Section 548(a)(1)(B)(i);

    (D) No, because the appreciation in the value of the property was entirely the result of market forces.

L lends $1.5 million to Y Corporation. Z Corporation is an affiliate of Y. Z guarantees repayment of the $1.5 million loan. After the guarantee, Z Corporation's assets are worth less than the amount it owes. One year later, Z files a chapter 7 bankruptcy petition. Assume the trustee brings a Section 548 (a)(1)(B) action against L.

    122. What is the most important issue in the case?

        (A) Whether L provided a reasonably equivalent value to Y;

        (B) Whether Z's guarantee was lawful under the relevant corporate law;

        (C) Whether Y became insolvent as a result of the transfer;

        (D) Whether L's loan to Y indirectly benefitted Z.

Subtopic D. Defenses to Fraudulent Transfers

X Corp. is in chapter 7 bankruptcy. About six months before the filing, X sold an office building to Y Corp. for $200,000. In exchange for the building, X received common stock in Y. Although X was insolvent at the time of the transfer, Y did not have actual knowledge of X's insolvency. Unbeknownst to both parties, the stock X received in exchange for the building had a value of $40,000. Facing its own difficulties and an SEC investigation, Y sold the building to Z Corp for value and Z had no knowledge of either X or Y's financial distress. Assume the trustee in bankruptcy can successfully bring a Section 548 action against Y.

    123. What is Y Corp.'s liability?

ANSWER:

Assume all of the same facts as in the previous problem.

    124. What is Z Corp.'s liability?

ANSWER:

X sold an office building to Y on April 1, 2008. The building's fair market value was $550,000, but Y paid $250,000 after he gave X cash on the spot. Prior to the sale, Y had read a report about X's cash flow problems in the *Wall Street Journal* and told business associates that he wanted to "take advantage of X's bind to make a killing." "Besides," he told others, "X's creditors are not my concern." After the sale, Y installed central air conditioning and refurbished the building's facade in accordance with local historic preservation codes. A year and a half after the sale, X filed chapter 7 bankruptcy and the trustee successfully sued Y to recover the building under Section 548 of the Code.

    125. Will Y be able to recoup the cost of the air conditioning system and the cost for refurbishing the facade?

        (A) No, because Y would not be considered a good faith transferee;

(B) No, because such a transferee can never recoup the cost of improvements;

(C) Yes, because such a transferee can always recoup the cost of improvements;

(D) It depends. The central air conditioning would be considered an improvement, but not the preservation costs.

Subtopic A. Turnover and Section 542

The "Friendly Skies" Airline Corporation ("Friendly") borrowed millions from First State Bank ("Bank") to purchase a brand new fleet of planes. The Bank took an Article 9 security interest in the planes. Shortly thereafter, Friendly defaulted on the loan and the Bank repossessed the planes. Two days later, Friendly filed for chapter 11 bankruptcy. The Bank had not yet resold the planes. The debtor in possession in Friendly's chapter 11 case filed a motion requesting that the Bank turn the planes over to it immediately.

126. Will the bankruptcy court grant the debtor in possession's motion?

   (A) Yes, because Section 542(a) gives the court the authority to grant the motion;

   (B) Yes, but only because this is a chapter 11 case;

   (C) No, because the Bank repossessed the planes prior to the filing;

   (D) No, because the property is of inconsequential value or benefit to the estate.

Corporation A ("Corp A") has a checking account at Solid State Bank ("the Bank"). Corp A files for chapter 7 bankruptcy. After the filing and in the ordinary course of business, the Bank honors (i.e., pays) a check written by Corp A to one of Corp A's creditors. The Bank had neither actual notice nor actual knowledge of the commencement of Corp A's bankruptcy filing.

127. Can the trustee in Corp's bankruptcy recover the value of the check from the Bank?

   (A) Yes, because this is a preferential transfer under Section 547;

   (B) It depends on whether the check was honored within 90 days after the filing;

   (C) Yes, because the Bank's notice or knowledge is irrelevant;

   (D) No, because of Section 542(c).

Subtopic B. Statutory Liens and Section 545

Acme, Inc. ("Acme") executed a promissory note to Bank in the amount of $150,000. Acme granted Bank a security interest in Acme's current and after-acquired business machinery, equipment, inventory, and accounts receivable. Bank perfected the security interest. Acme failed to pay the state corporate income tax for two years in a row. Acme then filed for chapter 7 bankruptcy. The state filed a proof of claim for the unpaid taxes. In the course of liquidating Acme's property, the trustee sold the business machinery, equipment, and inventory. Under state tax law, "if any owner of personal property surrenders or transfers such property to another before the tax thereon is paid, whether the transfer is by voluntary repossession or by any other voluntary act in reduction or satisfaction of indebtedness, then a tax lien shall attach to the property so surrendered or transferred. Such lien shall be due and payable immediately and shall be given priority over all other claims against the property."

128. The trustee in Acme's bankruptcy case has filed a motion to avoid the state's tax lien. Will the trustee prevail?

(A) Yes, because Section 545(1) allows the lien to be avoided;

(B) No, because the state tax provision trumps bankruptcy law;

(C) It would depend upon whether the promissory note to the Bank was secured or unsecured;

(D) No, because Acme did not agree to give the state a lien on its property.

Subtopic C. Reclamation and Section 546

Hallco ships widgets to Fragile, Inc. on February 2, 2007. The invoice price of the widgets is $5,000. On February 20, Fragile files for chapter 11, leaving Hallco's invoice unpaid.

129. Which of the following best describes the most likely set of remedies that Hallco has on February 21?

(A) Hallco is a general unsecured creditor, and only has a right to receive whatever every other unsecured creditor receives;

(B) Hallco has a right to reclaim the widgets delivered on February 2, but only if it acts within the next 20 days;

(C) Hallco has a priority claim for $5,000, but no right to reclaim; or

(D) Hallco has a priority claim for the $5,000, and a right to reclaim the goods if it acts within the next 20 days.

Subtopic D. Postpetition Transactions and Section 549

Robert Barr borrowed $20,000 from an auto finance company ("finance company") to purchase a car. The debt was unsecured. Robert defaulted on the loan and, shortly thereafter, he filed for chapter 7 bankruptcy. Prior to the bankruptcy filing, the finance company obtained a garnishment order. After the bankruptcy filing, the finance company garnished Robert's wages to pay the loan.

130. Is the garnishment payment voidable under Section 549(a)?

(A) Yes, because the garnishment payment is a postpetition transaction that meets the other requirements of Section 549(a);

(B) No, because the garnishment payment is fully legal;

(C) No, because garnishment payments are exempt from the reach of Section 549(a);

(D) Yes, because the finance company was acting in bad faith.

ABC Plumbing ("ABC") has a business checking account at Second National Bank ("Bank"). ABC files for chapter 7 bankruptcy. After the filing and in the ordinary course of business, Bank honors (i.e., pays) a check written by ABC to Industrial Supply Products ("ISP"), one of ABC's creditors. Bank has neither actual notice nor actual knowledge of the commencement of ABC's bankruptcy filing.

131. Can the trustee in ABC's bankruptcy recover the payment from ISP?

    (A) No, because payment was made in the ordinary course of business;

    (B) No, because ISP had no actual notice or knowledge of the filing;

    (C) Yes, because ISP is a transferee and not a transferor;

    (D) It would depend on whether ISP accepted the payment in good faith.

Assume all of the same facts as in the previous problem.

132. Why would it be important for the trustee to know the actual date when the check from ABC to ISP was honored?

    (A) Because if the check was honored more than 90 days after the date of the petition, then the transaction would not be voidable;

    (B) Because Section 549 has a separate statute of limitations;

    (C) Because the date of honor might be relevant to whether ISP acted in good faith;

    (D) Because the date of honor might be relevant to whether ABC committed fraud.

On June 1, Tom Smith filed for chapter 7 bankruptcy. On June 2, Tom sold Greenacre in Chester County to Mary Jones for $50,000. This price was for the "present fair equivalent value" of Greenacre. Mary had no knowledge of Tom's bankruptcy petition. Mary properly filed the land transfer in Chester County real estate records on June 3. A copy of the bankruptcy petition was filed in Chester County real estate records on June 4.

133. Can the trustee avoid the transfer of Greenacre?

    (A) Yes, because Section 549(c) would authorize such avoidance;

    (B) No, because Section 549(c) protects the transfer;

    (C) Yes, because Section 545(2) would authorize such avoidance;

    (D) No, because this transfer was authorized by the bankruptcy court.

Subtopic E. Subordinating Tax Claims under Section 724(b)

In a chapter 7 bankruptcy, the estate owns property with a fair market value of $50,000. The property is sold for a price yielding $50,000 in net proceeds. The property is non-exempt. The property is subject to a valid tax lien in the amount of $40,000. The tax lien is not for real property taxes. The debtor has $40,000 in priority claims under Section 507(a)(1)- 507(a)(7). The debtor has $60,000 in general unsecured claims.

134. Explain the order of payment of the claims under Section 724(b).

ANSWER:

Assume all of the same facts as in the previous problem, except now assume an additional lien on the property: an Article 9 security interest in the property that secures a debt of $40,000 and that is senior to the tax lien.

135. Explain the order of payment of the claims under Section 724(b).

ANSWER:

Debtor files for chapter 7 bankruptcy. Prior to the filing, the debtor was assessed for an income tax obligation and a tax lien attached to all of the debtor's property. However, the state taxing authority never filed the lien in accordance with the perfection provisions of state law. When the debtor entered bankruptcy, the trustee noticed the unperfected tax lien and moved to avoid it under the Code's strong arm provisions in Section 544. The trustee was successful in her efforts to have the lien avoided and it is now time for the trustee to sell all of the property and pay the chapter 7 claims.

136. Will the state's tax claim be subject to Section 724(b)?

ANSWER:

Subtopic F. Avoiding Setoffs under Section 553(b)

On January 2, the Debtor owes the Bank $110,000 on an outstanding loan. The Debtor has $50,000 in its checking account at the Bank. On March 29, the Bank learns that the Debtor is in financial distress and demands that the Debtor immediately pay off the loan. On March 30, the Bank exercises its setoff rights. At that time, the Debtor owes the Bank $80,000 on the loan and the Debtor has $70,000 in its checking account. On April 2, the Debtor files chapter 7 bankruptcy.

137. Can the trustee recover any of the $70,000 setoff?

    (A) No, because the setoff right was valid under nonbankruptcy law;

    (B) Yes, to the extent of $70,000 under Section 553(b);

    (C) Yes, to the extent of $50,000 under Section 553(b);

    (D) Yes, to the extent of $20,000 under Section 553(b).

Individual Debtor has an outstanding loan to Bank #1. Debtor has a checking account at Bank #1. Within the 90 day period before bankruptcy, Debtor takes the money in the checking account out of Bank #1 and deposits it with Bank #2. Debtor has no loans with Bank #2. At all times, the funds in both accounts are non-exempt. Debtor files for chapter 7 bankruptcy.

138. Does Section 553(b) apply? Whether it does or not, is there anything that Bank #1 can do about this?

ANSWER:

On February 2, the Debtor owes the Bank $120,000 on an outstanding loan. The Debtor has $70,000 in its checking account at the Bank. On April 29, the Bank exercises its setoff rights. The day before, the Bank heard a rumor that the Debtor was about to be indicted by federal prosecutors. On the date of setoff, the Debtor owes the Bank $100,000 on the loan and the Debtor has $50,000 in its checking account. On May 2, the Debtor files for chapter 7 bankruptcy.

139. Can the trustee recover any of the $50,000 setoff?

(A) No, because the Bank had legitimate concerns about the Debtor due to rumors about the federal indictment;

(B) No, because of the operation of Section 553(b);

(C) No, because all of this happened prepetition;

(D) Yes, because of the operation of Section 553(b).

Subtopic G. Section 550: Recovering Property or Cash

Dan Debtor is a businessman. He is eighty-nine (89) years old. He is not married and has no wife or children. He decides to divest himself of many of his assets, including a parcel of real property called "Greenacre." He gives Greenacre to his long-time personal secretary, Adelaide. The fair market value of Greenacre is $800,000. Dan files for chapter 7 bankruptcy. Assume that the transfer from Dan to Adelaide was avoidable under Section 548 of the Code.

140. Which of the following statements is correct?

(A) The trustee can recover Greenacre from Adelaide;

(B) The trustee cannot recover Greenacre from Adelaide because Greenacre is real property;

(C) The trustee cannot recover Greenacre from Adelaide because Dan was motivated by a desire to reward his long-time personal secretary;

(D) The trustee cannot recover Greenacre from Adelaide.

Assume the same facts as in the previous problem. Assume that Dan also gives Adelaide a set of original pencil sketches by Picasso. The sketches have a market value of $1.2 million. He conveys the sketches to her before he files chapter 7. Six months after the filing, the sketches are destroyed in a fire. Assume that the transfer of the sketches was avoidable under Section 548 of the Code and that the trustee now seeks to recover their value from Adelaide.

141. Can the trustee recover the value of the sketches from Adelaide?

(A) Yes, with court approval;

(B) Yes, but only if the trustee can show that Adelaide was negligent in protecting the property;

(C) No, because it would be very difficult to determine the value of the sketches;

(D) No, because there is no evidence that Adelaide tried to hide the property.

Subtopic H. Section 550: Immediate or Mediate Transferees

Debtor ("D") runs a car dealership. Within 90 days of filing for chapter 7 bankruptcy, the Debtor makes a transfer of a portion of its used car inventory to an unsecured creditor by the name of Ace Car Sales ("A") to pay a debt. The used cars were not subject to a security interest, but were wholly the property of D. Soon after acquiring the inventory, A transfers the used cars to Bob's Car Sales ("B"). Bob's Car Sales then transfers the cars to used cars to C's Car Sales ("C"). Assume that the transfer of the used cars to Ace Car Sales is avoided by the trustee under Section 547 of the Code. Assume that both Bob's Car Sales and C's Car Sales took for value and in good faith and without knowledge of the voidability of the transfer to A.

142. Can the trustee recover anything from B?

(A) Yes, because B is liable under Section 550(a)(2) as the immediate transferee;

(B) Yes, because B is liable under Section 550(a)(1) as the initial transferee;

(C) No, because B can use the Section 550(b)(1) defense;

(D) No, because the cars are now in C's possession.

Assume the same facts as in the previous problem.

143. Can the trustee recover anything from C?

(A) Yes, because C is liable under Section 550(a)(2) as the mediate transferee;

(B) No, because C can use the Section 550(b)(1) defense or the 550(b)(2) defense;

(C) No, because C can use the Section 550(b)(2) defense;

(D) Yes, because C is too far away from the initial transfer.

Assume all of the facts in the previous two problems, except this time assume that C cannot show good faith.

144. Can the trustee recover anything from C?

(A) Yes, because C is not protected by either Section 550(b)(1) or Section 550(b)2);

(B) Yes, because C's chain of title would be cloudy under state law;

(C) Yes, because good faith would always be required under state law;

(D) No, because the trustee would have the burden of proof.

Assume that a bankruptcy trustee can show that multiple transferees are liable under Section 550.

145. Can she recover from all of them even if that would result in a recovery that exceeds the property or its value?

ANSWER:

Subtopic I. Section 550: Other Defenses

Debtor makes a payment to creditor X. The payment is wired directly to Bank #1 and then Bank #1 immediately transfers the payment to another bank ("Bank # 2") at which X has deposits. After the Debtor files for chapter 7 bankruptcy, the trustee avoids the payment to X as a fraudulent transfer under Section 548 of the Code.

146. Who is the initial transferee under Section 550(a)?

   (A) Bank #1, because it received the funds;

   (B) Bank #1, because the payment was wired directly to it;

   (C) X, because both banks are considered conduits instead of transferees;

   (D) Bank #2, because it received the funds on the second deposit.

Debtor makes a $20,000 payment to creditor Z. The payment is paid to Z through an accounting firm that has done some accounting work for Z. The accounting firm keeps a portion of the payment ($12,000) as its fee for work that the accounting firm did for Z. After the debtor files for chapter 7 bankruptcy, the trustee avoids the transfer as a preference under Section 547(b) of the Code.

147. Who is the initial transferee under Section 550(a)?

   (A) Z, because the payment is made directly to Z;

   (B) The accountant because she cannot use the conduit exception;

   (C) Neither Z nor the accountant because both acted in good faith;

   (D) None of the above.

Assume the Debtor ("D") makes a cash transfer to X. The cash transfer satisfies Y's debt to X. In an unrelated transaction, X transfers the cash to Z. Z takes for value, in good faith and without knowledge of the voidability of the transfer. D files for chapter 7 bankruptcy and the trustee avoids the transfer to X as a preference under Section 547 of the Code.

148. Which party or parties can use the Section 550(b)(1) defense?

   (A) Only Z;

   (B) Only X;

   (C) Only Y;

   (D) Either Z or X.

Subtopic J. Section 551: Recovery for the Benefit of the Estate

A computer store is in financial distress. Its computers are subject to an Article 9 security interest held by First National Bank ("the Bank"). The Bank's security interest was timely and properly perfected. The computers are also subject to a tax lien for unpaid state sales taxes. Applicable state law gives the tax lien priority over the Bank's security interest. The computer store files for chapter 7 bankruptcy. The trustee avoids the tax lien under Section 545 of the Code.

149. What is the effect of the trustee's action?

(A) It removes the computers from the reach of the bankruptcy estate;

(B) The Bank's security interest becomes unperfected;

(C) The trustee steps into the shoes of the holder of the state tax lien;

(D) The trustee assumes secondary rights held by the state tax lien claimant.

Assume a chapter 7 trustee avoids a prepetition security interest under Section 544(a)(1) of the Code. The trustee was able to avoid the security interest because it was not properly perfected under state law. There is another prepetition security interest in the same property that was created after the first security interest, but properly perfected.

150. Which of the following statements is true?

(A) Section 551 allows the trustee to defeat both security interests;

(B) Section 551 allows the trustee to defeat the second security interest;

(C) Pursuant to Section 551, the avoided lien held by the estate remains subject to the same state law defect and is likely subordinate to the second security interest which was timely perfected;

(D) Pursuant to Section 551, the avoided lien held by the estate is no longer subject to the same state law defect and the trustee can defeat the second security interest.

Subtopic A. Basic Operation of a Discharge

Debtor ("D") owes Auto Finance Corporation ("AFC") $40,000 on a prepetition auto loan. The car which secures the debt is worth $35,000. D files for chapter 7 bankruptcy and receives a discharge.

151. Pursuant to Section 524(a), which of the following statements is correct?

   (A)   The debtor's personal liability for the debt is discharged;

   (B)   The discharge means that AFC cannot act to collect the $5,000 deficiency;

   (C)   AFC can continue to enforce its lien on the car in accordance with its legal and contractual rights;

   (D)   (A) and (C) only;

   (E)   (A), (B), and (C).

Assume all of the same facts as in the previous problem. Assume further that at the conclusion of the bankruptcy case, AFC sues Debtor in state court.

152. What is the most likely result?

   (A)   Debtor will pay the entire $40,000 owed and have no defense;

   (B)   Debtor will respond that its claim was discharged to the extent of $5,000 and will assert the discharge as a defense;

   (C)   Debtor will force AFC to appear in bankruptcy court to pursue its claim;

   (D)   AFC will argue that the loan was agreed to in the ordinary course of business and is thus not dischargeable under the Code.

Individual debtor files for chapter 7 bankruptcy. After the petition is filed, the debtor incurs several more debts.

153. Would any of the postpetition debts be affected by Section 524(a)?

ANSWER:

Business partners (Business Partner #1 and Business Partner #2) individually guarantee each other's debts on a business loan. Business Partner #1 files an individual chapter 7 bankruptcy and receives a discharge.

154. Will Business Partner #2's liability on his guarantee be discharged as a result of Business Partner #1's filing?

ANSWER:

Subtopic B. Discharge in Chapter 7

Frannie Mae, an individual, files for chapter 7 bankruptcy and she receives a discharge. One of her unsecured creditors continues to pursue her to collect on a debt that was discharged. When Frannie's lawyer tells the creditor's collection agent about the bankruptcy discharge, the agent says, "Oh, no. That is not correct. It was up to Frannie to prove to us that she was entitled to a discharge by a statement in writing sent to the creditor's office. Since she never did that, we can continue to pursue the debt."

155. Is the agent correct?

ANSWER:

Debtor filed for chapter 7 bankruptcy. At the time of the filing, debtor had twelve unsecured debts, including a debt to a credit card company. The credit card company alleged that the debtor fraudulently incurred the credit card debt in a way that prevented discharge on this particular debt under Section 523(a)(2). The credit card company followed all of the proper procedures to object to discharge. The bankruptcy court ruled in favor of the credit card company and the Debtor did not appeal. The debtor received a Section 727 discharge and the bankruptcy case was closed.

156. What happened to the other eleven debts?

   (A) The other eleven debts were discharged;

   (B) All twelve debts were discharged;

   (C) All twelve debts were not discharged;

   (D) The other eleven debts were not discharged.

Individual debtor files for chapter 7 bankruptcy on March 10. Debtor then borrows $50,000 from creditor on April 8. Debtor receives a discharge on May 16.

157. Would the $50,000 debt to creditor be affected by the debtor's discharge?

   (A) It would depend on whether the debtor disclosed to the trustee that he/she intended to incur more debt postpetition;

   (B) Yes, because the creditor did not object;

   (C) Yes, because the debt exceeded $10,000;

   (D) No, because of Section 727(b).

Subtopic C. Discharge in Chapter 11

XCM, Inc. is a high-tech startup company that provides real-time financial accounting, bookkeeping, and consulting for Fortune 500 companies. XCM relies on software provided by another high-tech company, GetSmart, Inc. XCM has contracts with about one hundred companies and everything goes smoothly until a software bug in GetSmart's products creates big problems for XCM and its clients. XCM also makes the mistake of expanding too rapidly and has some very expensive office leases that are a real drag on its own finances.

XCM files for chapter 11 bankruptcy. Shortly thereafter, one of XCM's creditors successfully sought relief from the automatic stay in order to foreclose on brand new office equipment that the bankruptcy judge ruled was not necessary to an effective reorganization and in which the XCM had no equity.

After seven months in chapter 11, XCM has its plan confimed. Prior to confirmation, the debtor in possession recovered $500,000 in fraudulent transfers from XCM's major creditors. After confirmation, the bankruptcy clerk officially closes the case.

158. Which of the following events operates as a bankruptcy discharge in XCM's case?

    (A) The confirmation of the chapter 11 plan;

    (B) The debtor in possession's recovery of fraudulent transfers;

    (C) The lifting of the automatic stay on the office furniture;

    (D) The official closing of the case.

Acme, Inc. manufactures widgets. It wildly overestimated the demand for its latest widget and that, combined with a serious SEC investigation into its most recent initial public offering have landed it in chapter 11. After several months, Acme's largest creditors were able to force Acme to liquidate the company and close operations. Rather than convert the case to a chapter 7 liquidation, however, Acme ends up staying in chapter 11 and filing a liquidating plan. The plan calls for Acme to terminate its business after the chapter 11 plan is consummated. The plan is confirmed.

159. Is Acme eligible for a chapter 11 discharge?

    (A) No, because Acme stayed in chapter 11 rather than converting to chapter 7;

    (B) No, because of Section 1141(d)(3);

    (C) Yes, because of Section 1141(d)(3);

    (D) It would depend on the outcome of the SEC investigation.

Assume all of the same facts as in the previous problem.

160. Are any of the Section 523 exceptions to discharge applicable in Acme's chapter 11 case?

ANSWER:

Wayne Futon is a Las Vegas hotel and casino magnate. It seems that his customers were not the only ones doing some risky gambling. Both Wayne and his hotel and casino empire end up in chapter 11 bankruptcy. Wayne files as an individual and his hotel and casino company file as a corporation. One year later, both his individual and the corporate case conclude with confirmation of their respective chapter 11 plans. In the corporate case, the discharge comes into effect once the plan is confirmed.

161. When does the discharge go into effect in Wayne's individual case?

    (A) At the same time — upon confirmation of the plan;

    (B) Once Wayne submits an affidavit certifying that he has paid substantially all of his debts;

    (C) Once a majority of creditors agree the Wayne has made a good faith effort to comply with the plan;

    (D) Upon the court's granting of a discharge on completion of all payments under the plan.

"MMNeatK," a wealthy rapper and music producer, ends up in an individual chapter 11 bankruptcy case. MMNeatK counts among his close friends some people who are connected to the drug trade and organized crime. It appears that MMNeatK might be indicted by federal authorities as a co-conspirator to some of the alleged unlawful activity. After consulting with the lawyer who is handling his criminal case, MMNeatK starts to get nervous about what the feds might find "if they go digging around in my affairs."

Unbeknownst to both his bankruptcy lawyer and his criminal defense lawyer, MMNeatK starts directing his associates to shred financial documents that could implicate him in criminal activities. He then goes to his bankruptcy lawyer and informs him (but not his criminal lawyer) of the shredding. MMNeatK tells his bankruptcy lawyer, "Well, the feds might come after me for this, but I'm still going to get out of my debts in bankruptcy if I just go along with what the bankruptcy judge says, right?" You are MMNeatK's bankruptcy lawyer.

162. What do you need to tell MMNeatK?

ANSWER:

Assume all of the same facts as in the previous problem. Assume that in addition to the document shredding problem, you also find out that MMNeatK is facing another problem: a prepetition court judgment in a civil suit for assault and battery against an obsessive fan who provoked a fight with MMNeatK in a nightclub. In discussing this matter, MMNeatK tells you that he's pretty sure he can get "this lawsuit cancelled in bankruptcy" because he saw a commercial on TV that said that bankruptcy lets people "block most of their creditors cold, kind of like the block I threw on that creep in the nightclub."

163. Is the civil court judgment dischargeable in MMNeatK's chapter 11 case?

    (A) Probably not, because Section 523(a) applies in an individual chapter 11 case;

    (B) Probably yes, because Section 523(a) does not apply in an individual chapter 11 case;

    (C) It would depend on whether the plaintiff in the lawsuit was awarded punitive damages at trial;

(D)   It would depend on whether MMNeatK knew about the lawsuit when he made the decision to file an individual chapter 11 case.

Subtopic D. Discharge in Chapters 13 and 12

Kip Kipper works as an information technology associate at a large corporation. Due to huge medical expenses incurred by his spouse, he files for chapter 13 bankruptcy. He earns a gross salary of $4,000 per month. Kit works with his bankruptcy lawyer to propose a budget covering his basic expenses and his wife's medical needs going forward. He proposes a plan under which his general creditors would receive payment of 20% of their claims. The plan meets confirmation standards under Sections 1322 and 1325 and is confirmed.

One of Kip's creditors thinks it got a raw deal in the chapter 13 case and it wants to challenge Kip in court. The creditor's lawyer reads Section 1325(a) of the Code and says to Kip's creditor, "The way I read the statute, Kip can't do this to you because Section 1328 says that the court shall grant the debtor a discharge of all debts provided for by the plan. Your debt was not provided for in the plan because Kip is only paying 20%. What about the other 80%? No payment is being made on that, so your debt is not really provided for."

164.   Is the creditor's lawyer reading Section 1328(a) correctly?

ANSWER:

Leona Merriweather files for chapter 13 bankruptcy. She proposes a plan to pay her creditors over a five-year period. The plan is confirmed and she begins to comply. Two years later, she returns to her lawyer's office with the following complaint. She has several close friends who filed for chapter 7 bankruptcy around the same time she filed her chapter 13 case. She thinks they are doing much better than she is. For one thing, they've all told her that they've already received a discharge of their debts. She knows for a fact that the chapter 7 friends had less overall debt than she had, but she is pretty sure that is the only difference between their cases and hers.

Leona is frustrated and suspects that her attorney may have missed something when he handled her case. She goes to another attorney, explains her situation, and requests that the second attorney look into her situation.

165.   What is the second attorney going to need to explain to Leona?

(A)   The chapter 7 debtors had less overall debt, so that is why they received their discharge sooner;

(B)   Chapter 7 specifies when a discharge occurs and it is thirty (30) days after the first date set for the first meeting of creditors;

(C)   Chapter 13 requires that a discharge be granted only after the debtor completes all payments under the plan and Leona has not done that yet;

(D)   Both (B) and (C).

Harry Markim was a championship soccer player for many years in the United States professional league. He has traveled the country many times over in pursuit of his sport. In the course of so doing, he has had many romantic relationships and has fathered eight children. He does not believe in marriage, so he is not legally married to either of the two women with whom he has had children.

After his soccer-playing days concluded, Harry invested in several failed business, including a now defunct sports bar. He has done some preliminary research and thinks he might be able to qualify for a chapter 13 bankruptcy (he does not want to risk asset liquidation and thinks a chapter 13 might give him a better chance to hold on to, among other things, some prized sports memorabilia). He has a part-time job as a television commentator for a cable soccer network, so he has regular income and he could qualify under the chapter 13 debt limits.

Harry is very interested in seeing if chapter 13 will help do something about the child support claims. He believes that he should have to pay something and regrets his past wild behavior, but he also thinks that showing a good faith effort to pay back most of his debts in chapter 13 should mean that he gets some relief from the child support claims.

166. Will chapter 13 help Harry achieve his main goal?

ANSWER:

Kyle Crisp was the bookkeeper for a very successful, adult, semi-pro football league. The league employed excellent coaches and had an outstanding reputation in the community. The league even produced some very successful professional players. Unfortunately, Kyle was stealing from the league treasury for about a year. Since he was the only one who recorded and monitored the funds, he was able to hide his activity for some time. It also helped that Kyle had a background in banking and that he had a reputation as a honest person. Once the league discovered the fraud, league officials fired Kyle and then promptly filed criminal charges.

The league pressured the prosecutor to resist any kind of plea deal and Kyle was convicted by a jury. He was sentenced to two years in jail and one year probation. He was also required to pay back all of the stolen funds by a payment to the state. The state then transferred the funds to the league.

Kyle is now out of jail and he wants to start fresh. The league is now more successful than ever and he thinks it doesn't need a cent more money from him. He comes to you seeking advice about whether he can get a bankruptcy discharge if he files for chapter 13 bankruptcy.

167. Can Kyle get a discharge from his obligation to the league?

(A) It depends on whether the league has a legitimate need for further payment from Kyle;

(B) It depends on whether Kyle is sufficiently remorseful;

(C) No;

(D) Yes.

Samantha Seacrest is a website designer who runs a small design company out of her home. She has been struggling financially during a severe economic downturn. She also incurred a lot of credit card debt after a recent divorce and related family crisis. She decides that her best option might be chapter 13 because she has regular income and it would enable her to keep a home that has been in her family for generations.

When starting her business, Samantha incurred an unsecured loan for the purchase of a very expensive computer system that allows her to run her business from a home office while still having the latest and fastest software. The term of the loan is six years which works perfect for her because it keeps her monthly payments reasonable. All of her past payments have been made on time. If she files for chapter 13, she will propose a five-year plan and provide for payment on the computer loan in accordance with Section 1322(b)(5) of the Code.

168. If Samantha does decide to file for chapter 13 bankruptcy, what is likely to happen to the debt on the computer loan?

   (A)   She can discharge it as long as she continues to use it for her business and not for personal, family, or household use;

   (B)   She can discharge it as long as she makes future payments in a timely manner;

   (C)   It will not be discharged because the payment period on the computer loan is likely to be longer than her chapter 13 plan repayment period;

   (D)   It will not be discharged unless Samantha can show that repayment on the computer loan would cause her undue hardship.

Janey Farmer and her family owned and operated a farm in the Midwest. A severe drought and a pest infestation caused great difficulty for Janey and her family. The farm was struggling financially. The farm reluctantly filed for chapter 12 bankruptcy and proposed a confirmable plan that met all legal standards under chapter 12. Six months after the chapter 12 plan was confirmed, Janey and her family auditioned for a reality television show about family farmers ("The Real Farmers of Madison County") and they were selected for the show. Once the show started, Janey and her family raised eyebrows around town when they renovated the house attached to the farm, bought a brand new truck, and took a trip to see the Grand Canyon.

The farm's creditors are now very distressed and believe that the terms of the chapter 12 plan are being violated. They now want to know if they can use Section 727 of the Code to block an attempt by the farm to discharge its debts.

169. Can the creditors use Section 727 of the Code to block an attempt by the farm to discharge its debts?

   (A)   Yes, because Section 727 applies in chapter 12;

   (B)   No, because Section 727 does not apply in chapter 12;

   (C)   It would depend on whether Janey and her family actually intended to defraud their creditors;

   (D)   Both (A) and (C).

Subtopic E. Discharge and Multiple Cases

Rachel has personal debts of $260,000, and a mortgage of another $300,000, secured by her house worth $350,000. In addition, she guaranteed on an unsecured basis the debt of a business she incorporated in the amount of $1,000,000. That business failed, and the bank holding the guaranty (the same bank as holds her mortgage) made a demand that Rachel make good on her guaranty.

Rachel's response was to file chapter 7 in January of 2005. There were no problems, and she received her chapter 7 discharge in May of 2005.

It is now May of 2007. Rachel is having personal troubles, and is behind four months on her mortgage. She files a chapter 13 to reinstate her mortgage loan. She files an otherwise confirmable plan that indicates she will remain current on her mortgage and will cure the default over the three-year life of her proposed plan (her annualized current monthly income is less than the applicable median family income). The bank objects to her plan, and moves to dismiss her case.

170. Which of the following best describes the most likely outcome?

  (A) Rachel will be able to confirm her plan, and receive her discharge at the end of her payment plan;

  (B) Rachel's case will be dismissed because she has more debt that chapter 13 allows debtors to have;

  (C) Rachel will not be able to confirm her plan because she is ineligible for a discharge;

  (D) Rachel will be able to confirm her plan, but will not receive a discharge of the debt under her plan.

Subtopic F. Discharge and Financial Education

Harry filed chapter 7 bankruptcy on March 1, 2006 without the benefit of an attorney. He has filed everything he is required to file, and attended his first meeting of creditors under Section 341(a). His trustee had no questions and no creditor appears then or since. Harry wants his discharge, but he also wants to keep his car, which he bought two years ago, and has three years to go before it is paid off. In his statement of intention, he stated he wished to reaffirm this debt under Section 524(c). He has taken no other actions with respect to his case.

After 70 days have passed since his creditors' meeting, Harry asks the clerk of the court why he hasn't received his discharge, she tells him it is because his file is deficient and that there is a "hold" on it. She doesn't tell him much more because "that would be practicing law." Harry is very frustrated.

171. Which of the following are the most likely reasons why Harry has not received his discharge?

  (A) Harry has not had the mandatory hearing regarding his discharge under Section 524(d);

  (B) Harry has not listed all of his creditors in the papers he has filed with the court;

  (C) Harry has not completed a course in financial education;

  (D) Harry has not submitted his required promise to not file bankruptcy again for eight years.

Individual debtor files for chapter 7 bankruptcy. The debtor's state has not "opted-out" of the federal bankruptcy exemptions and the debtor wants to claim several items of exempt property under Section 522(d).

172. What does the debtor need to do to claim the property as exempt?

    (A) Nothing immediately. The debtor has thirty (30) days after the filing to claim exemptions.

    (B) Contact the chapter 7 trustee and ask the trustee to inventory the property;

    (C) List the property claimed exempt on required schedules;

    (D) (B) and (C).

Sarah Smile is a personal life coach and motivational speaker who travels the country promoting her personal philosophy. She blends self-help with spiritual insights from "New Age" religions. She often speaks to large paying crowds. Her company charges a fee for participation in her weekend seminars and publishes books and articles. Her company employs about ten people. Sarah has three minor children and is divorced.

A serious personal injury accident occurs at one of Sarah's weekend events and several people suffer critical injuries as a result. Because of some sloppy attention to corporate form, Sarah is at substantial risk of personal liability if any of injured participants decide to file a lawsuit. Additionally, it appears that Sarah took on substantial business debt to finance her operations and substantial consumer debt to finance an opulent life-style. Her business and personal creditors are hounding her and there is great concern about the potential lawsuits. Her lawyers have recommended that she file an individual chapter 7 bankruptcy case.

Sarah files for chapter 7 bankruptcy. She owns a house, valued at $2.1 million and not subject to a mortgage. She owns several cars, all of which she paid for in cash. She has household goods and personal property worth $500,000 and a set of ancient philosophy texts that Sarah used in her speeches and in her seminars. The books are worth about $175,000.

Before her bankruptcy lawyer files her list of property claimed exempt, Sarah disappears. She takes some of her followers with her and she leaves no word with anyone as to their location. Her bankruptcy lawyer discovers several items of property that Sarah could exempt in her chapter 7 case.

173. Which of the following best describes the most likely outcome?

    (A) Sarah's children will file a list of exemptions;

    (B) Sarah will lose her exemptions;

    (C) Sarah will not lose her exemptions if she can show good cause for failure to file a list;

(D)   One of Sarah's employees will file a list of exemptions.

Tom Tuna files for chapter 7 bankruptcy. Three years before the bankruptcy, Tom was a plaintiff in a successful class action securities fraud lawsuit. Tom listed his award of money damages from the lawsuit in his list of claimed exemptions under Section 522(l). Tom's state has "opted-out," so Tom can claim only his state's exemptions.

Prior to Tom's chapter 7 filing, his state's legislature reformed the state exemption laws and specifically removed securities fraud damage awards from the list of property exempt under state law. Tom did not know about the state law action. Now that Tom is in chapter 7, the trustee has a right to challenge Tom's claim of an exemption in the award.

174.   What should the trustee do?

(A)   File an objection within thirty (30) days of the filing of Tom's chapter 7 case;

(B)   File an objection within sixty (60) days of the filing of Tom's chapter 7 case;

(C)   File an objection within thirty (30) days after the first meeting of creditors;

(D)   File an objection within (60) days after the first meeting of creditors.

Assume all of the same facts as in the previous problem. Assume further that neither the trustee nor the creditors object within the required time frame or request an extension to do so. Assume further that no amendments or supplemental schedules are filed.

175.   What is the likely result?

(A)   The creditors still have a right to object and should do so;

(B)   The creditors still have a right to object, but the trustee does not;

(C)   The exemption could stand;

(D)   The bankruptcy judge will intervene since there is no colorable basis for the claimed exemption.

Husband and wife each file for chapter 7 bankruptcy. They file individually, but their cases are jointly administered pursuant to Bankruptcy Rule 1015(b). The state in which they reside has very generous exemptions in some categories, but it omits some property that the federal exemptions allow.

The state has not opted-out, so debtors are free to choose either the state or the federal exemptions. The couple are correctly told that under Section 522, each spouse will be entitled to separate exemptions. The wife suggests to the bankruptcy lawyer handling both cases that perhaps it might make sense for the husband to select the state exemptions and for the wife to use the federal exemptions so that they can maximize their exempt property.

176.   Can each spouse choose a different set of exemptions?

ANSWER:

Subtopic B. Examples of Exemptions

In February of 2007, Frank moves from Indiana, a state with a $15,000 homestead exemption, to South Dakota, a state with an unlimited state homestead exemption. Eighteen months later, in October 2008, he files for chapter 7 bankruptcy in South Dakota due to an extended layoff at his new job.

When leaving Indiana, Frank sold his house for $100,000 in cash (he had no mortgage). He bought a house in South Dakota with those sale proceeds, and it is now worth perhaps $110,000. He claims the entire house value as exempt; his trustee objects. Assume that Indiana requires a person to reside in a house in Indiana to claim a homestead exemption, and further assume that both Indiana and South Dakota have "opted out" under Section 522(b) — that is, they do not allow their residents to claim any of the federal exemptions under Section 522(d).

177. Which of the following best expresses the likely outcome of the exemption contest?

   (A) Frank will win, and will be able to exempt the entire $100,000;

   (B) Frank will lose, and will be to exempt only $15,000 of the value of his house;

   (C) Frank will lose, and will not be able to exempt any part of the value of his house;

   (D) Frank will lose, but will be able to exempt the applicable exemption amount in the federal exemption statute found at Section 522(d).

Jan moves to Nevada in January of 2006. She is a doctor, and in December of 2008, a large tort judgment is entered against her. She files bankruptcy in January of 2009. Her house is worth $450,000, and she has a $300,000 mortgage on it. Nevada's homestead is $350,000 at the time of her bankruptcy filing.

When Jan bought her house in 2006, approximately $25,000 of the proceeds used for her down payment came from the sale of non-exempt assets she held; at the time, she had no major creditors, and did not anticipate any. She schedules her exemption as $150,000; her trustee objects. Assume Nevada has opted out of the federal scheme of exemptions.

178. Which of the following best describes the most likely outcome?

   (A) Jan will be able to exempt $150,000 as her homestead exemption;

   (B) Jan will be able to exempt $146,450 as her homestead exemption;

   (C) Jan will be able to exempt $100,000 as her homestead exemption;

   (D) Jan will not be able to claim any homestead exemption.

A chapter 7 debtor filed her bankruptcy petition on April 8, 2010. The debtor invested in real estate partnerships over the years and in 2009, the real estate market hit a rough patch. The partnerships were highly leveraged. Between March 3, 2003 and March 5, 2005, debtor initiated a series of transactions. She made double payments on her home mortgage. She opened several lines of credit at banks around town and then accessed the credit lines to make further payments on her mortgage. Her financial advisor recommended this practice as a good way to build up equity in her home and take advantage of rising home prices.

The debtor also sold a sailboat and applied the sale proceeds to the mortgage. She told the purchaser that she wanted to give up sailing because it took up too much time and money and besides, she said, "I'm not losing a lot of sleep over whether my creditors lose anything. They are all big corporations with deep pockets. They aren't little old ladies living on a pension or the little guys."

The debtor lives in a state with a very large homestead exemption and the transactions initiated by the debtor in 2003 and 2005 will enable her to claim as large an exemption as possible. The debtor's state has opted-out, so debtors in her state must use state exemptions only.

It is now November 11, 2010. The debtor's creditors are pretty annoyed at the debtor's actions over the years and want to try to block the debtor's attempt to claim an exemption in her home.

179. What is the most important issue in the case?

    (A) Whether the debtor's state has the right to have a very large homestead exemption;

    (B) Whether the 2003 and 2005 transactions happened too long ago to affect the bankruptcy case;

    (C) Whether the debtor acted with fraudulent intent;

    (D) Whether the creditors acted prudently in extending credit to the debtor.

Subtopic A. General Distributions under Chapter 7

Section 726 governs the distribution of property to creditors in bankruptcy. However, it does not apply in all bankruptcy chapters or cases.

180. Section 726 applies in which of the following types of bankruptcy cases?

   (A) Liquidation cases involving individuals;

   (B) Liquidation cases involving corporations and other business entities;

   (C) Both (A) and (B);

   (D) Both liquidation and reorganization cases, as long as a trustee has been appointed in the case.

You are an experienced bankruptcy lawyer. Your eldest child, a daughter, decides to go to law school and follow in your footsteps. She passes the bar exam, hangs out her shingle and starts taking bankruptcy cases. Unfortunately, she did not take a bankruptcy course in law school. Through your connections and a bit of luck, your daughter is hired to be counsel to a bankruptcy trustee in a small corporate liquidation case.

Your daughter starts working on the case and one day, she calls you and says, "I'm studying the bankruptcy code and I'm at the part where the trustee sells the property and begins to distribute the proceeds from the sale to the various creditors. I'm pretty sure if a creditor has a lien on the property, they get paid first. But, I don't see that anywhere in Section 726."

181. Where would your daughter find statutory support for the idea that lienholders get paid first?

   (A) Section 725;

   (B) Section 726;

   (C) Section 522;

   (D) Section 541.

Universal Nail Corporation ("UNCO") is in chapter 7 bankruptcy. Tom Turner ("Turner") was president and the sole stockholder of UNCO until ten years ago, when he transferred fifty (50) percent of the stock to the sales manager. Six years after that sale, he withdrew from the business and sold his remaining fifty (50) percent to the corporation, taking back a promissory note secured by assets of the company. He was to be paid in installments over ten years with interest. The sale provided no benefit to UNCO.

Four years after the transaction, UNCO defaulted on the note and became insolvent. Upon a motion by UNCO, the bankruptcy court ruled that Turner's claim was to be subordinated under Section 510(c) of the Code.

182. Where will Turner's claim rank under Section 726?

    (A) Before secured creditors;

    (B) After secured creditors, but before administrative claimants;

    (C) After administrative claimants, but before general unsecured creditors;

    (D) After general unsecured creditors.

Corporation X files for chapter 7 bankruptcy. The trustee collects the non-exempt property and liquidates it. The following creditors have claims: Creditor A has a claim for postpetition interest on a prepetition claim; Creditor B has an allowed unsecured claim that was not timely filed. Creditor B did not know of Corporation X's bankruptcy; Creditor C has an allowed unsecured claim that was filed late. Creditor C had knowledge of Corporation X's bankruptcy; Creditor D has a claim for punitive damages.

183. What is the order of distribution under Section 726?

    (A) (1) A, (2) B, (3) C, (4) D;

    (B) (1) B, (2) C, (3) D, (4) A;

    (C) (1) D, (2) B, (3) C, (4) A;

    (D) (1) D, (2) A, (3) B, (4) C.

Subtopic B. Administrative Priorities and Sections 503 and 507

Debtor, a corporation, makes plastic plumbing tubes that can be installed in residential and commercial buildings. The debtor falls into financial crisis and on May 1, files for chapter 7 bankruptcy. Three days before the filing, a creditor delivers plastic to the debtor. The plastic is used to make the plumbing tubes. The creditor requests that the court grant an administrative expense under Sections 726, 507(a)(2), and 503(b) for the cost of the plastic that was delivered before the filing. The chapter 7 trustee objects.

184. What is the likely result?

    (A) The creditor's request will be denied because the expense was incurred before the bankruptcy filing;

    (B) The creditor's request will be denied because this is a chapter 7 case;

    (C) The creditor's request will be granted because plastic is a necessary ingredient in the debtor's product;

    (D) The creditor's request will be granted because the creditor is a trade creditor.

Eve's Olive Oil company has a contract with an olive grower. Under the contract, the grower delivers, on unsecured credit, olives each week. The olive grower files for chapter 7 bankruptcy. The trustee elects to maintain the contract with Eve's Olive Oil. This is known as the "assumption of the contract" under Section 365 of the Code (see Chapter 7 of this book for more on that.).

Following the assumption of the contract between Eve's Olive Oil and the grower, Eve's Olive Oil has a claim in the olive grower's bankruptcy.

185. What type of claim does Eve's Olive Oil have?

    (A) A general unsecured claim;

    (B) A superpriority administrative claim;

    (C) An administrative claim;

    (D) A reclamation claim.

Atlantic Gas and Electric ("AGE") is a utility company that, due to very poor management, ends up in chapter 7. AGE has power lines and transformer boxes in several counties throughout the state in which AGE is located. State officials want to remove the power lines and transformer boxes in one county in particular. They essentially want to return that county to the condition it was in prior to the installation of the power lines and transformer boxes.

The state has hired a private company to remove all of the power lines and transformer boxes in that county. The lines would have to be dug up, removed and hauled away. The transformer boxes have to be removed and then what remains would have to be covered over with concrete.

The state now wants to know whether it could get an administrative expense priority for the cost of removing the lines and the transformers.

186. What is the most important issue in determining whether the state could have an administrative expense claim in AGE's bankruptcy case?

    (A) Whether the benefit to AGE's bankruptcy case from removing the power lines and transformer boxes is too indirect to be considered an actual, necessary cost of preserving the estate;

    (B) Whether the expense incurred in the removal is a prepetition or postpetition expense;

    (C) Whether AGE intended to abandon the power lines;

    (D) Whether the state qualifies for the special priority given to governmental claimants under Sections 507 and 503.

National Motors ("NM") is in chapter 11 bankruptcy. NM got there after years of quality problems with its vehicles, a massive recall, and fierce price competition from its chief rival. The chapter 11 case continued for three years when it became quite apparent that National Motors could not survive as a going concern. The case was converted to a chapter 7 case. New attorneys were hired by the trustee. They were approved by the court to work on the liquidation.

When it came time for the assets of National to be distributed to creditors, the new attorneys submitted a claim for the payment of their fees.

187. Who will get paid first? The chapter 11 attorneys or the chapter 7 attorneys?

(A) The chapter 11 attorneys because they were hired first;

(B) The chapter 11 attorneys because the case began in chapter 11;

(C) The chapter 7 attorneys because they were the most recently hired;

(D) The chapter 7 attorneys because they need an incentive to work on the liquidation.

Subtopic C. Wage, Tax, and Family Law Priorities

A small electronics company filed for chapter 7 bankruptcy on October 1, 2009. The company has five employees. All five employees file claims in the chapter 7 case. The claims include:

Employee A files a claim for $8,000 for salary earned in August 2009.

Employee B files a claim for $18,000 for severance pay pursuant to a contract signed by the company's duly authorized representative and employee B on June 2, 2009. Assume the employee's right to payment arose on that date the contract was signed.

Employee C files a claim for $14,000 for sick leave pay earned during the months of November 2009, and December 2009.

Employee D files a postpetition claim for backpay arising out of a disability discrimination lawsuit.

188. Which of the above claims would qualify under Section 507(a)(4) as priority claims? If any so qualify, explain the extent of priority.

ANSWER:

Tony Bandani is a stand-up comedian who had a lot of success in the comedy business two decades ago. Since then, his act has grown stale and he gets very few profitable bookings. During his run of good fortune, he spent a lot of money on cars and made some very bad real estate investments. Tony is now in chapter 7. He filed his petition on June 1, 2009. Among the claims filed in his bankruptcy case is a state property tax claim in the amount of $10,000.

Pursuant to state statute, the state property tax claim was assessed on November 1, 2008. It was last payable on the last day of the calendar year in which the tax claim was assessed.

189. Is the property tax claim entitled to priority under Section 507(a)(8)(B)?

(A) Yes, because it met the criteria of that section;

(B) Yes, but only to the extent of $5,000;

(C) Yes, but only if the state can show that the debtor willfully evaded payment;

(D) No, because the state did not attempt to convert the claim into a lien.

Assume all of the same facts as in the previous problem. Assume further that Tony has two more tax claims to worry about. Both of these are federal tax claims.

Claim 1 is a tax claim from the IRS is for withholding of social security taxes that Tony was obligated to withhold from the wages of his long-time personal assistant. The personal assistant was Tony's employee.

Claim 2 is for employment taxes on wages earned by that same employee.

190. Are these tax claims entitled to priority under Section 507(a)(8)?

    (A) Claim 1 is entitled to priority, but claim 2 is not;

    (B) Both claim 1 and claim 2 are entitled to priority;

    (C) Claim 1 is entitled to priority. We need to know more facts about claim 2;

    (D) Claim 2 is entitled to priority; We need to know more facts about claim 1.

Harry and Sally obtain a divorce in 2003. The divorce decree calls for Harry to make support payments of $500 per month to Sally until 2008.

In 2007, Harry files a chapter 7 bankruptcy. His income is below the applicable median family income. Harry's schedules and statements reveal non-exempt assets of $3,000, and an exempt homestead of $100,000. Sally is listed as a creditor owed $5,000 of back support payments, and this is an accurate figure. There is no other priority unsecured debt, and Harry has about $100,000 of general unsecured debt. The trustee has collected the $3,000, but has not sought to sell the house.

191. Which of the following best describes what Sally will receive in distribution from the bankruptcy estate?

    (A) $3,000, plus the first $2,000 from the trustee's sale of Harry's house (which Sally can force the trustee to sell);

    (B) $3,000, plus the ability to force the sale of Harry's house;

    (C) $3,000, less the amount of the trustee's expenses in collecting the $3,000, plus the ability to force the sale of Harry's house;

    (D) An amount equal to $3,000 divided by $105,000.

Zack owes $15,000 in back child support to Debra. Zack files for chapter 7 bankruptcy in 2008; his income is below the applicable median family income. His statements and schedules accurately disclose that he has no non-exempt assets to distribute to creditors.

Debra is mad. After Zack files, she convinces a state assistant attorney general to file a state court procedure to terminate Zack's driver's license for non-payment of child support; this procedure is permitted by state law.

Zack drives a truck for a living. If Debra is successful, Zack will have no way to earn any money.

192. If Zack seeks a bankruptcy court order enjoining Debra and the State Assistant Attorney General from proceeding, which of the following best describes the most likely outcome?

    (A) Debra will win because her actions were exempt from the automatic stay;

    (B) Debra will win unless Zack can show the traditional grounds for an injunction, and that the Bankruptcy Code preempts the state statute regarding license terminations;

(C) Debra will not be held in contempt for violation of the automatic stay, but Zack will win on the injunction against her activities;

(D) Zack will win damages for Debra's blatant and willful violation of the automatic stay.

Subtopic A. Grounds for Denial of a Discharge

Bill Bickerman and Larry Lane were business partners in a video game enterprise. They were both extremely talented programmers with an uncanny sense for the latest game trends. After Bill and Larry produced and marketed their latest hit video game, their business relationship soured and Bill ended up suing Larry. The lawsuit alleged that Larry had converted thousands and thousands of dollars that should have gone to Bill.

Larry responded by claiming that any money that went to him was legally his, pursuant to their business agreement. Nonetheless, Bill recovered a judgement against Larry on July 1, 2007. One month later, Larry executed a deed of trust in favor of Acme, Inc. on property Larry owned in another state. Larry claimed that the deed of trust was intended to be security for a large debt he owed to Acme, but there was no written documentation of the debt.

Bill continued to do discovery to try to find out what assets Larry owed and the location of those assets, but such discovery was difficult. Larry filed for chapter 7 bankruptcy on May 1, 2008. After the filing, Bill objected to Larry's discharge under Section 727(a)(2).

193. What is the most important issue in the discharge objection?

   (A) Whether there was a transfer of property of the estate;

   (B) Whether there was a transfer of property of the debtor within one year of the filing of the petition;

   (C) Whether there was a transfer or property of the debtor;

   (D) Whether there was intent to hinder, delay, or defraud creditors.

Debtor X owns Blackacre in fee simple absolute. Debtor X files for chapter 7 bankruptcy. Within a year of the filing, Debtor X creates with Y a tenancy-in-common in fee simple absolute in Blackacre. Y is not a relative of X.

Assume X created the tenancy-in-common for the purpose of hindering, delaying, or defrauding creditors. The creditors in Debtor X's bankruptcy object to Debtor X's discharge under Section 727(a)(2). The Debtor argues that the creation of the tenancy-in-common with Y does not constitute a transfer.

194. What is the most likely outcome?

   (A) The creditors will prevail because the creation of the tenancy-in-common in Blackacre constitutes a transfer;

   (B) The creditors will not prevail because the creation of the tenancy-in-common in Blackacre does not constitute a transfer;

(C) The Code does not define what constitutes a transfer, so the question would have to be determined with reference to state law;

(D) The creditors will not prevail because Y is not a relative of X.

Individual chapter 7 debtor files on January 10, 2000. Debtor receives a discharge on May 1, 2000. Same debtor files chapter 7 on June 15, 2008. Assume no misconduct or problems in the second filing.

195. Would the debtor be barred from receiving a discharge in the second bankruptcy?

    (A) No, because the debtor was granted a discharge in a case that was commenced on January 10, 2000;

    (B) No, because the second filing occurred after May 1, 2008;

    (C) Yes, because Section 727(a)(8) says the debtor cannot file again;

    (D) Yes, because the debtor received a discharge on May 1, 2008.

Assume the same facts as in the previous problem. Assume further that creditors of the debtor now want to file a chapter 7 involuntary petition against the debtor.

196. Will Section 727(a)(8) prevent that?

ANSWER:

Tom Bateson filed for chapter 7 bankruptcy on October 1, 2007. Tom owned and ran three businesses: (1) Tom Bateson Electronics (TBE), (2) Tom Bateson Air Conditioning Company (TBAC), and (3) Tom Bateson Carpet Cleaning Service (TBCS).

Tom was the sole shareholder for each of these corporations. He used checking accounts of TBE to pay personal expenses. His personal funds were sometimes co-mingled. When he filed his bankruptcy petition, Tom listed some of the corporate debts. No corporate records were kept for TBAC or TBCS, Tom explained, because he could only afford to pay an accountant enough to keep track of the books for TBE.

Between May and September of 2007, there were asset sales of varying dollar amounts from TBE to TBAC, but no dollar amounts were recorded for the transactions.

The creditors in Tom's bankruptcy want to object to his discharge under Section 727(a)(3). Tom argues that he should be excused from the obligations under that statute because, during the time he was sloppy with his records, he was sliding into bankruptcy.

197. Is Tom's defense a valid one?

    (A) Probably, yes. If Tom's financial condition were better, he would have kept better records;

    (B) Probably, yes. Section 727 is supposed to be construed strictly against the creditor and liberally in favor of the debtor;

    (C) Probably, no. Insolvency alone is not a defense to an obligation to keep financial records;

(D) Probably no. Section 727(a)(3) does not allow the debtor to provide an explanation for failing to keep records.

Sally Cheatoff started an investment fund for wealthy individuals. The fund produced a decent return when the economy was good. When the economy took a turn for the worse, Sally felt pressure to produce better earnings. The problem was that the clients she had also had less money to invest and her office overhead and other expenses were increasingly out of control.

Sally decided that the only way to keep her fund going would be to take money from new clients, pool it, and then use that same money to pay returns to old clients.

Sally perpetrated this scheme for two years before she was discovered and prosecuted for violations of state and federal securities fraud, as well as common law fraud. The penalties included substantial fines. Sally filed a chapter 7 bankruptcy petition.

Sally lives in a state with an unlimited homestead exemption and she elects to claim that exemption as well as other exemptions under her state's law.

198. Will Sally be able to get a discharge under Section 727?

    (A) Probably not, because of Section 727(a)(12);

    (B) Probably yes, because there is no indication that Sally did anything improper once her bankruptcy case started;

    (C) Probably yes, although the specific debts to the fraud victims might be nondischargeable under Section 523;

    (D) Probably not. The state has an unlimited homestead exemption and thus Sally is merely taking advantage of an exemption to which she is legally entitled.

Subtopic B. Procedure for Denial of a Discharge

Sam Smith files for chapter 7 bankruptcy. Sam is a carpenter by trade. Sam has ten creditors, including the local hardware store where Sam charged tens of thousands of dollars in wood supplies for his business. The local hardware store is owned and operated by George Brown. George files a proof of claim on behalf of the store in Sam's chapter 7 case.

Sam and George have done business with each other for many years. George purchases his store's inventory of wood from Lumber Merchants, Inc. Sam does not do any business with Lumber Merchants.

Lumber Merchant's chief accountant has heard a fairly persistent rumor that Sam has transferred a lot of his personal assets to family and friends since the bankruptcy filing. He's concerned that George's store is not going to see a dime in Sam's bankruptcy and that such non-payment could have a negative impact on Lumber Merchants.

Lumber Merchants wants to object to Sam's discharge under Section 727 of the Code.

199. Can Lumber Merchants do this?

    (A) No, because Lumber Merchants is not a creditor of Sam;

    (B) No, because Lumber Merchants does not have any direct proof that Sam has acted improperly;

    (C)   Yes, because Lumber Merchants will be affected by the outcome of Sam's bankruptcy case;

    (D)   Yes, because Lumber Merchants is a creditor of George's store.

Assume all of the same facts as in the previous problem. Assume George sends a letter to the U.S. Trustee. The letter contains allegations that Sam has indeed transferred property to his family and friends since his chapter 7 filing. Attached to the letter are two signed affidavits, one from Sam's former wife and the other from his former mother-in-law. He sends the letter certified mail and follows up with a request for a meeting with the U.S. Trustee. The meeting takes place and the representative from that office assures him that the matter will be investigated.

Three months go by and George doesn't hear anything back from the U.S. Trustee. A few months after that, George receives a final order from the bankruptcy court notifying him that Sam received a discharge of all of his prepetition debts, including the debt to George's store.

George goes to a bankruptcy lawyer and asks why Sam got a discharge even though George sent the letter to the U.S. Trustee and even had a meeting with someone from that office.

200.   What is the lawyer likely to tell him?

    (A)   The lawyer will probably tell him that Sam received a discharge because the U.S. Trustee did not find George's evidence convincing;

    (B)   The lawyer will probably tell him that the affidavits were not notarized and that this explains why Sam received a discharge;

    (C)   The lawyer will probably tell him that George should have filed a complaint to object to Sam's discharge;

    (D)   The lawyer will probably tell him that he should have done more to make sure that the U.S. Trustee followed through on its investigation.

Assume all of the same facts as in the previous two problems.

201.   When did Sam's Section 727 discharge likely occur?

    (A)   When the trustee liquidated Sam's non-exempt assets and filed his report with the court;

    (B)   Sometime after the expiration of the creditors' time for objection;

    (C)   Sometime after Sam's bankruptcy case was officially closed;

    (D)   Sometime after Sam certified to the court that he could not pay his debts.

Subtopic C. Revoking the Discharge

Debtor filed for chapter 7 bankruptcy. Debtor filed the necessary petitions, schedules, and statements. There were no misstatements in the debtor's petitions, schedules, or statements. There were no objections to discharge and the debtor received a Section 727 discharge.

Two years after the debtor received a discharge, the U.S. Trustee designated the debtor's case for an audit under 28 U.S.C. Section 586(f). The debtor made a material misstatement during the audit and the U.S.

Trustee can prove that it was indeed a material misstatement. The creditors now request that the court revoke the debtor's Section 727 discharge.

202. What is the likely outcome?

    (A) The creditors will prevail because they can prove that the debtor made a material misstatement;

    (B) The creditors will prevail because the U.S. Trustee was the entity that conducted the audit;

    (C) The creditors will not prevail because the debtor's material misstatement does not automatically result in revocation of a discharge;

    (D) The creditors will not prevail because there were no misstatements in the debtor's petitions, schedules, and statements.

Subtopic A. Dismissal for Abuse and Section 707(b)

It is now November 1, 2008. Fred is in financial trouble. He seeks and obtains credit counseling, and also seeks the advice of a lawyer. After receiving this advice, it appears that a realistic budget would allow him to pay about $500 a month towards his $25,000 of unpaid unsecured debts. His lawyer tells him, truthfully, that under the means test form he would only show an ability to pay about $95 a month (Fred was laid off for most of the last six months, and only recently obtained a stable job that pays relatively well). Fred's median income last year exceeded his state's "median family income" for his family size.

203. If Fred files, and the Office of the United States Trustee (or bankruptcy administrator) seeks to dismiss Fred's case under Section 707(b), which of the following best describes the most likely outcome?

   (A) Fred will *not* be able to stay in chapter 7 because his relatively high ability to repay his debts means that his filing will be presumed abusive;

   (B) Fred will likely *not* be able to stay in chapter 7 because, while his case would not be categorized as presumed abuse, the totality of the circumstances would indicate that allowing his case to go forward would be an abuse;

   (C) Fred will likely be able to stay in chapter 7 because, while his case would not be categorized as presumed abuse, the totality of the circumstances *do not* indicate that allowing his case to go forward would be an abuse;

   (D) Fred will have no problem prevailing on the motion.

Same facts as in the last question, except now assume that the applicable income for Fred was below his state's median income.

204. If Fred files a chapter 7 bankruptcy case, and a creditor (but not the Office of the United States Trustee (or bankruptcy administrator)) seeks to dismiss Fred's case under Section 707(b), which of the following best describes the most likely outcome of the creditor's motion?

   (A) Fred will *not* be able to stay in chapter 7 because his relatively high ability to repay his debts means that his filing will be presumed abusive;

   (B) Fred will likely *not* be able to stay in chapter 7 because, while his case would not be categorized as presumed abuse, the totality of the circumstances would indicate that allowing his case to go forward would be an abuse;

(C) Fred will likely be able to stay in chapter 7 because, while his case would not be categorized as presumed abuse, the totality of the circumstances *do not* indicate that allowing his case to go forward would be an abuse;

(D) Fred will have no problem prevailing on the motion.

Subtopic B. Redemption and Section 722

Margaret drives her car to and from work everyday. She files for chapter 7 bankruptcy. Her car is worth $6,000. Margaret still has $10,000 to pay on her secured car loan. The original loan amount was $12,000. Margaret wants to redeem the car in the chapter 7 case. Assume all requirements for redemption under Section 722 are met.

205. What amount does Margaret have to pay the secured creditor in order to redeem the car?

   (A) $6,000;

   (B) $10,000;

   (C) Some amount between (A) and (B), depending on what the bankruptcy judge believes would be an equitable adjustment of the debt;

   (D) $12,000.

Charles owns a car valued at $5,000. The car is subject to a $3,575 lien. Under the applicable exemption laws, Charles may exempt a $2,425 interest in the car. Charles wants to redeem the car under Section 722. Assume all of the requirements for redemption under Section 722 are met.

206. What amount does Charles have to pay the secured creditor in order to redeem the car?

   (A) $2,000;

   (B) $5,000;

   (C) $3,575;

   (D) $2,425.

Virginia is a full-time emergency room physician and an amateur fiction writer. She does not write for profit. She has never submitted any of her stories to publishers, but she has registered for copyrights on them with the U.S. Copyright Office. Due to overuse of credit cards, Virginia ends up in chapter 7. Prior to bankruptcy, she had offered her copyrights as collateral for a personal loan from the local bank. Now she wants to use Section 722 to redeem the copyrights.

207. Can Virginia do this?

   (A) No, because the copyrights are not tangible property;

   (B) No, because the copyrights are not real property;

   (C) No, because the copyrights are not for her personal, family, or household use;

(D) No, because the loan was a business loan.

Charlotte is a chiropractor. She is very good at what she does and would like to expand her business at several other locations in town. The Wholistic Chiropractic Center ("WCC"), a competitor across town, is thinking about selling its business to Charlotte. Negotiations ensue and finally a deal is struck. Under the terms of the deal, Charlotte is to buy WCC's business and assets for $100,000. Charlotte doesn't have all of the cash she needs to do the purchase outright, so WCC agrees to finance it.

Charlotte gives WCC a lien on the medical and office equipment included in the purchase of WCC's assets. Charlotte has title to the equipment and she is the sole user. Charlotte eventually defaults on the loan and files for chapter 7. Charlotte seeks to redeem the equipment and WCC objects. The medical and office equipment is exempt under applicable law.

208. How likely is it that Charlotte will be able to redeem the equipment under Section 722?

ANSWER:

Barry files for chapter 13 bankruptcy. After about a year in chapter 13, Barry seeks to convert his chapter 13 case to a chapter 7 case and the court orders the case to be so converted. Barry then decides to redeem an automobile. Assume that all of the requirements for redemption are met.

209. Will the valuation of the allowed secured claim in the chapter 13 case still apply or will there have to be a new valuation for the chapter 7 case?

ANSWER:

Subtopic C. Reaffirmation and Section 524

Jay files for chapter 7 bankruptcy in June of 2006. His income is below the applicable median family income. Jay owns a 2004 PT Cruiser, and owes Fran's Auto Sales about $20,000 on it. It is worth maybe $15,000. Fran has a perfected security interest in the automobile. Jay's filed statements and schedules show that he has about $550 left over at the end of each month without counting any car payments.

Fran approaches Jay after filing and gets him to sign an agreement obligating Jay to pay the entire unpaid balance on the same terms as the original contract. This means approximately $530 monthly payments for the next four years. No attorney is consulted, and no court approval is sought.

After he gets his discharge, Jay realizes he can't keep up the payments. He surrenders the car to Fran, who takes it and then promptly sues him for the $5,000 deficiency, relying on the postpetition contract.

210. Which of the following best describes the most likely result of this lawsuit?

(A) Fran will be able to recover the deficiency since she had a perfected security interest in the car;

(B) Fran will not be able to recover the deficiency unless her lawsuit is brought in the same federal court that granted Jay his discharge;

(C) Fran will not be able to recover the deficiency, but will suffer no other consequences;

(D) Fran will not be able to recover the deficiency, and Jay will be able to recover his costs of defending Fran's lawsuit since it violated the discharge injunction.

Same facts as the previous question, except now Fran requires Jay to obtain, and he does obtain, court approval for the postpetition agreement.

211. Which of the following describes the most likely result of Fran's lawsuit under these revised facts?

(A) Fran will be able to recover the deficiency but only if the agreement had several pages of disclosures as required by Section 524(k);

(B) Fran will not able to recover the deficiency unless her lawsuit is brought in the same federal court that granted Jay his discharge;

(C) Fran will not be able to recover the deficiency, but will suffer no other consequences; or

(D) Fran will not be able to recover the deficiency, and Jay will be able to recover his costs of defending Fran's lawsuit since it violated the discharge injunction.

Jane Honda is a personal trainer, aerobics instructor, and yoga teacher. She worked part-time at the local gym, but made most of her income by teaching classes in aerobics and yoga out of her own studio. She was quite popular and taught three and sometimes four classes, six days a week. Two months ago, Jane had a serious accident while skiing with friends. She broke her right leg, right arm, and suffered a severe back sprain. This has taken a heavy toll on her business and she has no personal disability insurance, nor does she have any disability insurance through the gym (since she was only part-time there).

The accident, subsequent reduction in income, and a recent divorce have brought Jane to the brink financially. Jane decided to file a chapter 7 petition and hired an attorney to handle her case. Jane owns a small home with a $200,000 mortgage.

Jane had been in chapter 7 for about a week when she received a letter from the bank holding the mortgage on her home. The bank, noting that she was current on her payments, proposed that she reaffirm her mortgage. When the bank did not hear anything back from Jane in response to the letter, a bank officer called her at home to confirm that she had received the letter and to see if she had any questions.

212. Should Jane mention the letter and the phone call to her bankruptcy attorney?

(A) Yes, because the bank obviously wants to strike a deal that could be to her benefit;

(B) Yes, because the bank's actions could be considered a violation of the automatic stay;

(C) Yes, because the rule is that only the debtor can start a discussion with the creditor about reaffirmation;

(D) Yes, because while the letter would be okay, the phone call would be considered intrusive and thus a violation of the automatic stay.

Hope Andrews files for chapter 7 bankruptcy. Among the debts she lists on her schedule is a $2,750 unsecured debt to an orthodontist, Dr. Roberts. Hope and her husband have five children, three of whom have had treatment from Dr. Roberts (The $2,750 bill is for child #4.). She has always appreciated Dr.

Robert's expertise, kind manner, and flexibility when it comes to payment (i.e., he takes late payments and allows payment on credit.).

After her bankruptcy attorney explains the bankruptcy discharge and her options for dealing with all of her creditors in chapter 7, Hope tells her attorney that she would like to reaffirm the $2,750 bill, both because she likes Dr. Roberts personally and because she wants to stay in his good graces in the event that child #5 needs braces too.

213. Can Hope reaffirm the debt to Dr. Roberts?

(A) No, because the debt is unsecured. Reaffirmations are only for secured debt;

(B) No, because Hope's reasons for wanting to reaffirm are not objectively reasonable;

(C) Yes, but it would have to be a voluntary repayment under Section 524(f);

(D) Yes, as long as the parties comply with Section 524.

Subtopic A. Types of Nondischargeability Claims

Wally Clark filed for chapter 7 bankruptcy on August 1, 2002. Wally has had some difficulty keeping up with his federal and state tax returns over the years. For the taxable year 2001, Wally's federal income tax return was last due on April 15, 2002. Wally filed his return on May 1, 2002 and he at no time sought an extension of time to file. Now that Wally is in chapter 7, he wants to know if he can get his 2001 federal income tax debt discharged in bankruptcy.

214. Can Wally get his 2001 federal income tax debt discharged in bankruptcy?

    (A) Yes, because he filed his return within 30 days of April 15;

    (B) No, because his return was filed late and within 2 years of his bankruptcy filing;

    (C) No, because all federal income taxes are *per se* nondischargeable;

    (D) Yes, because he does not appear to have been willful and malicious in his actions.

Chris Crank and David Denning are very good friends. They went to high school together, played on the high school soccer team, and served as "best man" at each other's weddings. Chris runs a successful insurance company franchise, selling auto, home, and life insurance policies to families around town. David is a trained chef and restauranteur. His restaurants have been successful. David is now convinced that what he'd really like to do is open a cooking school and he'd like for Chris to lend him some of the money to start the school.

Chris asks David to provide a written financial statement before he lends him any money. David objects and says he "is really offended" that Chris would "insult me by suggesting that my school will be a bust and that you won't get repaid." Chris relents and tells David that he at least needs to have David tell him what assets he owns so that he "can make some kind of rational decision on this."

David orally tells Chris that he owns two homes in the area, as well as four multi-family rental properties. David also tells Chris that he will use the rental properties and "some other stuff I own" as collateral for the loan. David tells Chris, "You know me. We've been friends for years. I'm good for the money." In fact, David owns no real property whatsoever and most of his personal property is already encumbered with purchase money loans, but Chris doesn't know this.

Chris lends David the money. The cooking school is a failure and David ends up in chapter 7. Chris files an objection to discharge of David's debt to Chris under Section 523(a)(2)(A).

215. Will the debt be nondischargeable under Section 523(a)(2)(A)?

    (A) Probably yes, because David's statements did not relate to his financial condition;

    (B) Probably yes. Given the close relationship between David and Chris, it is fair to say that David acted maliciously in incurring the debt;

    (C) Probably no, because David's statements clearly relate to his financial condition;

    (D) Probably no, because David's statements were oral.

"Shorty" Winston was an elderly farmer who maintained a herd of cattle on land that he owned. The land was marked by rivers and heavily wooded terrain. Over the years, Shorty had done most of his banking business with First Bank. Shorty ran into financial difficulties one year and asked First Bank to grant an extension on the maturity of a recent promissory note. First Bank did so. Under the agreement on the extension, Shorty agreed to provide periodic financial statements and let First Bank inspect the cattle. First Bank never actually inspected the cattle, preferring instead to rely on a handwritten "cattle count book" that Shorty kept.

About a year later, First Bank conducted a routine audit of its outstanding promissory notes. First Bank discovered that the number of cattle fell far short of the number listed in the "cattle count book." Moreover, First Bank discovered that Shorty never sent the required financial statements. Instead, he sent inventory reports to First Bank. The reports were false. Shorty filed for chapter 7 bankruptcy and First Bank objected to the discharge of its debt under Section 523(a)(2)(B).

   216. Which of the following statements is false?

    (A) Shorty obtained credit by use of a statement in writing;

    (B) The false inventory reports qualify as statements respecting Shorty's financial condition;

    (C) First Bank does not have to show that Shorty had an intent to deceive;

    (D) First Bank has to show reasonable reliance.

Husband and wife were attorneys who ran their own two-person law firm. The law firm specialized in patent law. They chose to run the firm as a traditional partnership. After about ten years, husband and wife encountered marital difficulties and decided to divorce. They also agreed to dissolve the law firm partnership. The husband intended to move to France and paint watercolors of the French countryside. The wife intended to continue practicing law and her prospects for future income were promising. The couple had no children.

The law firm dissolved with six months remaining on its office lease and both the husband and the wife were legally liable for the remaining rent. As a part of the divorce settlement, the wife agreed to pay that debt. The parties labeled that obligation as a support obligation in the divorce decree and the decree was approved by a family court judge.

Unfortunately, the wife mishandled a difficult and very expensive patent lawsuit and was immediately sued for malpractice. While the litigation dragged on, her clients abandoned her and no new ones came in the door. She filed for chapter 7 bankruptcy.

   217. Will the wife's obligation arising from the lease be nondischargeable under Section 523(a)(5)?

    (A) No, because the debt arose out of the rent obligation and is thus actually not for support;

(B) Yes, because the lease was a joint obligation during the marriage;

(C) Yes, because the parties characterized the obligation as a support obligation and the family court approved the divorce decree;

(D) No, because the husband obviously does not need alimony or child support.

Barbara Rates received her Ph.D. in archeology at one of the nation's top universities. She has recently moved to a new city to take a tenure track job teaching archeology at a highly regarded liberal arts college. Barbara has never been great at managing finances and in order to finance her undergraduate and graduate studies, she took out a lot of student loans. Her student loans total about $175,000.

Severe budget cutbacks at the liberal arts college have resulted in Barbara losing her tenure track position. To make matters worse, she is now in chapter 7. The main reason she is in chapter 7 is that while she was a Ph.D. student, she got into the habit of routinely financing expensive archeological expeditions rather than soliciting grant funding. She always felt that getting grants made her work "less objective" since "grants always have strings attached." She often plans ambitious and fairly expensive research jaunts because, as she put it, "that is how you make your mark." Barbara has made very few payments on her student loans even during the time she has been employed.

Barbara has been offered a full-time position teaching archeology at the local community college, but she won't take the position because she doesn't think it is suitable for someone, as she puts it, "with my academic pedigree." At the same time, she is thinking seriously about asking her lawyer to file a motion seeking to have her student loans discharged on the grounds of undue hardship under Section 523(a)(8) of the Code.

218. Assume you are Barbara's lawyer and she has asked you to file a motion to have her student loans declared dischargeable on the grounds of undue hardship. What do you need to explain to her?

ANSWER:

Subtopic B. Nondischargeability Procedure

Aaron Lambert was an assistant bank manager at Second Bank. He was in charge of, among other things, securing and monitoring Second Bank's safe deposit boxes. Bank customers put many valuable items in the boxes: official documents, savings bonds, cash, rare coins, stock certificates, etc. Unbeknownst to the bank, Aaron developed a gambling habit that became increasingly serious. To cover his gambling debts, Aaron started stealing cash and other property from customers' boxes.

Second Bank found out about the stealing. Aaron was fired and, under threat of civil and criminal action, he confessed to the embezzlement. He also agreed to voluntarily repay all of the money he stole (about $85,000).

Aaron filed for chapter 7 bankruptcy. Second Bank filed a proof of claim in the bankruptcy, but took no further action in the case.

219. Will the debt Aaron owes to Second Bank be discharged in Aaron's bankruptcy?

(A) Yes, because Second Bank did not affirmatively object;

(B) Yes, because the debt is less than $100,000;

(C) No, because the debt arises out of embezzlement;

(D) No, because Aaron was acting in a fiduciary capacity when he stole the money.

Debtor files for chapter 7 bankruptcy. Debtor has a tax debt that is nondischargeable under Section 523(a)(1)(A). Prior to the filing, debtor borrowed money from a credit union to pay off the nondischargeable tax debt. The credit union files a proof of claim in the debtor's chapter 7 case, but does not object to the debtor's discharge of the debt to the credit union. The credit union then sues the debtor in state court to recover on the debt and argues that the debt is nondischargeable under Section 523(a)(14) of the Code.

220. Which of the following statements is true?

(A) The dischargeability litigation can occur only in bankruptcy court;

(B) The credit union did not object to the debtor's discharge in the bankruptcy case, so the credit union loses its rights to do so in state court;

(C) The debt is dischargeable because the debt at issue is owed to the credit union, not the taxing authority;

(D) The dischargeability litigation can occur either in state court or in bankruptcy court.

You are an attorney who specializes in debtor-creditor law and bankruptcy. One of your clients is a small, local credit union. The credit union has experienced a dramatic spike in the number of consumer debtors who are ending up in bankruptcy. The chairwoman of the credit union board is concerned about the effect of this spike on the financial condition of the credit union and she wants to meet with you to discuss the problem.

Prior to the meeting, the chairwoman sends you the following communication in an e-mail: "This is something we'll discuss in our upcoming meeting, but I think we ought to have a much stronger presence in the bankruptcy cases filed by our debtors. I think we should set up a system where we automatically object, on the grounds of fraud, to the bankruptcy discharge of almost all of our consumer debtors. As I see it, this would help us improve our recovery rates for present debtors and future ones. It would send the message that we are not going to be taken for a ride anymore. What do you think?"

221. What do you need to tell the chairwoman?

ANSWER:

Subtopic A. Chapter 13 Eligibility

Marty Nichols is a partner in a small interior design firm. As far back as college, Marty has always had difficulty managing his finances and recent health problems have not helped matters. Marty is thinking seriously about filing a chapter 13 bankruptcy. He doesn't know much about bankruptcy law, so he starts doing his own research. He comes across Section 109(e) of the Code. Marty is now worried that he might not be able to file chapter 13 because he sees that it applies only to "individuals." Further research reveals that partnerships are not considered "individuals" under the Code. Since he's a partner in his design firm, he's pretty sure he won't be able to file chapter 13.

222. Is Marty correct?

ANSWER:

Carl is a former automobile assembly line worker who is now retired. Carl fixes cars in his spare time, both because he enjoys it and because it helps supplement his pension. Carl is in financial distress and is considering filing either chapter 7 or chapter 13. He'd prefer to file chapter 13 because he thinks it is the "better way to go morally." Carl has $325,000 in unsecured debt (mostly from a judgment against him in connection with an uninsured slip and fall on his property) and a $275,000 mortgage.

To his most loyal car repair customers, Carl offers a 30-day, $5,000 warranty on all repairs. Three repairs are currently under warranty for a total amount of $15,000, but the warranties are set to expire in ten days. There are no other warranties pending.

223. Is Carl eligible to file for chapter 13 bankruptcy if he were to file today?

(A) Yes, because he is currently under the statutory debt limit;

(B) No, because he is not currently under the statutory debt limit;

(C) No, because he does not have "regular income" as that term is defined in the Code;

(D) No, because we do not know yet whether his customers will have problems with their cars.

Husband and wife have joint unsecured debt of $250,000 and joint secured debt of $3,000,000. The husband is thinking about filing for chapter 13 bankruptcy and wants to completely exclude from his debt calculations the joint $3,000,000 secured debt so that he can get under the chapter 13 secured debt limit of $1,081,400. The husband argues that since he is the only one filing for bankruptcy, the joint debt shouldn't count.

224. Is the husband correct?

ANSWER:

Amanda Grimes filed for chapter 7 bankruptcy on June 1, 2002. The case was uneventful and Amanda received a discharge on August 1, 2002. Amanda is back in financial distress, mainly due to a stubborn problem with substance abuse. It is now 2008. Amanda has regular income from a home-based catering business. Her unsecured and secured debt are under the respective statutory ceilings. Amanda heard on a talk-radio show the other day that "you can only file bankruptcy once every 8 years."

Assume you are a bankruptcy lawyer and that Amanda comes to you seeking advice. She tells you what she heard on her radio program and she wants to know if it is true and if so, how it applies to her situation.

225.   What do you need to tell her?

ANSWER:

Subtopic B. Chapter 13 and Co-Debtor Stay

Marietta is a recent college graduate who is having difficulty finding work in her chosen field. She has a job as a hostess at an upscale restaurant, but she needs more income. She decides to start a home-based business selling decorative candles. She takes out a loan from Third Bank to start the business and her father-in-law co-signs for the loan. She buys inventory from the candle company and starts attending home decorating fairs and craft shows.

The candle company goes out of business and Marietta finds herself in financial distress. She gets a demand from Third Bank to pay off the entire loan balance immediately. Marietta makes no payments. The initial demand is followed by phone calls and e-mails from Third Bank demanding immediate payment.

Marietta files for chapter 13 bankruptcy and Third Bank ceases contact with Marietta to collect the debt. Instead, her father-in-law (who is not in bankruptcy at all) starts getting the letters, phone calls, and e-mails from Third Bank demanding immediate repayment in full.

226.   Which of the following statements is false?

    (A)   Marietta would qualify for chapter 13 because she has regular income;

    (B)   Third Bank should continue to refrain from taking action against Marietta to collect on the loan;

    (C)   The automatic stay in Marietta's case also applies to her father-in-law;

    (D)   The automatic stay in Marietta's case does not apply to her father-in-law.

Sally and Sam are a young married couple. They borrow money from Second Bank to buy their first home. Sam's parents co-sign on the mortgage. Sally and Sam file jointly for chapter 13 bankruptcy. They propose a plan to pay Second Bank's mortgage claim in full. The plan meets all other requirements and is confirmed. After about one year in chapter 13, Sally and Sam convert their joint case in chapter 13 to a joint case in chapter 7. They agree to reaffirm the mortgage debt in the chapter 7 case.

227.   Will the chapter 13 co-debtor stay remain in effect in the chapter 7 case?

    (A)   Yes, because Sally and Sam proposed full payment on the mortgage in the chapter 13 case;

    (B)   Yes, because Sally and Sam are reaffirming the mortgage in the chapter 7 case;

    (C) No, because the case was converted to chapter 7;

    (D) It depends on whether Sally and Sam are acting in good faith in both cases.

Assume all of the same facts as in the previous problem, except that this time, Sally and Sam receive no consideration for the mortgage and the case is not converted to chapter 7. Assume instead that Sam's parents receive the consideration and that the case remains in chapter 13.

228. How, if at all, does this change the result in the previous problem?

    (A) The creditor can seek relief from the co-debtor stay and will likely win;

    (B) The creditor can seek relief from the co-debtor stay, but will likely lose;

    (C) The result does not change at all;

    (D) It depends on whether Sally, Sam, and his parents committed fraud in securing the mortgage.

Subtopic C. Chapter 13 and Property of the Estate

Debtor is a high school gym teacher. Debtor files for chapter 13 bankruptcy on May 1.

229. Is the money the debtor earns from work she does as a gym teacher after May 1 considered "property of the estate" in the debtor's chapter 13 filing?

    (A) No, because of Section 541(a)(1) and (a)(6);

    (B) Yes, because of Section 1306(a)(2);

    (C) No, because the money is a regular part of her income;

    (D) No, because of Section 1306(a)(1).

Jack Dodge is in a car accident. The accident was not his fault. The accident sets him back financially. Jack files for chapter 13. After the filing, Jack receives a check from his insurance company for the damage to his car.

230. Which of the following statements is true?

    (A) The insurance proceeds would be property of the estate under Section 541(a)(6);

    (B) The insurance proceeds would not be property of the estate because the accident happened before the filing;

    (C) The insurance proceeds would be property of the estate under Section 1306(a)(1);

    (D) The insurance proceeds would not be property of the estate because the accident was not Jack's fault.

CHAPTER 13 ISSUES: PLAN AND PLAN CONFIRMATION

Subtopic A. Chapter 13 Plan Provisions and Sections 1322 and 1325

Edgar files for chapter 13 bankruptcy in July of 2006. His "current monthly income" is $1,000, but that is only because he was out of work for five months, and just last month started a new job that pays $6,000 per month (and you may assume that this level of income is well below any applicable state median family income). He has about $4,000 in expenses per month.

His plan as filed indicates that he is willing to pay $100 per month for three years toward a chapter 13 plan. Among the debts listed in his plan is a debt of $100,000 to Zoe, which represents a judgment Zoe obtained against Edgar for fraud in state court several months ago. Zoe objects to what Edgar is doing.

231. With respect to his plan, which of the following best describes the most likely outcome?

    (A) He will be unable to confirm his plan since he has $2,000 in disposable income and only proposes to pay $100;

    (B) He will be able to confirm his plan, and will be able to discharge Zoe's debt upon completion of all of his plan payments;

    (C) He will be able to confirm his plan, but under no circumstances will he be able to discharge Zoe's debt, regardless of whether he completes his plan payments or not;

    (D) He will be able to confirm his plan, and will be able to discharge Zoe's debt unless Zoe timely files and successfully prosecutes an adversary proceeding seeking to declare the debt to be nondischargeable.

Ben files chapter 13 bankruptcy. Ben owes Continental Bank $450,000 secured by a first mortgage on Greenacre. Greenacre is presently worth more than $450,000. Ben proposes a chapter 13 plan under which he would surrender Greenacre to Continental Bank.

232. Which of the following best describes the most likely outcome of Ben's decision to surrender Greenacre?

    (A) Continental Bank will object to Ben's decision and argue that the Code does not allow it;

    (B) The bankruptcy court will convert the case to a chapter 7 case since chapter 13 is not really appropriate for a debtor who wants to surrender property subject to a secured debt;

    (C) Ben's decision will be acceptable to the court because of Section 1325(a)(5)(C);

    (D) Ben's decision will be acceptable to the court because of Section 1322(b)(2).

Clarence Dowdy files for chapter 13 bankruptcy on May 1, 2010. Clarence owes $20,000 to a finance company on a car that he uses for work. He took out the loan on the car on December 1, 2009 and the loan enabled him to purchase the car. Clarence wants to keep the car and confirm his chapter 13 plan. The car is worth $12,000.

233. How would you describe the car payments that Clarence will have to propose under his plan in order for it to be confirmed?

   (A) Payments with a present value of $20,000;

   (B) Payments with a present value of $12,000;

   (C) Payments that would allow the finance company to receive more than it would have received in chapter 7;

   (D) Both (A) and (C).

Antonin is four months behind on his home mortgage payments to the Security National Bank. His mortgage payments are $2000 a month. He files for chapter 13 bankruptcy. Antonin's default on his mortgage meant that the entire loan balance was due and payable immediately. His plan proposes to pay the mortgage debt in full over the life of the plan and to pay an additional $200 a month to cure the default within 40 months.

234. Can Antonin's plan be confirmed?

ANSWER:

Subtopic B. Chapter 13 Plan Confirmation and Section 1328

Ally Forest files for chapter 13 bankruptcy. Ally proposes a plan wherein she would pay 20% of her monthly income over a period of two years and eight months. Her annualized current monthly income is below the applicable median family income. She cannot pay more than the 20% she proposes in her plan and this amount would pay her unsecured creditors 2% of their claims. If Ally's non-exempt property were liquidated under chapter 7, there would not be enough proceeds to pay anything to general unsecured creditors.

Ally filed chapter 7 six years ago and she promptly received a discharge. Two years ago, Ally won a very large lawsuit against her former employer for wrongful termination. She used the proceeds of that lawsuit to invest in a failed real estate venture. She told her bankruptcy lawyer and others that she was filing for chapter 13 "because I want those big banks to keep their grubby hands off my lawsuit money" and "because this time, I want to do the right thing and pay off anyone who would really be hurt if I didn't pay them back."

235. What issues are the most important ones in Ally's chapter 13 plan confirmation?

   (A) Whether her plan satisfies the "best interests test" and whether her plan is being proposed in good faith;

   (B) Whether her plan meets the "disposable income test" and whether her plan is being proposed in good faith;

(C)   Whether her plan is being proposed in good faith;

(D)   Whether she can file for chapter 13 since she previously filed for chapter 7.

Assume the same facts as in the previous problem. Assume the bankruptcy judge finds that Ally's plan does not meet the disposable income test and refuses to confirm the plan.

236.   What does the judge's refusal to confirm the plan probably mean for Ally's chapter 13 case?

(A)   It probably means that the case will be dismissed;

(B)   It probably means that the case will be converted to a chapter 7 case;

(C)   It probably means that Ally will have to amend the plan and resubmit it;

(D)   It probably means that Ally will not receive a chapter 13 discharge.

Jane Napier filed for chapter 13 bankruptcy. At the time of the filing, Jane was undergoing treatment for a non-fatal disease at her local hospital. Jane incurred postpetition expenses in connection with her treatment and the hospital thus had a postpetition claim against Jane. Rather than to have its claim treated as a postpetition expense, the hospital elected to prove its claim in the estate so that it could be guaranteed payment under Jane's plan. Jane obtained prior approval from the trustee of the debt to the hospital.

237.   Which of the following statements is false?

(A)   If Jane receives a chapter 13 discharge, the balance of her unpaid debt to the hospital after the chapter 13 distribution will be discharged;

(B)   Jane's debt to the hospital probably would qualify as a "consumer debt";

(C)   The hospital would not have to file a proof of claim since Jane obtained prior approval from the trustee of the debt to the hospital;

(D)   If the trustee's approval could have been obtained and was not, then Jane's debt to the hospital would be nondischargeable.

Randy Jackson files for chapter 13 bankruptcy. He proposes a plan that meets all of the legal standards for confirmation under Section 1325. Two years after plan confirmation, a major earthquake strikes his town. The earthquake destroys his home and his business. Randy then finds out that he has a serious illness that will likely render him permanently disabled.

Randy requests a discharge under Section 1328(b). Randy can prove that the distribution to the unsecured creditors in his chapter 13 case is equal to the present value of what unsecured creditors would have received in a chapter 7 case.

Among the unsecured creditors in Randy's bankruptcy case is his former business partner. Randy punched the business partner in the face when the two were having a heated argument (several years prior to Randy's chapter 13 filing). The former business partner obtained a civil judgment against Randy for personal injury. The former business partner filed a claim in Randy's bankruptcy case and also objected to his discharge under Section 523(a)(6).

238.   What is the most likely outcome of Randy's request for a discharge under Section 1328(b)?

(A) Randy will likely be granted a discharge under Section 1328(b), but the debt to his former business partner will not be discharged;

(B) Randy will likely not be granted a discharge under Section 1328(b), and the debt to his former business partner will not be discharged;

(C) Randy will likely not be granted a discharge under Section 1328(b), and will be ordered to modify his plan instead. The debt to the former business partner will not be discharged unless Randy modifies the plan;

(D) Randy will likely be granted a discharge under Section 1328(b), and the debt to his former business partner will be discharged.

Liza Levy filed for chapter 13 bankruptcy. Liza's chapter 13 case proceeded normally and she requested a discharge under Section 1328(a). Liza has completed all of her payments under the plan. Liza was not married and had no dependents, so she had no domestic support obligations at all. She completed the instructional course on personal financial management. There was no reasonable cause to believe that Section 522(q)(1) applies.

Before Liza filed her chapter 13 case, she was sued by her neighbor, Stan Sebor. Liza got into a dispute with Stan over his construction of a wooden fence that encroached ten feet onto Liza's property. Stan refused to move the fence even after Liza presented him with a survey that documented the intrusion. After months of heated arguments, Liza decided to take matters into her own hands and tear down the fence herself. Shortly thereafter, Stan sued Liza for willful and malicious injury to his property and he recovered a judgment in civil court. Stan objected to the discharge of his claim in Liza's bankruptcy case. Liza received a discharge under Section 1328(a).

239. Is Liza's debt to Stan dischargeable?

(A) No, because Liza willfully and maliciously destroyed Stan's property;

(B) Yes, because Liza willfully and maliciously destroyed Stan's property instead of causing personal injury;

(C) No, because Stan should not have built a fence that encroached on Liza's property in the first place;

(D) Yes, because Stan sued Liza before she filed her chapter 13 petition.

Subtopic C. Chapter 13 and Postconfirmation Issues

Margaret Morris filed for chapter 13 bankruptcy. Margaret was a smart and capable person, but she had a somewhat difficult personality and a chaotic home life. She had a very spotty work record, although she seemed to be a steady contributor at her new job in the accounting department of a local paper supplier.

Margaret proposed a chapter 13 plan that met all of the requirements for confirmation. Right before plan confirmation, she told her lawyer that she was in line for a promotion at work. The promotion would make it possible for her to earn as much $50,000 a year more than she had previously been earning. Her lawyer advised Margaret to reveal the possible promotion to her creditors and to the trustee so that they could take this into account in evaluating whether her plan needed to be resubmitted. Reluctantly, Margaret took her lawyer's advice and did just that.

When Margaret contacted her two largest creditors, one didn't return her phone call and took no further action in her bankruptcy case. The other creditor, upon hearing Margaret talk about the potential promotion said, "Sure, you think you're going to get a promotion with your employment record? In this tough economy? You must be dreaming. Thanks for nothing." That creditor also took no action in her bankruptcy case. Margaret contacted the trustee and was told that someone would be back in touch with her. She never heard anything back.

Margaret's plan was confirmed and she began making payments contemplated under the plan. One year later, she indeed received the promotion she had talked about earlier. Now, her creditors have filed a request for chapter 13 plan modification under Section 1329. Courts in Margaret's jurisdiction hold that a confirmed chapter 13 plan constitutes res judicata when it comes to any circumstances that existed or were foreseeable at the time of confirmation.

240. Which of the following best describes the most likely outcome of the creditors' request for modification of Margaret's chapter 13 plan?

(A) The modification will likely be granted because it would be unfair not to give Margaret's creditors the benefit of her increased income;

(B) The modification will likely be granted because the creditors had no reason to know that Margaret's was going to be promoted;

(C) The modification will likely be denied because Margaret's promotion was foreseeable;

(D) The modification will likely be denied because only the trustee can request modification.

Karen Haywood filed for chapter 13 bankruptcy. Everything went smoothly and her plan was confirmed. Karen began to make payments under the plan. Karen worked as a customer service representative at the local utility company. She had health insurance through her company. One year after her plan was confirmed, however, she was laid off from her job and when she lost her job, she lost her health insurance. She is confident that she can find another job in her field within six to eight months, but in the meantime, she has to purchase health insurance.

Karen wants to stick with her chapter 13 case and not convert to chapter 7 because she feels morally obligated to complete her plan even if her unemployment means it will take her a little longer to do so.

You are representing Karen in her chapter 13 case. You are reluctant to request modification of the entire plan because you think she got a great deal the first time around and you are nervous that she won't be so lucky if creditors get another chance to extract more money. Karen comes to you seeking advice as to whether she can at least change her chapter 13 plan "a bit" so that she can buy health insurance.

241. Can Karen modify her chapter 13 plan so that she can buy health insurance?

ANSWER:

Chad Hawkins filed for chapter 13 bankruptcy on March 13, 2005. Chad's plan was confirmed four months later and he began making payments under the plan. Chad made all of his plan payments and was granted a chapter 13 discharge under Section 1328(a). The date of discharge was June 10, 2008.

In September of 2008, Chad's creditors learned that his chapter 13 discharge was obtained through fraud and they can easily prove the fraud in court. On July 1, 2009, Chad's creditors requested a revocation of his discharge under Section 1328(e) of the Code.

242. Which of the following best describes the most likely outcome of the creditors' request?

   (A) The request will likely be granted because the creditors can easily prove their allegations in court;

   (B) The request will likely be granted because the creditors' request is timely;

   (C) (A) and (B);

   (D) The request will likely be denied because the creditors' request is not timely.

Subtopic A. Chapter 11 Eligibility

243. Which of the following entities *may not* file a chapter 11 bankruptcy petition?

   (A) A non-profit corporation;

   (B) A limited liability corporation;

   (C) A sole proprietorship;

   (D) An S corporation.

Billy Smith is a mixed martial arts fighter who has had some success in that field. Unfortunately, Billy's fighting gifts did not translate to financial acumen. He used the profits from his success to buy several expensive homes and invest in real estate. He also bestowed lavish gifts on family and friends. Another matter to deal with is a products liability suit being brought against a steroid product that Billy endorsed.

Billy is now in major financial distress. Billy consults with a business lawyer. The business lawyer tells Billy that his best option would be to file an individual chapter 11 bankruptcy petition and then to propose in his chapter 11 plan that he liquidate all of his assets in much the same way as he would if he were to file chapter 7. That way, the lawyer explains, he can maintain control of his assets while still getting most of the benefits of a chapter 7.

244. How would you rate the usefulness of the business lawyer's advice?

ANSWER:

Assume the same facts as in the previous problem. Assume further that Billy has a separate corporation called "Too Bad To Fail" ("TBTF"). TBTF promotes mixed martial arts events, manages the careers of individual fighters, and sells a line of fitness wear with the logo TBTF®.

245. Would Billy be able to follow the business lawyer's advice if TBTF filed chapter 11 instead of Billy?

ANSWER:

Subtopic B. Chapter 11 Trustees, Committees and Examiners Under Sections 1104 and 1106.

The Yankee Mustard Company ("YMC") makes mustard and distributes it nationwide. The company is now in chapter 11 due to the gross mismanagement by its former CEO, Wally Clinka ("Clinka"). Before the chapter 11 petition was filed, Clinka, in an effort to stave off the total demise of YMC, hired Susan

Spiegel ("Spiegel") to run the company. Spiegel and Clinka served together on several corporate boards over the years and they belong to many of the same social clubs. Clinka thinks highly of Spiegel's qualifications and experience.

Prior to her appointment, Spiegel insisted on a clause in her employment contract that provided that she was not to report to or receive instructions from Clinka. She also requested another contract term providing that he was not to exercise any management or authority over her running of the company. Both provisions were included in her contract. Apparently, Clinka has made suggestions to Spiegel from time to time about how to handle various corporate issues, but he has not insisted that she adopt his views, nor has she done so.

Spiegel has run the company capably thus far and she has been free from taint. However, the U.S. Trustee and several parties in interest are skeptical that she will continue to do so in the future. They have filed a motion for the appointment of a trustee pursuant to Section 1104 of the Code.

246. Which of the following statements best describes the most likely outcome of the motion?

(A) The motion will probably succeed because Section 1104(a) requires the court to examine the misdeeds of past management in considering whether to order the appointment of a trustee;

(B) The motion will probably succeed because Spiegel was selected by Clinka and the contract provisions might not be honored by Clinka in the future;

(C) Both (A) and (B);

(D) The motion will probably fail because Section 1104(a) requires the court to focus on current management and Spiegel is currently free from taint.

Lucky's is a restaurant chain based in the Midwest. Lucky's has 50 restaurant locations. The restaurants emphasize casual dining and a family-friendly atmosphere. The restaurants serve the standard American fare (chicken dishes, pasta, steak, salads, pizza, etc.).

Lucky's recently expanded to seventy-five locations and also decided to expand its menu. Lucky decided to add vegan dishes to its standard fare. To make the additions, Lucky's hired twenty-five new menu planners and about one hundred new cooks. All of the new cooks (and many of the old ones) had to be put through extensive training on vegan cooking. The expansion to seventy-five locations was based on market projections of a likely increase in dining out among Midwestern families and the menu changes were based on recommendations from a restaurant consulting firm.

As it turns out, the projections for an increase in dining out have not come to fruition, partly due to an overall downturn in the economy. Neither did the new menu prove to be a big hit, although the reasons for that are unclear. Another possible problem has been the choice of locations for the new restaurants. Some locations worked well and others did not.

Lucky's is now in chapter 11. The same managers who ran Lucky's before the bankruptcy filing are also running it now that it is in chapter 11. A group of creditors has moved for the appointment of a trustee under Section 1104(a)(1).

247. How likely is it that the creditors' group will prevail on its motion?

(A) Not likely, because the current managers have probably not engaged in gross mismanagement;

(B) Not likely, because the current managers have not engaged in fraud;

(C) Very likely, because the current managers have mismanaged the debtor's affairs;

(D) Very likely, because the current managers should not be given a "second chance" to ruin the company and thereby possibly harm creditors.

Liston Steel, Inc. ("LSI") is in chapter 11 bankruptcy. The creditors and the United States Trustee move for the appointment of a trustee under Section 1104(a)(1) and the court grants the motion. The creditors and the United States Trustee then confer and propose to the court that it appoint Jane Jones as the trustee. One year before the chapter 11 filing, Jane was the Vice President for Corporate Affairs at LSI. In that post, she had top responsibility for all marketing and public relations matters at LSI. She served in that post for five years. Jane has an M.B.A. from a top ten business school (graduating first in her class) and, prior to taking her post at LSI, she had worked on corporate strategy and on financial matters for other companies in the steel industry. She left LSI after she gave birth to her first child. She always intended to return to the corporate world.

Jane is thrilled at the prospect of being appointed a trustee in LSI's chapter 11 case because it would give her the opportunity to use her expertise to help the debtor reorganize and it would allow her to get back into the industry without making a long-term commitment to any particular company.

248. How likely is it that Jane will get the appointment?

ANSWER:

Hudnut, Inc. is a tool-making company. Hudnut is in chapter 11. A trustee has not been appointed. The United States Trustee has appointed a committee of general unsecured creditors pursuant to Section 1102 of the Code. The committee has investigated Hudnut's assets and liabilities and the operation of its business. The committee has solid information on the business and financial affairs of Hudnut. It appears that there are plausible claims for corporate fraud and malfeasance that could be pursued against the former officers and directors of Hudnut.

The committee has ideas about how Hudnut can overcome its past failures and what a successful plan of reorganization might look like. There are at least two corporations in Hudnut's industry that are thinking seriously about acquiring Hudnut's assets in a Section 363(f) bankruptcy sale. Now, the committee needs to develop an effective strategy for achieving its goal of maximizing value for the general unsecured creditors. Hudnut's major secured lender has approached the committee with a proposal to work together on a possible reorganization plan that would challenge the debtor in possession's plan.

249. Which of the following activities would be legally permissible strategies for the committee to pursue?

(A) Initiate litigation against former director and officers of Hudnut for corporate fraud and malfeasance;

(B) Work with the major secured lender on the proposed plan that would challenge the debtor in possession's plan;

(C) Align itself with one of the potential acquirers of Hudnut's business;

(D) All of the above;

(E) None of the above.

Assume all of the same facts as in the previous problem. Assume further that three unsecured creditors who are not on the unsecured creditors' committee would like more information relating to a possible sale of Hudnut's assets to a potential acquirer. The committee is concerned that some of the information might be highly confidential, non-public, and proprietary and it has thus denied the request. The committee has told the three unsecured creditors that if they want more information, they will need to get a court order.

250. What is likely to happen next?

(A) The three unsecured creditors will take their demand for information to court;

(B) The committee will cease to distribute any further information about the possible sale to any entity that is not a committee member;

(C) The three unsecured creditors and the committee will devise a method for providing the requested information;

(D) Pursuant to Section 1102, the bankruptcy judge will conduct an *in camera* inspection of the requested information to determine whether any of it is actually confidential, non-public, or proprietary.

Acme Industries is in chapter 11. A trustee has not been appointed in the case. An unsecured creditors' committee has been appointed by the United States Trustee and is actively working on the case.

You represent Second Bank, a creditor that extended unsecured credit to Acme. Second Bank is on the committee. Second Bank has not previously served on a creditors' committee. Second Bank has the following question for you.

251. Which of the following activities can Second Bank *not* engage in now that it is serving on the committee?

(A) Decline to extend postpetition credit;

(B) Seek to acquire assets of Acme;

(C) Give interviews to business journalists about Acme's prospects for a successful reorganization without first seeking permission from the other committee members;

(D) (B) and (C).

(E) (A), (B), and (C).

Section 1104(c) of the Code provides that, in certain cases, the bankruptcy court can order the appointment of an examiner. Other possible actors in a chapter 11 case include: a trustee (where appointed), a debtor in possession (where a trustee has not been appointed), and a creditors' committee (where appointed), and the United States Trustee.

252. If appointed in a chapter 11 case, an examiner typically plays a role most closely analogous to which of the following?

   (A) A debtor in possession;

   (B) A trustee;

   (C) A creditors' committee;

   (D) The United States Trustee.

Subtopic C. Exclusivity and Section 1121

Dueller Madsen, Inc. makes large concrete pipes and tubing used in major municipal projects. Dueller Madsen files a voluntary chapter 11 petition. Dueller Madsen files its chapter 11 reorganization plan 45 days after the order for relief. Dueller Madsen had negotiated most of the key features of its plan prior to filing, but the plan has not been accepted. No trustee has been appointed. Dueller Madsen is not a small business debtor.

253. For how many more days is Dueller Madsen entitled to maintain exclusivity during the acceptance and solicitation period required by the Code?

   (A) 135 days;

   (B) 15 days;

   (C) 45 days;

   (D) 75 days.

Weinrick, Inc. filed a voluntary petition for chapter 11 bankruptcy. Weinrick made wooden and plastic musical instruments for use in schools throughout the United States. Weinrick has long had difficulty adapting its manufacturing and shipping processes to the current needs of its customers (i.e., music stores, school band programs, etc.). Weinrick was in chapter 11 only a short time before the creditors moved for the appointment of a trustee. A trustee was appointed 90 days after the order for relief. Assume that the debtor has not submitted a chapter 11 reorganization plan. Assume that Weinrick was not a small business debtor.

254. What was the effect of the appointment of a trustee on the debtor's exclusive period for filing a chapter 11 reorganization plan?

   (A) Weinrick has 30 days of exclusivity left;

   (B) Weinrick's exclusive period for filing a plan terminates;

   (C) Weinrick's exclusive period for filing a plan terminates if a party in interest in the case can show cause;

   (D) Weinrick has 90 days of exclusivity left.

Corporate debtor files for chapter 11 bankruptcy. The debtor is not a small business debtor. Creditors have serious concerns about current management and about the prospects for a successful reorganization. The creditors move for the appointment of a trustee. The request is denied. The creditors then move to reduce the debtor's exclusivity period under Section 1121(d)(1) of the Code.

255. Which of the following pieces evidence, if proved, would be effective in helping the creditors establish cause to reduce the debtor's exclusivity period under Section 1121(d)(1)?

(A) Evidence that the debtor is managing to pay its trade creditors on time;

(B) Evidence that the debtor has made little or no progress in arranging long-term financing;

(C) Evidence that the debtor's business is large and complex;

(D) Evidence that the debtor has demonstrated good faith in its dealings with creditors.

Subtopic D. Non-Recourse Claims and Section 1111(b)

Grant Bank is a secured creditor in a chapter 11 bankruptcy case. Grant Bank has a non-recourse mortgage on Blackacre. The mortgage secures a debt of $800,000. Blackacre is zoned for the development of small parcels, but there is a rezoning application pending with the city which would allow for the development of larger parcels. Blackacre is currently valued at $600,000, but its value is expected to rise after the rezoning application is granted because the development of larger parcels will bring a higher price when the property is eventually sold.

The chapter 11 reorganization has placed Grant Bank's claim in its own class. Grant Bank makes an election to have its claim treated under Section 1111(b).

256. What will be the likely result of Grant Bank's election?

(A) Grant Bank will lose its $200,000 deficiency claim;

(B) Grant Bank will lose its voting rights as an unsecured creditor;

(C) Grant Bank's will lose its right to receive a distribution on its unsecured claim;

(D) (A) and (B) only;

(E) (A), (B), and (C).

Assume all of the same facts as in the previous problem. Assume now that Grant Bank's mortgage document contains, among other things, two provisions. Provision 1 states: "In no event shall Grant Bank have the right to recover any deficiency from the debtor as a personal liability on this debt." Provision 2 states: "Furthermore, in no event shall any insolvency code, statute, or similar provision under state or federal law operate so as to bifurcate Grant Bank's claim on this debt." Assume also that the mortgage has a higher interest rate solely because it was a non-recourse loan.

257. Will Grant Bank's claim be affected by Section 1111(b)?

(A) No, because of mortgage provision 1;

(B) No, because of mortgage provision 2;

(C) Yes, because Section 1111(b) overrides mortgage provision 1 and mortgage provision 2;

(D) Yes, as long as Grant Bank makes its Section 1111(b) election within 180 day the filing of the petition.

Greenacre is property of the estate in a chapter 11 bankruptcy case. Greenacre is subject to a $1 million secured debt. The value of Greenacre is $500,000. Greenacre's value is depressed because of the recent discovery on the property of hazardous waste left over from a time when Greenacre was used as the site of a truck manufacturing plant. Greenacre's owner has been under federal and state environmental statutory mandates to remove the hazardous waste from the property. Fortunately, the waste was stored in drums under the land's surface and thus the potential long-term damage to Greenacre is minimal. The owner intends to meet all federal and state mandates requiring removal of the waste. Current estimates are that the value of Greenacre will appreciate once the environmental hazard is removed.

The secured debt on Greenacre has been placed in its own class in the chapter 11 case. The secured debt on Greenacre is non-recourse. The creditor holding the secured debt on Greenacre elects treatment under Section 1111(b).

258. What is the effect of the secured creditor's Section 1111(b) election on the debtor's chapter 11 plan?

(A) The plan must provide assurances to the secured creditor that the debtor will comply with nonbankruptcy rules and restrictions relating to the debtor's future use of the property;

(B) The plan must provide for the payment equal to the value of Greenacre ($500,000);

(C) The plan must provide for an immediate liquidation sale of Greenacre;

(D) The plan must provide for at least the full face value of the secured claim ($1 million).

Subtopic E. Dismissal or Conversion under Section 1112

Max Battata filed for chapter 11 bankruptcy. In verified schedules attached to his chapter 11 petition, Max stated that the value of his home was zero. He also denied that he had transferred property during the year preceding the filing. Neither statement was true. In fact, the home had substantial value and Max transferred it to a newly created revocable trust for no consideration seven months prior to filing his chapter 11 case. Max admitted that the purpose of the transfer was to keep the property safe from creditors.

Max has now filed a motion to convert his chapter 11 case to a case under chapter 7. Assume that Max's disposable income is low enough to allow him to file under chapter 7 (i.e., he does not have enough disposable income to make payments under a chapter 13 plan). Assume further that Max's debts are primarily consumer debts.

259. Can Max convert his case from chapter 11 to chapter 7?

(A) Probably yes, because Max would be able to meet the means test in Section 707(b);

(B) Probably yes, because Section 1112(a) does not provide otherwise;

(C) Probably no, because there is evidence that Max is a bad faith debtor;

(D) It would depend on whether Max filed his motion within 180 days of the chapter 11 filing.

Sarah Robinson filed for chapter 11 bankruptcy one year ago. At the time of the chapter 11 filing, Sarah was the most talented cartoonist on staff at a kids' television network. While she was enjoying a lucrative income and was in constant demand for her innovative cartoon work, Sarah lived way beyond her means and she ended up in chapter 11. Sarah was an only child. Both of her parents are deceased and she has no significant connections to any cousins, aunts, or other extended family members.

Since filing her chapter 11 case, Sarah and her attorney now realize that chapter 11 was not the optimal chapter for her situation. They believe that chapter 13 would work better for her. However, Sarah has contracted a serious and chronic nerve disorder that severely restricts her ability to work and she will likely be so restricted for the foreseeable future. Sarah has not applied for any unemployment benefits. Nor can she obtain any assistance from her extended family. Sarah wants to convert her case from chapter 11 to chapter 13. She meets the chapter 13 debt limits under Section 109(e).

260. What is the main obstacle to Sarah's being able to convert from chapter 11 to chapter 13?

ANSWER:

Candell's Soup Company ("CSC") is in a chapter 11 involuntary bankruptcy case. CSC has been poorly managed for years and has thus failed to take advantage of trends in consumer demand for quick, easy meals. CSC's creditors filed the involuntary chapter 11 case against CSC in order to force it to reorganize. CSC's creditors believe that the fundamental business of CSC is salvageable. CSC's creditors think that a reorganization, not a liquidation, would maximize value for creditors.

CSC's creditors moved for the appointment of a trustee in the case, but the motion was rejected. The debtor in possession (mostly the same management team that has run the company over the last three to five years) remains in control. The debtor in possession has concluded that the creditors are wrong. The debtor in possession sincerely believes that a quick and efficient liquidation of the company's assets is the optimal outcome for CSC. The debtor in possession has filed a motion to convert the case to a case under chapter 7.

261. What is the most important issue the court will need to decide in determining whether to grant the debtor in possession's motion?

   (A) Whether cause exists for the conversion;

   (B) Whether CSC's creditors filed the involuntary chapter 11 in bad faith;

   (C) Which entity, as between CSC's creditors and the debtor in possession, is in a superior position to judge what is the optimal solution for the company;

   (D) Whether the debtor in possession filed the motion for conversion in good faith.

The ChockyWocky Cookie Company ("CCC') makes chocolate chip cookies and has a string of franchise stores in malls and tourist destinations throughout the United States. After a burst of rapid expansion and a slump in consumer demand, CCC ends up in chapter 11 bankruptcy. CCC struggles to effectuate a reorganization plan and finally its creditors file a motion to dismiss the case for cause. The creditors are not willing to consent to any continuances and no compelling circumstances exist that would prevent the bankruptcy court from meeting any time limits with respect to the motion.

262. What is the time limit, if any, for the court to commence a hearing on the creditors' motion to dismiss?

(A) 30 days;

(B) 60 days;

(C) 90 days;

(D) There are no set time limits, but the movant can request such limits if it can show that a failure to promptly hear the matter could result in diminution of the estate.

Gordon's Steakhouse, Inc. (Gordon's) is a chain of family-friendly restaurants throughout the United States. Gordon's is a well-run company from a managerial perspective and is financially solvent (i.e., its assets exceed its liabilities). Nonetheless, Gordon's is seriously contemplating filing for chapter 11 bankruptcy. The sole reason for the filing is that Gordon's is facing a large claim for trademark infringement brought against it by a rival national chain restaurant. Gordon's recently adopted, as its new trademark, a symbol of a cow standing at a barbeque grill with a hat and apron cooking steaks over an open flame. The rival restaurant chain contends that Gordon's willfully and maliciously stole its trademark and it has sued Gordon's in federal court. Gordon would be filing chapter 11 to frustrate the prosecution of the trademark claim.

Before, during, and after the possible chapter 11 filing, Gordon's expects to continue normal business operations. Moreover, it has not defaulted on any of its credit obligations, including its leases. Gordon's creditors are distressed at the prospect of being subjected to chapter 11 and want no part of it. They are prepared to promptly file a motion to dismiss the chapter 11 case.

Assume that Gordon's proceeds with its chapter 11 filing and that the creditors promptly file a motion to dismiss the case under Section 1112 of the Code.

263. How likely is it that the creditors will prevail on their motion?

(A) Not likely, because Gordon's action is not listed among the possible grounds for cause to dismiss in Section 1112(b)(4);

(B) Very likely, because Gordon's is technically solvent and thus has no need for chapter 11 relief;

(C) Not likely, because there is no Code section that expressly authorizes a court to dismiss a chapter 11 case on the grounds that it was not filed in good faith;

(D) Very likely, because the requirement of good faith is an implied condition for the filing of a chapter 11 case.

Corporate debtor files for chapter 11 bankruptcy. Corporate debtor requests dismissal under Section 1112(b) on the grounds of cause. After notice and a hearing, the dismissal is granted.

264. Which of the following is *not* an effect of the dismissal?

(A) The dismissal prejudices the debtor with regard to the filing of a subsequent petition;

(B) The debtor is released from the bankruptcy case;

(C) Property of the estate is revested in the entity in which the property was vested immediately before the filing;

(D) The nonbankruptcy law collection rights of creditors are no longer stayed.

Subtopic F. Benefit and Labor Claims under Sections 1113 and 1114

The Acme Paper Company ("Acme") has been in business for forty-five years. Throughout most of those years, Acme has been profitable. Recently, however, the company has taken a downturn financially, mostly due to three factors: 1) increased competition from foreign firms, 2) higher energy and labor costs, and 3) the trend toward electronic communications and digital data storage.

Acme has always had a unionized workforce and the union has negotiated a collective bargaining agreement with Acme that has more favorable terms for workers than any other company in the industry. Included in the collective bargaining agreement is a employee benefit pension plan that is similar in terms of its generosity to Acme's workers. The provisions on vesting are very favorable to Acme's workers and the overall financial contribution made to the worker's pensions exceeds industry norms by approximately 20%.

Acme would like to file for chapter 11 bankruptcy and then immediately move to modify the employee benefit pension plan to bring it more in line with the financial condition of the company and in accordance with industry norms.

265. Would Section 1113 of the Code govern Acme's attempt to modify the employee benefit pension plan?

(A) Yes, because the employee benefit pension plan is a part of the collective bargaining agreement;

(B) Yes, because the employee benefit pension plan is not within the industry norm;

(C) No, because employee benefit pension plans are not included in Section 1113;

(D) No, because Acme's filing would be dismissed as a bad faith filing.

Dearheart, Inc. is in financial trouble; indeed, it is insolvent. It has a contract with its former employees that permits it unilaterally to modify the benefits it provides those retirees, and it does so during July of 2007. The modifications do not assist it any, and in August of 2007 it files for chapter 11. It moves to assume the contract with its retirees, as modified before the filing. There are no defaults under the agreement as modified. A ragtag group of former employees oppose the change.

266. Which of the following best describes the most likely outcome of the motion?

(A) Dearheart will be able to assume the contract without making any changes;

(B) Dearheart will be able to assume the contract only if it restores the contract to its premodification status;

(C) Dearheart will be able to assume the contract only if the court finds that, on balance, Dearheart needs the modifications to survive in business more than the retirees need the benefits lost through modifications;

(D) Dearheart will be unable to assume the contract.

Spernco Industries ("Spernco") filed for chapter 11 bankruptcy. Six months prior to the filing, Spernco reduced its workforce. Under the reduction plan, fifty of its employees were terminated. Five of the terminated employees were given a severance package. The severance package included separation pay, a car allowance, and payment of health insurance premiums. Spernco described the payment of the health insurance premiums as "part of an early retirement package." The severance plan package was not covered by a collective bargaining agreement.

When Spernco filed chapter 11, it stopped making the health insurance premium payments to the five employees. The five employees filed suit in bankruptcy court. The employees argued that Section 1114 of the Code applied to the health insurance premium payments.

267. Are the employees making a credible argument in light of the language of Section 1114?

ANSWER:

Subtopic G. Small Business Debtors

Consolidated Food Corporation ("CFC") is a fast food chain with five restaurant locations, all of which are located in a small town. Due to market downturns and serious labor problems, CFC has had quite serious cash flow difficulties of late. One of its trade creditors, Midwest Beef Supply, has threatened to withhold shipments unless CFC makes timely payments on future deliveries. CFC's president, Sherry Barber ("Barber"), recently loaned CFC $2 million to help stabilize and improve cash flow. The loan hasn't helped much and CFC continues to struggle.

CFC files a petition for chapter 11 bankruptcy. At the time of the filing, CFC has not repaid any of the $2 million it owes Barber and CFC owes $1 million in unsecured and secured debt to other creditors.

268. Would CFC be considered a "small business debtor" under the Code?

(A) Yes, because CFC is not a national chain. All of the stores are local;

(B) No, because CFC has not elected "small business debtor" status under the Code;

(C) No, because CFC is over the applicable debt limit;

(D) Yes, because CFC is under the applicable debt limit.

Assume all of the same facts as in the previous problem. Assume that CFC goes into chapter 11 as a small business debtor. Six weeks later, the United States Trustee appoints an unsecured creditors' committee.

269. What is the effect of the United States Trustee's appointment of an unsecured creditors' committee?

(A) CFC must withdraw its original chapter 11 petition and file a non-small business chapter 11 petition within 90 days;

(B) CFC is no longer a small business debtor, but it does not need to file another petition;

    (C)   The bankruptcy court will hold an immediate hearing on whether CFC will remain a small business debtor;

    (D)   CFC is no longer a small business debtor and the debtor in possession must meet with the unsecured creditors' committee within 120 days of the appointment of the committee.

Blatt Tomato Company ("BTC") files for chapter 11 bankruptcy. BTC is a small business debtor under Section 101(51D). BTC begins to work on its plan of reorganization, but faces several crises of various kinds. It is now 150 days after the filing of the chapter 11 petition and BTC has not submitted its plan.

270.   For how many more days does BTC have the advantage of exclusivity?

    (A)   90 days;

    (B)   30 days;

    (C)   180 days;

    (D)   60 days.

Subtopic H. Individuals and Chapter 11

Rex Rockney is an actor who stars in action movies. The movies are highly profitable at the box office and Rex enjoys a very luxurious lifestyle. Unfortunately and incredibly, Rex has spent more money than he earns over the past several years. He is now in chapter 11 bankruptcy. When Rex entered bankruptcy, he had substantial debts for alimony to his three ex-wives. His chapter 11 plan makes provisions for him to pay these debts in full over the life of the plan. Rex's film career continues to thrive. He has now hired a new accountant who imposes strict controls on Rex's disposable income.

After Rex went into chapter 11, he got married again. He married a fellow film star, Andrealina Storm. Andrealina has stared in a couple of successful movies, mostly in supporting roles. She earns much less than Rex and the expected trajectory of her career pales in comparison to Rex's, particularly when it comes to earning potential. The marriage between Rex and Andrealina lasted five months. Neither Rex nor Andrealina have any children. As a part of the divorce settlement, Rex agreed to pay Andrealina $1 million in alimony payments over the course of two years.

Although the two rarely see each other in person, a lot of bitterness remains from their brief marriage and abrupt divorce. Rex would like to stop making payments to Andrealina altogether and take his chances that the bankruptcy court would, as he puts it, "call him on it." Rex's thinking is that he shouldn't have to pay Andrealina anything because he is in bankruptcy and she is capable of earning money on her own. Rex comes to you and asks you whether he ought to just stop paying Andrealina and if so, what the risks of that course of action might be. Rex's chapter 11 plan has not yet been confirmed.

271.   What do you need to tell Rex in order to properly advise him in this situation?
ANSWER:

Assume all of the same facts as in the previous problem, except now assume that Rex's plan has been confirmed. Assume further that Rex heeds your advice and continues to pay Andrealina as agreed. Assume further that Rex is very close to making all of his payments in accordance with his chapter 11 plan and that he has fulfilled all other duties required of an individual chapter 11 debtor. Now, Rex wants to know when he gets his discharge.

272. What do you need to tell him?

(A) He will receive a discharge when he is granted a discharge upon completing all of his plan payments;

(B) The discharge occurred by operation of law at the time his chapter 11 plan was confirmed;

(C) The discharge occurs no later than sixty days after the creditors certify to the court that he has made his last payment under the plan;

(D) He receives a discharge when his case is officially closed by the clerk of the bankruptcy court.

Sammy Wentworth is a rock concert promoter. He handles some of the biggest acts in the world of rock music and makes a very good income. Due to severe financial fallout from lawsuits filed against him by several rock music artists, he files for chapter 11 bankruptcy on August 14.

273. Is the money Sam earns after August 14 considered "property of the estate" in his chapter 11 case?

ANSWER:

Subtopic I. Single Asset Real Estate Cases

TopFlight, Ltd. is a limited partnership whose only asset is an office building in the middle of the city. The office building is subject to a mortgage in favor of United Bank. The office building has a 45% occupancy rate. Many of the tenants are in default on rent. There are other buildings in the immediate area that have the same problems.

TopFlight is in serious financial difficulty. It has little or no cash flow. As a result, it cannot make its regular payments, nor can it pay the interest that is rapidly accumulating on the debt. TopFlight also cannot remain current on property taxes. United Bank is threatening foreclosure. TopFlight files for chapter 11 bankruptcy in order to stall the foreclosure. Since the mortgage debt is rising and the market value of the building is declining, United Bank is undersecured. The building is worth $9 million and the debt has ballooned to $17 million. TopFlight has few unsecured creditors and the claims of those creditors are small compared to United Bank's claim.

The debtor proposes a plan in which United Bank will be paid $9 million with interest over a thirty-five year period. Under the plan, the $8 million unsecured deficiency is classified separately. United Bank intends to vote against the plan, but the bankruptcy court will probably confirm it if it meets essential confirmation requirements. United Bank wants to foreclose on the property as soon as possible so that it can sell it quickly and thus reduce any further financial loss. TopFlight, on the other hand, believes that a rental market rebound is close and wants to keep the office building in its portfolio so that it can profit when the good times return. Assume that TopFlight has been in bankruptcy for twenty-eight days.

274. Which of the following would be the best legal strategy for United Bank to pursue if it wants to frustrate TopFlight's plans?

(A) File a foreclosure action in state court;

(B) Challenge the constitutionality of TopFlight's bankruptcy filing;

(C) Argue that TopFlight obtained the mortgage through fraud;

(D) Seek to have the automatic stay lifted on the grounds that the chapter 11 filing was not filed in good faith.

Assume all of the same facts as in the previous problem. Assume that United Bank files a motion to have the automatic stay lifted on the grounds that the chapter 11 filing was not filed in good faith. Assume further that United Bank's motion is denied by the bankruptcy judge. Assume that TopFlight has now been in chapter 11 for forty-five days and that TopFlight' case is still a single-asset real estate case.

275. How many more days does TopFlight have to either a file a plan or begin making monthly payments to United Bank?

(A) 15 days;

(B) 75 days;

(C) 45 days;

(D) None of the above.

Advent, Inc. ("Advent") is a high tech start up company that creates and develops software for navigation components on commercial airplanes. Until recently, Advent leased office space for $20,000 a month. Advent's software has been extremely profitable and the business has been successful. Advent recently used its surplus income to buy an office building so that it would not have to continue paying rent to a landlord who was only marginally cooperative in meeting Advent's specialized needs. Advent had no trouble finding tenants to occupy the offices that Advent was not using. Advent financed the purchase by offering a mortgage to the Second Bank. At that time, the building was worth $12 million. Advent paid $2 million in cash and took out a $10 million mortgage for the difference. Advent owned no other real property.

Advent developed and marketed a new software product it believed would revolutionize commercial air navigation. Advent invested most of its resources (both human and financial) in the development of the new product and it bet that the product would bring huge financial rewards. Unfortunately, the new software product contained a serious latent defect and Advent's investment went sour. The failed product caused Advent's financial position to become quite precarious, but it continued on with its main business.

Meanwhile, Advent's purchase of the office building presented other problems. Advent did a lousy job as a landlord. Additionally, many of the tenants who signed leases defaulted when the economy went into a downturn. Advent has filed for chapter 11 bankruptcy. The office building is now worth $7 million and the mortgage is now $9 million.

276. Will Advent's filing be considered a single asset real estate case under the Code?

(A) No, because Advent is a high tech company and not a manufacturing company;

(B) No, because the mortgage debt of $9 million exceeds the applicable statutory limit;

(C) No, because Advent continued to conduct substantial business other then being a landlord;

(D) Yes, because Advent focused most of its attention before the filing on a single asset, the new software product.

Maple Street Homes, Inc. ("MSI") is a large home builder. MSI owns an eighty-five percent interest in each of twenty-five affiliated companies. Each of the affiliated companies owns separate real estate development projects for the construction of single-family homes and condominiums. Each affiliate researches and purchases land, conducts planning and construction of homes, markets and sells the homes and maintains each development. MSI and its affiliated companies have filed for chapter 11 bankruptcy. MSI's creditors want the bankruptcy court to rule that MSI's filing should be treated as a single asset real estate case under Sections 101(51B) and 362(d)(3).

277. What would be the best argument in favor of the creditor's legal position?

(A) The debtors own the underlying real property. Thus, they qualify as single asset debtors because even if they have other substantial operations, those operations are tied to the eventual sale of the land;

(B) Sections 101(51B) and 362(d)(3) should cover virtually all debtors who purchase, sell, market, or lease real estate since those creditors in those situations are usually exposed to volatile market risks;

(C) Sections 101(51B) and 362(d)(3) should cover debtors whose real estate activities might have potential for fraud and MSI's corporate structure gives rise to concerns of that nature;

(D) MSI's business model resembles a manufacturing operation, not a passive investment activity.

Subtopic A. Claim Classification under Section 1122

A corporate debtor in chapter 11 has two types of unsecured, nonpriority claims, among others. Claim 1 consists of severance payments for terminated employees for work rendered prior to the chapter 11 filing. The terminations occurred after the filing. A majority of courts in the applicable jurisdiction hold that such payments do not qualify as administrative expenses under the Code because the payments are based on prepetition services. Claim 1 is not entitled to priority payment under Section 507(a)(4).

Claim 2 consists of pension benefit payments and these payments are addressed in a separate contract. A majority of courts in the applicable jurisdiction hold that payments under the pension benefits do not qualify as administrative expenses because the payments are for services provided prior to the filing. Claim 2 is not entitled to priority payment under Section 507(a)(5).

Neither claim 1 nor claim 2 would be considered a small claim. The corporate debtor wants to place claim 1 and claim 2 in separate classes for purposes of the chapter 11 plan process.

278. Can the corporate debtor in chapter 11 put claim 1 and claim 2 in separate classes for the purposes of Section 1122?

   (A) Probably no, because both claims are unsecured, nonpriority claims;

   (B) Probably yes, because the claims are not substantially similar;

   (C) Either (A) or (B) could be correct;

   (D) It would depend on whether the severance payments and pension benefits payments were reasonable.

Assume all of the same facts as in the previous problem. Assume the corporate debtor places claim 1 and claim 2 in separate classes and one or both groups of claimants challenge the corporate debtor's action.

279. Which of the following would be a persuasive reason for separate classification under Section 1122 as applied to the facts in this situation?

   (A) It would be administratively convenient;

   (B) It would create an impaired class that would vote in favor of the plan;

   (C) The claimants have different incentives when it comes to what they will accept as payment under the plan because they have different legal rights;

   (D) It would result in a faster plan confirmation.

Eliza Thompson is the president and largest shareholder of Berger, Inc. ("Berger"). Eliza holds 2,000 shares of preferred stock in Berger. A few years ago, Berger was nearly insolvent and Eliza loaned Berger $750,000 to help with cash flow. Berger is in financial distress once again and recently filed for chapter 11 bankruptcy. Berger has paid back $500,000 of the loan. A trustee has been appointed in Berger's chapter 11 case and a plan has been proposed. The plan places Eliza's interest as a preferred shareholder and Eliza's $250,000 claim against Berger in the same class.

280. Does Eliza have any grounds under Section 1122 to object to this?

   (A) No, because both the interest and the claim can be traced to Eliza;

   (B) Yes, because interests held by shareholders and claims held by creditors cannot be placed in the same class;

   (C) No, because Eliza is a preferred shareholder and not a common shareholder;

   (D) Yes, because otherwise, insiders would have no incentive to assist their own companies when those companies are in financial distress.

Alaxis is a limited partnership that is in chapter 11. It owns an office building. The building is valued at $20 million. Colonial Bank has a non-recourse mortgage on the building to secure a $30 million dollar loan that Colonial Bank provided to Alaxis. There are no other secured creditors in Alaxis's chapter 11 case.

Assume that Colonial Bank is legally entitled to make the Section 1111(b) election to have its entire claim treated as a secured claim. Colonial declines to elect this treatment. (If you are unclear on what this means, go back and review the questions and answers in subtopic D of chapter 20). Colonial Bank now has a $10 million deficiency claim. To the extent of the deficiency, Colonial Bank is the largest unsecured creditor in Alaxis's chapter 11 case. The debtor in possession proposes to classify Colonial Bank's unsecured deficiency claim separately from the claims of the general unsecured creditors. Colonial Bank objects.

281. How likely is it that the debtor in possession's separate classification proposal will be approved by the bankruptcy court?

   (A) It is unclear because the cases on the topic are divided;

   (B) It is unclear because we do not know whether Alaxis's deficiency claim will get smaller or grow bigger between now and the time of plan confirmation;

   (C) Very likely, because if Colonial Bank did not want separate classification, it should not have declined treatment under Section 1111(b);

   (D) Very unlikely, because Colonial Bank's deficiency claim is exactly like the claims of the general unsecured creditors.

Subtopic B. Chapter 11 Plan Provisions and Section 1123

A chapter 11 corporate debtor has the following classes of priority claims: a Section 507(a)(3) class of claims (administrative expense claims); a Section 507(a)(4) class of claims (employee wage claims); a Section 507(a)(5) class of claims (employee benefit contribution claims), and a Section 507(a)(7) class of claims (consumer deposit claims).

282. Which of the above classes of claims does *not* need to be designated pursuant to Section 1123(a)(1) and why?

    (A) The Section 507(a)(3) class because a majority of a class having such claims cannot restrict the minority to treatment that is inconsistent with Section 1129(a)(9);

    (B) Both the Section 507(a)(4) and 507(a)(5) classes because those classes consist of employee claims;

    (C) The Section 507(a)(7) class because those claims have a small dollar amount;

    (D) The Section 507(a)(4) class because a majority of a class having such claims cannot restrict the minority to treatment that is inconsistent with Section 1129(a)(9).

Assume all of the same facts as in the previous problem. The chapter 11 corporate debtor proposes a plan to pay the Section 507(a)(5) class of priority claims in deferred cash payments and the Section 507(a)(7) class of priority claims in full on the effective date of the plan.

283. Which of these classes of claims must be specified under Section 1123(a)?

    (A) The Section 507(a)(5) class of claims only;

    (B) The Section 507(a)(7) class of claims only;

    (C) Both, because one is unimpaired and the other is impaired;

    (D) Neither, because they are both Section 507(a) priority claims.

Brad Markey files an individual chapter 11 case. Brad is a former real estate broker who once had many home deals and who made himself wealthy in the process. Unfortunately, Brad has fallen on hard times financially and has filed chapter 11. Brad went into bankruptcy with a lien on a luxury automobile. The car is now worth $35,000. Brad's debt on the car is $50,000. The First Capital Bank loaned Brad the money to buy the car. Brad uses the car solely for his real estate business. When he is not working, he uses public transportation because he is an avid environmentalist.

For business and legal reasons, Brad wants to specify First Capital Bank's allowed secured claim on the car ($35,000) separately from its allowed unsecured claim ($15,000). Under the plan, both classes of claims would be impaired. First Capital Bank objects.

284. How likely is it that Brad will be able to separately specify these two classes of claims?

    (A) Very likely, because the two classes of claims are not substantially similar;

    (B) Very likely, because Brad is not using the car for personal, family, or household use;

    (C) Very unlikely, because the same creditor holds each claim;

    (D) Very unlikely, because First Bank has a purchase money security interest.

Third Bank has a mortgage on an office building. The office building is owned, operated, and managed by Taylor, Inc. ("Taylor"). Taylor is in chapter 11 and the office building is its only asset. Taylor's chapter 11 case would be considered a single asset real estate case under the Code. The debtor in possession has proposed a chapter 11 plan under which Third Bank's mortgage will be modified and restructured. The modification and restructuring would otherwise be restricted or prohibited under federal laws that govern bank and borrower regulations.

Third Bank objects to the plan pursuant to Section 1123(a)(5) and argues that since the plan proposes actions that would be otherwise restricted or prohibited under federal law, the plan violates Section 1123(a)(5) and thus cannot be confirmed.

285. What would be the debtor in possession's best argument in response?

   (A) Section 1123(a)(5) is a permissive provision, not a mandatory one;

   (B) The Bankruptcy Code can preempt other federal law in certain circumstances;

   (C) The Bankruptcy Code expressly preempts other federal law in single asset real estate cases;

   (D) Section 1123(a)(5)(E) specifically allows for the modification of liens.

Subtopic C. Nonimpairment under Section 1124

Summit Industries ("Summit") produces a variety of iron materials for use in decorative railings that one would find on large stairways and balconies in commercial buildings. Green River State Bank has a personal property security interest in the inventory, accounts, and equipment of Summit pursuant to Article 9 of the Uniform Commercial Code.

Summit has defaulted on its obligations to Green River State Bank and Green River State Bank has seized the inventory and equipment pursuant to its state law collection rights. Green River State Bank has not yet sold the collateral, but it does intend to do so quickly.

Summit files for chapter 11 bankruptcy prior to any sale of the collateral. The debtor in possession then files a motion asking Summit to turn over the collateral (under Section 542 of the Code) so that the collateral can be utilized in its reorganization efforts. Green River State Bank turns over the collateral and is unable to successfully move to lift the automatic stay. The debtor in possession proposes a chapter 11 plan that in no way alters the legal, equitable, or contractual rights of Green River State Bank. Green River State Bank, however, contends that its rights were altered because it was forced to turn over the collateral to the debtor in possession instead of being able to sell the collateral as it would be able to do outside of bankruptcy. Since its rights to sell the collateral were limited, Green River State Bank argues, its class of claim has been impaired under Section 1124(1) of the Code.

286. How likely is it that Green River State Bank will be able to successfully argue that its class of claim has been impaired?

   (A) Very likely, because Green River State Bank could not sell its collateral when it wanted to sell it;

   (B) Very unlikely, because the concept of impairment does not apply to personal property security interests. It only applies to real property security interests;

   (C) Very likely, because otherwise, secured creditors have reduced incentives to lend;

   (D) Very unlikely, because an alteration of rights by the Code does not constitute impairment under Section 1124(1).

Chapter 11 corporate debtor has three mortgages on its corporate property and the debtor in possession proposes a chapter 11 plan that has the following features. The first mortgage is restructured by extending the payment terms and modifying the interest rate. The second mortgage is not changed in any way. The third mortgage is also not changed in any way.

287. Are the second and third mortgages impaired by the chapter 11 plan?

    (A) Yes, because the first mortgage was restructured and modified;

    (B) No, only the second mortgage is impaired;

    (C) No, neither mortgage is impaired because neither has been changed;

    (D) Yes, both mortgages are impaired because there is little chance they will both remain unaffected by future events;

    (E) No, only the third mortgage is impaired.

A chapter 11 corporate debtor has two classes of common stock and two classes of preferred stock. Under the chapter 11 plan, the secured classes of claims and unsecured classes of claims are restructured and modified in significant ways. The restructuring and modification is expected to create a positive net worth for the corporate debtor as soon as the chapter 11 plan is confirmed. No new shares of stock are issued under the plan, nor are the classes of common and preferred stock affected by the plan.

288. Does the expected positive net worth for the corporate debtor under the plan mean that the classes of interests (i.e., the holders of the common and preferred stock) are impaired under the plan?

ANSWER:

Subtopic D. Disclosure and Voting on Chapter 11 Plans under Sections 1125 and 1126

You represent Spectrum Industries, Inc ("Spectrum"). Spectrum is in chapter 11. Spectrum's managers are eager to exit from chapter 11 as quickly as possible as they fear that a long process will leave them out of the competitive race to get their latest products out on the market. Spectrum has a very feasible chapter 11 plan and you anticipate that the plan will be quicky accepted by all or most of the impaired classes of claimants. Spectrum's chapter 11 case is not a pre-packaged chapter 11, nor is it a small business case. Spectrum has transmitted its written disclosure statement to its creditors and has filed its written disclosure statement with the court

Spectrum wants to start soliciting creditor acceptances of the plan before the written disclosure statement has been approved by the bankruptcy court. Spectrum asks you if this is permissible.

289. What should you say?

ANSWER:

Assume all of the same facts as in the previous problem, except that now assume that Spectrum is a "prepackaged bankruptcy."

290. Does that change your answer?

ANSWER:

Trilox Corporation ("Trilox") is in chapter 11. Trilox is not a small business debtor. Trilox has had ongoing issues with the state's Department of Environmental Protection ("DEP")when it comes to environmental issues. For example, Trilox is subject to a clean-up order from the DEP for hazardous waste that Trilox deposited on property near a state wildlife preserve five years ago. Additionally, Trilox is subject to ongoing monitoring by the DEP with respect to other property. DEP is a creditor in Trilox's chapter 11 case. Trilox transmits its written disclosure statement to DEP and other creditors.

DEP receives Trilox's written disclosure statement pursuant to Section 1125(a) and is not satisfied with the information provided. DEP insists on a written disclosure statement that complies with its own state's environmental rules and regulations.

291. Can the DEP insist on a written disclosure statement that complies with its state's environmental rules and regulations?

   (A) Yes, because nonbankruptcy law trumps Section 1125;

   (B) Yes, because environmental laws relate to the exercise of police power in furtherance of public health and safety;

   (C) No, because of Section 1125(d);

   (D) No, because the DEP does not have standing to be heard on the issue.

Assume all of the same facts as in the previous problem. Assume that DEP has another concern. The exclusivity period under Section 1121 is now over and the unsecured creditors' committee (of which DEP is not a member) has filed a competing plan in the case. DEP has received Trilox's written disclosure statement and it does not disclose or make reference to the competing plan in any way.

292. Can DEP insist that Trilox's disclosure statement disclose or make reference to the competing plan?

   (A) Yes, because otherwise, creditors cannot intelligently evaluate the written disclosure statement;

   (B) Yes, because DEP is not a member of the unsecured creditors' committee;

   (C) No, because of Section 1125(a)(1);

   (D) No, because there is no case law authority suggesting that DEP has a such a duty.

LifeEx makes fertilizer for use by consumers in their household yards and gardens. LifeEx is in chapter 11. LifeEx offers a one-year warranty to its consumers for all products sold. Thus, LifeEx has about 20,000 possible warranty claims when it enters chapter 11. None of the products sold has yet breached the warranty and none of the 20,000 claimants has yet filed a claim with LifeEx on the warranty. None of the claims has been estimated under Section 502(c). It is now time for a vote on LifeEx's chapter 11 plan.

293. Can any of the 20,000 consumers vote on LifeEx's chapter 11 plan?

ANSWER:

You represent a secured creditor in a chapter 11 case. The secured creditor has received the written disclosure statement and the plan. The secured creditor's class of claim is not impaired under the plan. Nonetheless, the secured creditor wants to vote on the plan just to make sure that it doesn't get disadvantaged and to make sure that it can continue to exercise some leverage over the chapter 11 debtor in the future. Your client wants to know if it can vote on the plan.

294. What should you tell your client?

   (A) It can vote on the plan because it has legitimate concerns about future treatment;

   (B) It cannot vote on the plan because its acceptance is conclusively presumed;

   (C) It cannot vote on the plan because it is a secured creditor;

   (D) It can vote on the plan because it has legitimate concerns about whether it can continue to exercise leverage over the chapter 11 debtor in the future;

   (E) Both (A) and (D).

Mason, Inc. ("Mason") is in chapter 11. Mason's schedule of creditors contains 300 creditors. There is a total of $5 million in debt. Mason's chapter 11 plan divides creditors into six classes. Class 4 has 100 creditors, with claims totaling $800,000. Seventy (70) of these creditors vote on the plan. Their claims total $500,000. Forty (40) class 4 creditors vote for the plan. Those who vote for the plan have claims totaling $170,000.

295. Did class 4 accept the plan under Section 1126(c)?

ANSWER:

Subtopic E. Consensual Confirmation of a Chapter 11 Plan under Section 1129(a)

Acme Corporation is in chapter 11. The debtor in possession seeks confirmation of a plan under which it will pay each general unsecured creditor 10% of its claim. Creditor A is in this class of general unsecured creditors. Creditor A is owed $400,000, so it will receive $40,000 on its claim and Acme proposes to pay this amount over 5 years with a payment of $8,000 per year. If Acme were liquidated under chapter 7, it would also receive $40,000 since such a liquidation would provide for each creditor to be paid 10% of its claim.

296. Does Acme's chapter 11 plan satisfy the "best interests test" of Section 1129(a)(7)?

ANSWER:

Go back to the previous problem. In this chapter and the previous one, when discussing impairment, voting, and confirmation issues in chapter 11, we've usually focused on *classes* of claims instead of *holders* of claims.

297. Why should we focus on *holders* of claims in applying Section 1129(a)(7)?

ANSWER:

A chapter 11 plan for an individual debtor is presented to the bankruptcy court for confirmation under Section 1129(a). Among other things, the plan provides for payment of a Section 507(a)(10) claim for personal injury as a result of a drunk driving incident. The plan does not provide for full payment of the claim, either in full on the effective date of the plan, or over time. The plan provides for full payment of all other priority claims. General unsecured creditors will not receive any payment according to the terms of the plan.

298. Can this plan be confirmed under Section 1129(a)?

    (A) No, because the plan would violate the absolute priority rule;

    (B) Yes, because this priority claim is nondischargable under Section 1141(d)(2);

    (C) No, because claims of this type should be paid in full whenever possible;

    (D) Yes, because this priority claim is not entitled to special treatment.

Subtopic F. Nonconsensual Confirmation of a Chapter 11 Plan (of Cramdown and Section 1129(b))

Vandelay Industries ("Vandelay") is seeking confirmation of its chapter 11 plan. The plan has ten classes of claims. All of the classes of claims are impaired. None of these impaired classes accepts the chapter 11 plan. Vandelay wants to use Section 1129(b) to invoke cramdown to gain confirmation over the objection of the impaired classes. Vandelay makes such a request.

299. Does Section 1129(b) apply?

    (A) No, because there has to be acceptance by at least one class of impaired claims in order for Section 1129(b) to apply;

    (B) Yes, because there would be no other way for the debtor to confirm the plan;

    (C) Yes, because there are ten or more classes of claims;

    (D) No, because all of the classes are impaired.

A chapter 11 corporate debtor has five classes of claims or interests. In seeking confirmation of its plan, the debtor proposes a feasible plan that distributes estate assets in the following manner: class of claim 1-additional real property as collateral for a secured loan; class of claim 2-additional personal property as collateral for a secured loan; class of interest 3-common stock to an equity holder; class of claim 4-cash and promissory notes for a secured loan; class of claim 5-cash and personal guarantees signed by the company's president for a secured loan. The debtor can also show that the plan is fair and equitable with respect to all classes.

Class 4 and class 5 reject the plan on the grounds that it discriminates against them because they are getting very different treatment. The debtor can show that the requirements of Section 1129(a) have been met and seeks to confirm the plan under Section 1129(b).

300. How likely is it that the dissenting creditors will be able to block plan confirmation?

    (A) Very likely, because in both cases, they are getting a future promise to pay which might not be worth much;

    (B) Very unlikely, because they are both getting cash. This offsets the risk of default on the notes and the guarantees;

    (C) Very likely, because if at least two classes of claims reject the plan, that constitutes *per se* discrimination under the Code;

    (D) Very unlikely, because different treatment does not prove unfair discrimination.

A corporate chapter 11 debtor proposes a plan and the plan has been rejected by a secured creditor. The debtor in possession now will need to obtain court approval over the objection of that secured creditor. There are ten other secured creditors and each secured creditor has its own class under the plan. The plan has been accepted by all other clases of impaired claims. The plan complies with all of the applicable requirements of Section 1129(a).

301. What facts does the debtor in possession need to know before it can properly analyze whether confirmation under Section 1129(b)(2) is possible?

    (A) Whether the debtor in possession could get a majority of the assenting secured creditor classes to overrule the dissenting secured creditor class;

    (B) The value of the collateral and the applicable interest rate;

    (C) Whether the secured creditor is eligible for the Section 1111(b) election and if so, whether the creditor has elected it;

    (D) (B) and (C) only;

    (E) (A), (B), and (C).

Assume all of the same facts as in the previous problem, except that now assume that the debtor in possession has modified the chapter 11 plan in response to the secured creditor's objection. The debtor in possession proposes to allow the secured creditor to retain a lien in the amount of its allowed secured claim. The plan further provides that the secured creditor will be provided with payment of its allowed secured claim.

The secured creditor then throws the debtor in possession another curve by making the Section 1111(b) election. Assume the secured creditor is eligible for the election and that the election is timely. Now, the debtor in possession has determined the following facts: The debtor in possession's loan amount to this secured creditor is $2,000,000. The loan is secured by mortgage on property worth $1,500,000. After making the Section 1111(b) election, the secured creditor continues to reject the plan.

302. What will the debtor in possession need to do to cram down the plan over the objection of the secured creditor?

ANSWER:

Subtopic G. Postconfirmation Issues

Holiday Cruise Lines, Inc. ("HCLI") files for chapter 11 bankruptcy after coming to terms with serious financial and operational issues. After nine months of plan negotiation and other challenges, HCLI emerges from chapter 11 with a confirmed plan.

303. Against which of the following entities is HCLI's confirmed plan binding?

(A) HCLI's common stock holders who had to extinguish their stock under the terms of the plan;

(B) A prepetition creditor of HCLI who was not scheduled;

(C) A prepetition creditor of HCLI who did not file a claim;

(D) A Section 507(a)(10) priority creditor whose class was impaired under the plan;

(E) All of the above.

Assume the same facts as in the previous problem, except that now assume that HCLI filed a liquidating plan instead of a reorganization plan and that HCLI intends to terminate the business at the consummation of its plan.

304. Is HCLI eligible for a discharge upon confirmation of its chapter 11 plan?

ANSWER:

Assume you represent a secured creditor in the chapter 11 bankruptcy of Medix, Inc. Medix makes vitamins and other health-related products for distribution to consumers. Medix filed for chapter 11 and then proceeded to put together a plan that your client did not believe was fair and equitable. Nevertheless, the bankruptcy court confirmed the plan over your client's objection because the debtor was able to use cram down under Section 1129(b). The chapter 11 plan is now underway, but has not yet been substantially consummated. Your client calls you on the phone and wants to know when you will "start working on the modifying the plan."

305. What should you tell your client?

(A) Secured creditors whose claims are crammed down can move to modify a plan, but only if they can show irreparable injury;

(B) Only the proponent of the plan can modify the plan;

(C) Only the court or the U.S. Trustee can modify the plan;

(D) Any creditor whose claim is impaired can move to modify the plan, but debtors are given 300 days under the Code to show that the plan is working before they can so move.

Subtopic A. Non-Discrimination under Section 525

Bob has worked for over ten years as a preschool teacher. He is one of the most popular teachers in the school. He really wants to run his own state-licensed preschool, so he leaves the preschool at which he currently working, takes a part-time job, and sets out to run his own school.

Bob undergoes the necessary training and related certifications, including personal interviews with representatives from the state agency that licenses preschools and other daycare establishments. The application also includes information about credit history, bank accounts, and other financial matters. One of the application forms also asks if an applicant has ever filed for bankruptcy and whether the applicant has received a discharge of his debts. It is state policy that anyone who is not current on domestic support obligations (including alimony, maintenance, and child support) cannot obtain a license to run a childcare facility, including a preschool. Bob's interviews go well and he fills out all of the applications, but Bob is not aware of the policy.

Five years ago, Bob filed for chapter 7 bankruptcy and he was not discharged from an alimony debt to his ex-wife. He is currently three months behind on his alimony payments to his ex-wife (mainly because he is pouring most of his money into getting the school up and running). The state licensing authority finds out about the delinquent alimony from its review of Bob's application and, solely on the basis of nonpayment of that debt, it rejects Bob's application for the license. Bob comes to you seeking legal advice.

306. Was the state's action in denying Bob the license legal under Section 525?

ANSWER:

Assume all of the same facts as in the previous problem, except that assume now that Bob filed for chapter 13 bankruptcy instead of chapter 7.

307. Would your answer to the previous question be different if Bob filed for chapter 13 bankruptcy instead of chapter 7?

    (A)   Yes, because in chapter 13, he would have at least been trying to pay his debts;

    (B)   Yes, because in chapter 13, the debt would have been dischargeable;

    (C)   No, because Section 525 applies in all chapters;

    (D)   No, because discrimination is wrong whenever it occurs.

Trudy Philmark applies for a government administered student loan and is rejected solely because of a prior bankruptcy filing. The administrators of the student loan program contend that since a student loan is not a "license, permit, charter, franchise or other similar grant," Section 525(a) does not apply to their decision.

308. Are the student loan administrators correct?

ANSWER:

Subtopic B. Lien Avoidance to Protect an Exemption under Section 522(f)

Mary Nixon has a home with a value of $400,000. Mary files for chapter 7 bankruptcy. She lives in a state that restricts its debtors to state law exemptions. Her exemption statute provides a $100,000 homestead exemption and Mary's home qualifies. Mary also has a $200,000 mortgage and a judgment lien on the home. The amount of the judicial lien is also $200,000. Mary's bankruptcy lawyer files a motion seeking to avoid the judgment lien under Section 522(f). The judicial lien does not secure a domestic support obligation. There are no other liens on the property. The motion to avoid the lien is granted.

309. What is the effect of lien avoidance in Mary's case?

ANSWER:

Assume all of the same fact as in the previous problem, except that now assume that the judgment lien secured a domestic support obligation arising from a divorce decree.

310. Would the result be the same if the judgment lien secured a nondischargeable domestic support obligation arising from a divorce decree?

ANSWER:

John Jett has a home with a value of $65,000. He lives in a state that restricts its debtors to state law exemptions. His exemption statute provides a $15,000 homestead exemption and John's home qualifies. John also has a $50,000 mortgage on the home. John got involved in a property dispute with a neighbor and the neighbor sued him for $28,000. So, now there is also a judicial lien on the home and the amount of the lien is $28,000. There are no other liens on the property. John's bankruptcy lawyer files a motion seeing to avoid the judgment lien under Section 522(f). The motion to avoid the lien is granted.

311. What would be the result?

ANSWER:

Olivia is an optometrist. She recently borrowed $450,000 from her local credit union to buy some new optical equipment. She, in fact, purchased the equipment with the proceeds of the loan. The credit union acquired an Article 9 security interest in the dental equipment. Olivia is now in chapter 7 and she wants to use Section 522(f)(1)(b) to avoid the credit union's security interest because it impairs her state law exemption for "tools of the debtor's trade."

312. Can Olivia use Section 522(f)(1)(B) to avoid the credit union's security interest?

(A) No, because Section 522(f)(1)(B) applies only to consumer debts under $250,000;

(B) Yes, because Olivia purchased the equipment for a legitimate business purpose;

(C) No, because the security interest is a purchase money security interest;

(D) Yes, because the problem states that the lien impairs her state law exemption.

Subtopic C. Revocation of Plan Confirmation

You were the chief bankruptcy counsel for Herbert Industries ("Herbert"). Herbert filed for chapter 11 bankruptcy. After eight months of seemingly endless planning and negotiating with creditors, Herbert got its plan confirmed. Several of the secured creditors were very unhappy with the entire chapter 11 process. Eventually, Herbert had to resort to cramdown under Section 1129(b) to get the plan confirmed over the objection of those creditors. Herbert never even came close to engaging in any improper or fraudulent behavior.

Herbert's new CEO is calling you because he's received a letter from the lawyer for a secured creditor whose class was not impaired under the plan. This particular secured creditor was not part of the group whose claims were subject to cramdown, but this secured creditor is nonetheless angry because it thinks that Herbert's new management is now unfairly favoring the group of creditors who were so difficult to deal with during the chapter 11 case.

Herbert's CEO reads you a letter over the phone in which the secured creditor's lawyer is threatening to request that Herbert's plan confirmation be revoked. The basis for revocation is that unless the plan is revoked, the secured creditor will suffer irreparable injury. The letter was delivered to Herbert's 120 days after the date of the entry of the order of confirmation.

313. How likely is it that Herbert's plan will be revoked?

(A) It is difficult know without more facts as to the nature of the secured creditor's allegations of irreparable injury;

(B) Unlikely, because only an entity whose class of claims was impaired under the plan can bring such a request;

(C) Very likely, because the facts fit the statutory criteria for plan revocation and the complaining creditor's move is timely;

(D) Very unlikely, because although the move is timely, fraud is the only basis for plan revocation.

Subtopic A. Jurisdiction and Venue of Bankruptcy Courts

Jergen, Inc. manufacturers bolts. It has many contracts with its vendors and its customers. Due to a fire at one of its plants, it was unable to meet some of its deadlines under its contracts with its customers, and the failure of the customers to pay had deprived it of cash, forcing it to file chapter 11 bankruptcy quickly.

Jergen files suit against Xeres in the same court in which its chapter 11 case was filed. Xeres is a company operating in the same town as Jergen, and the suit seeks to collect a $10,000 debt Xeres owes Jergen for bolts Xeres bought from Jergen last month.

314. Which of the following best describes Xeres' options?

   (A) Xeres will be able to have the matter heard in state court because there is no diversity of citizenship necessary to have a federal court hear the matter;

   (B) Xeres will be able to have the matter heard in state court only because the matter must be heard by a court with general jurisdiction, and only state courts judges have such jurisdicition;

   (C) Xeres will be able to have the matter heard either in state court or in federal district court because the matter must be heard by a court with general jurisdiction, or a court with federal jurisdiction staffed by a judge with Article III powers, and bankruptcy judges do not have such powers;

   (D) Xeres will have to defend in bankruptcy court.

Assume the facts from the prior question, and further assume that Xeres is located in another state in another district. Assume also that Xeres files an answer to Jergen's complaint that raises no jurisdictional issues or venue questions. Six months later, Xeres brings a motion to dismiss the action for lack of jurisdiction and because the action was filed in the wrong venue.

315. The most likely outcome will be:

   (A) Jergen will prevail;

   (B) Xeres will prevail, but only on the contention that the bankruptcy court lacks jurisdiction;

   (C) Xeres will prevail, but only on the contention that Jergen filed the action in an improper venue;

   (D) Xeres will prevail on either its contention that there is a lack of jurisdiction or on its contention that Jergen filed the action in an improper venue.

Fatma is a supplier to Jergen. It sues Jergen in state court in the state in which Jergen filed its chapter 11 case in order to liquidate and collect a $50,000 debt Jergen owed it prepetition.

316. Which of the following is the most likely?

(A) Jergen will have to defend in state court because there is no jurisdiction in the federal bankruptcy court;

(B) Jergen will remove the action to federal bankruptcy court and will litigate it as an adversary proceeding there;

(C) Jergen will object to the filing of the lawsuit as a violation of the automatic stay found in Section 362(a), and Fatma will be forced to file a proof of claim in Jergen's bankruptcy case;

(D) Jergen will object to the filing of the lawsuit as a violation of the automatic stay, and Fatma will be forced to file a new adversary proceeding in federal district court because there is no jurisdiction in federal bankruptcy court.

Fatma ceases its state court litigation and files a proof of claim in Jergen's bankruptcy. Jergen objects to it, and at the initial hearing on the objection, Fatma demands a jury trial on the matter.

317. The most likely outcome of this demand will be:

(A) Fatma will obtain a jury trial;

(B) Fatma will obtain a jury trial only if its claim is such that nonbankruptcy law would grant it a jury trial were the matter filed outside of bankruptcy;

(C) Fatma will obtain a jury trial only if local rules permit bankruptcy courts to hear jury trials, even if Jergen objects;

(D) Fatma will not be able to obtain a jury trial.

Randy is a defendant in a complex auto accident case pending in state court. His liability is premised on ownership of the car that caused most of the injuries. He carries insurance for this, and his insurance company is defending him (and there is no possibility of a judgment outside of his policy limits). Under state law pleading rules, he is a necessary party. The state court litigation is about to go to trial when Randy files an individual chapter 11 in the federal district in which the state court sits. Randy is trying save his real estate investing business. Randy then removes the entire action to the federal bankruptcy court in which he filed his chapter 11 case.

All other defendants and the plaintiffs move to remand the matter to state court, with the plaintiffs agreeing not to pursue their action beyond verdict; in essence they only wish to liquidate all claims in state court and not pursue Randy or any of his assets should they win. In addition, all parties other than Randy move for the bankruptcy court to abstain from deciding the matter.

318. What is the most likely outcome of the two motions?

(A) The bankruptcy court will remand the action, and not decide the abstention motion;

(B) The bankruptcy court will not remand the action and will deny the abstention motion;

(C)   The bankruptcy court will not remand the action and will grant the abstention motion;

(D)   The bankruptcy court will remand the action, and grant the abstention motion.

Subtopic B. Special Issues with Bankruptcy Professionals

Mellow, Inc. hired Bob as its insolvency lawyer 18 months ago. Bob has struggled mightily to avoid a chapter 11 for Mellow, but has been unsuccessful. In the process, Bob has racked up a hefty $50,000 bill for services rendered. Mellows pays the entire amount one hour before Bill files their chapter 11 case.

319.   If Bob's employment is challenged by a party in interest, which of the following is the most likely outcome?

   (A)   Bob will be able to continue to represent Mellow because of his longstanding representation and knowledge of Mellow's problems;

   (B)   Bob will not be able to represent Mellow;

   (C)   Bob will be able to represent Mellow only if Mellow does not contest Bob's bill;

   (D)   Bob will not be able to represent Mellow unless he disgorges the fee paid, and then waives the outstanding bill and agrees that the amount is forgiven.

Lucy represents Tagtag, Inc. in its chapter 11 bankrutpcy. Tagtag is a debtor in possession, but after some fraud was discovered, a creditor successfully moved to appoint a chapter 11 trustee. Lucy assisted the trustee for the remainder of the case, incurring over $100,000 in fees in doing so.

Lucy seeks court allowance for the $100,000 in fees. She prepares a fee application which fully discloses her time spent. Her fee is quite reasonable for the work done. The chapter 11 trustee supports her fee application.

320.   Which of the following describes the most likely disposition of the fee application?

   (A)   Lucy will receive all of her fees;

   (B)   Lucy will receive only those fees which represented a substantial contribution to the chapter 11 case;

   (C)   Lucy will receive an allowed amount of her fees to be paid pro rata with all other unsecured claims in Tagtag's case;

   (D)   Lucy will receive no fees.

Subtopic C. Bankruptcy Appeals

Heavenly, Inc. files a motion to have its plan of reorganization approved. The court denies the motion. Heavenly files a notice of appeal, and nothing more. The circuit in which Heavenly's case is located has adopted a Bankruptcy Appellate Panel.

321.   Which of the following best describes Heavenly's effort to have the District Court hear its appeal?

(A) The District Court will not hear the appeal because the order appealed from is interlocutory;

(B) The District Court will not hear the appeal because the Court of Appeals is the proper court to hear appeals from bankruptcy courts;

(C) The District Court will not hear the appeal because Heavenly did not make an election to opt out of having the Bankruptcy Appellate Panel decide the appeal;

(D) The District Court will hear the appeal.

A client asks if she may appeal an order of the bankruptcy court directly to the appropriate Court of Appeals.

322. The best answer is:

(A) Yes, without qualification;

(B) Yes, but the other side will have to agree;

(C) Yes, but the other side and the Court of Appeals will have to agree;

(D) No.

Subtopic D. International Aspects of Bankruptcy-Chapter 15

Juan is a Mexican citizen who lives in Mexico, and has most of his property there. He does, however, own on parcel of real property in Arizona. He files bankruptcy in Mexico, and properly lists his interest in the Arizona property. Frank has a mortgage on Juan's property in Mexico. He has started foreclosure proceedings. Teresa, who is Juan's sindico (Mexican equivalent of a bankruptcy trustee), has commenced chapter 15 proceedings in the District of Arizona, and has obtained a court order recognizing Teresa as a foreign representative in a foreign mail proceeding.

323. Which of the following best describes what Frank may do in his foreclosure action?

(A) Frank may do anything proper under nonbankruptcy law, including going to foreclosure on Juan's property;

(B) Frank may do anything until he receives formal notice of the recognition by certified mail or any other similar notification process;

(C) Frank may do anything until he receives notification that his particular foreclosure proceeding has been stayed;

(D) Frank may do only what he could do if Juan had filed a domestic bankruptcy.

Assume the same facts as the last question, but assume now that Juan is a citizen and resident of Spain, and is in insolvency proceedings there. Assume further that Juan had business dealings in Mexico, and that Mexican ancillary proceedings were initiated there, and that the representative of that proceeding initiates the chapter 15 proceeding. Assume finally that Juan still owns the property in Mexico, and that it is used in the Mexican business dealings.

324. Which of the following best describes what Frank may do in his foreclosure action?

(A) Frank may do anything proper under nonbankruptcy law, including going to foreclosure on Juan's property;

(B) Frank may do anything until he receives formal notice of the recognition by certified mail or any other similar notification process;

(C) Frank may do anything until he receives notification that his particular foreclosure proceeding has been stayed;

(D) Frank may do only what he could do if Juan had filed a domestic bankruptcy.

PRACTICE FINAL EXAM: QUESTIONS

General Instructions: This is an open-book examination. There are nine questions. You are expected to prepare a short essay (i.e., usually two or three paragraphs) for each question. Your answers should cite the relevant Code sections and/or other applicable nonbankruptcy law. This examination should take approximately two hours to complete.

1. Debtor leases space in a commercial building (assume the building is not a shopping center) for a period of four years, at a rental of $120,000 per year, and operates an upscale womens' clothing store on the premises. After three years, Debtor files chapter 7 bankruptcy. When Debtor files, the market rental for similar space has increased to $124,000 per year. The bankruptcy trustee seeks to assign the lease to another tenant and make the $4,000 profit. The new tenant will sell clothing, gear, and other supplies for extreme sport enthusiasts. The lessor opposes such an assignment, citing a use clause in the lease which provides that "the lessee shall use the premises only for sale of common household goods to affluent consumers." The Debtor is not in default under the lease. What result?

ANSWER:

2. Mary was a wheat farmer in North Dakota. Due to extremely heavy rains in her part of the state, she could not plant a crop in 2004 and, as a result, she suffered substantial financial losses. On September 7, 2005, Mary filed chapter 7 bankruptcy. On September 17, 2005, Congress passed the Omnibus Consolidated Appropriations Act which funded a Crop Disaster Program. Between November 2005 and April 2006, Mary received $78,478 in payments under the Program. The trustee then filed a motion to force Mary to turn over the money. What result?

ANSWER:

3. Janie operates a bar under a lease limiting use to operation of a "restaurant and lounge bar." The bar is not in a shopping center. The lease also prohibits "any practices that may be a nuisance or objectionable to other local merchants." Janie has spread her business interests a little too thin and the bar has been struggling as of late. After filing a chapter 11 bankruptcy, Janie realized she could attract more people into her bar on Monday and Wednesday nights by showcasing several local rock bands at her bar. The promotional appearances were advertised on local radio stations. Several local merchants complained to the landlord that the increased crowds at the club were becoming very disruptive and threatened to endanger patronage of surrounding businesses. The landlord, fed up with the debtor's tardy rental payments and spurred on by the other merchants (who were also tenants of his) wants to get an injunction on a nuisance theory against Janie to stop the rock events. Although a few rental payments have been tardy, Janie is not in default under the lease. Advise the landlord.

ANSWER:

4. Developer sold a beachfront lot to Michael Brown under an installment contract requiring the payment of $100,000 per year for five years. Title was to remain in the developer until completion of payments. After Brown made two annual payments, developer filed for chapter 11 bankruptcy and sought to reject the contract. Brown had looked forward to building his vacation home on the lot as soon as he could afford to, and he is very upset. Advise Brown.

ANSWER:

5. Debtor is a school for adults interested in learning to sail small watercraft. The school, "ComeSailAway," files for chapter 7 bankruptcy. The company employees include: 1 office manager, 3 instructors (including the schools's director) and 2 boat hands/custodians. The assets of the company include: the main office building, a fleet of small watercraft it leases from a local boat manufacturer, training equipment, and a trademark interest in its name, ComeSailAway®. The claims filed in the bankruptcy case include the following:

1. Postpetition claims for lease payments on the waterfront prior to the Debtor's decision to reject the leases.

2. A mortgage on the main office building.

3. A postpetition claim for current property taxes and insurance on the main office building.

4. A claim by two instructors at the school who had not been paid for two months prior to the bankruptcy. Each instructor earned $4,000 a month.

5. A claim by WEBSOLUTIONS, Inc. WEBSOLUTIONS designed a website and web-based training programs for the Debtor. The work was completed prior to the filing.

6. A claim by the trustee's legal counsel.

7. The Debtor had agreed to serve as the host site for training seminars run by a private company for instructors seeking to become certified sailing teachers. The Debtor plans to reject that contract.

8. A claim arising out of a breach of contract lawsuit (under state law) successfully brought against the school's director by a book publisher. The director had promised to write a book for the publisher. The book was to be entitled, "Sailing For Dummies."

In what order will the Debtor's property be distributed?

ANSWER:

6. Debtor owned Whiteacre, an unencumbered parcel of real property purchased a few years earlier for $600,000. The market value of Whiteacre was recently appraised at $620,000 to $640,000. Debtor, needing cash to pay creditors, advertised the sale of Whiteacre at a price of $610,000 payable within 10 days. Buyer offered to pay $580,000 immediately. Debtor griped that the amount offered was far below market value. Buyer replied: "Look, I am not in business for my health. Take it or leave it." Several others expressed an interest in the property at the price of

$590,000 but no one was able to raise the cash in 10 days. Debtor, swallowing his pride, sold to Buyer for $580,000 and used the proceeds to pay creditors. At the time of the sale, Buyer knew that Debtor was being hounded by creditors, but did not have actual knowledge that Debtor was insolvent. Two months later, Buyer resold Whiteacre to Buyer #2 for $620,000. Buyer #2 lived in the area, but had no knowledge of the transaction between Debtor and Buyer. Shortly after that sale, Debtor filed chapter 7 bankruptcy. Can the trustee avoid any transactions?

ANSWER:

7. Bank Creditor made an unsecured $180,000 working capital loan to a Business Debtor on January 6. According to the terms of the loan, it was to be repaid in two equal installments, with one payment due thirty days after January 6 and the other payment due thirty days after that. On February 7, Debtor repaid $160,000 after the Creditor sent the Debtor an e-mail message in which the Creditor expressed concerns regarding the Debtor's debt-to-asset ratio on a recent balance sheet report. On March 8, Creditor lent an additional $150,000. On April 9, Debtor filed chapter 11 bankruptcy. Assume that at all relevant times, assets of the Debtor were sufficient to pay each general creditor 85 cents on the dollar. Can the trustee avoid any transactions?

ANSWER:

8. Chapter 11 reorganizing Debtor owes Creditor $1,000,000 and Creditor has a security interest in equipment worth $600,000. Creditor requests relief from the automatic stay and Debtor offers adequate protection payments of $10,000 a month to cover the anticipated decline in value due to the debtor's continued use of the equipment. After the Creditor is granted adequate protection in the form of the payments, the bankruptcy court denies the motion to lift the stay. Eight months later, the reorganization fails and the equipment is worth $200,000 due to the Debtor's continued use. The Debtor returns the equipment to the Creditor. The Debtor has made $80,000 in adequate protection payments. Advise Creditor on its next move.

ANSWER:

9. John Smith owed $40,000 to GreenTree National Bank ("GreenTree") on a unsecured loan. John filed chapter 7 and scheduled the debt. John received a discharge. GreenTree did not file a claim or otherwise take part in the bankruptcy case because GreenTree received an official notice from the bankruptcy court that stated that John had no non-exempt assets. After the bankruptcy case was closed, GreenTree sued John on the loan debt in state court. John pleaded discharge in bankruptcy. GreenTree alleged that the loan was obtained by written fraudulent statements concerning John's financial condition under Section 523(a)(2)(B). John filed a motion for summary judgment. What result?

ANSWER:

Answers

1. **The correct answer is (B).** The Bankruptcy Code is structured by chapters, with each chapter having its own scope and application. Chapters 7, 11, 12, 13, and 15 each create a specific type of relief for a specific type of debtor. Under Section 103(a), chapters 1, 3, and 5 are generally applicable to all cases. As a consequence, Section 1307 cannot apply to a chapter 11 debtor, unless there is something in chapter 11 which specifically incorporates it into chapter 13 (and there is not). Since there is nothing in chapter 11 incorporating Section 1307(b), (B) is the correct response.

   Answer (A) is incorrect because Section 1307(b) does not state that it applies to individuals; it applies only to chapter 13 debtors. Even though only individuals can be chapter 13 debtors, that is different than saying Section 1307(b) applies to all individuals. It is important to read and note carefully the exact scope of each section of the Code. Chapter 13 provisions presumptively apply only in chapter 13 cases, pursuant to Section 103(i).

   Answer (C) is incorrect because being an individual (which the Code never defines, but uses to mean a flesh and blood human, as opposed to an artificial entity, such as a corporation or limited liability company) is not used by the Code to organize relief. In reading the Code, you must develop a sense of when characteristics may be applied in new contexts and when they may not. In this case, the status of being an individual does not carry over from one chapter to another.

   Answer (D) is a red herring. Section 1307(b) doesn't require a waiver to be effective. It just invalidates any waivers of the right to dismiss that a chapter 13 debtor agrees to. The key is to note that Alf is not a chapter 13 debtor, and thus there is a strong presumption that nothing in chapter 13 applies to Alf.

2. **The correct answer is (D).** Avoiding powers actions are found in chapter 5 of the Code. Under Section 103(a), chapter 5 is applicable in all chapter 7, 11, 12, and 13 cases. (It is also applicable in a chapter 9 cases by a municipality, but only because it is incorporated by Section 901(a).) As a consequence, **Answer (A) is incorrect**, since it assumes that the chapter 5 provisions are not applicable in chapter 11.

   Since Alf is a debtor in possession as well as a debtor, he has all the powers of a trustee, including all powers of a trustee under chapter 5. *See* Section 1107(a). Thus, **Answer (C) is incorrect**. There is also no requirement that, acting as a debtor in possession, he obtain any court permission, thus making **Answer (B) incorrect** as well.

3. No. You can tell from the numbering that Section 727 only applies in chapter 7. Since Garry has filed a chapter 13 case, Section 727 is inapplicable to Garry's case.

4. **The correct answer is (C).** In every chapter 7 case, a case trustee is appointed. Typically, an interim trustee is selected from a list or "panel" of pre-qualified trustees, and their appointment is confirmed at the first meeting of creditors held under Section 341(a) of the

Bankruptcy Code. It is that "trustee in bankruptcy" who has all the obligations and powers under Section 704 of the Bankruptcy Code and standing to bring avoidance actions, such as the setting aside of the preference Debbie made.

Answer (B) is incorrect. The Office of the United States Trustee, although it has a similar name, does not have the standing to bring the action. (In extremely rare cases, the Office of the United States Trustee may appoint itself the trustee, pursuant to 28 U.S.C. Section 586(a)(2), but that power is almost never used. If appointed, the Office of the United States Trustee becomes the case trustee.). The Office of the United States Trustee, or just simply the U.S. Trustee, is part of the Department of Justice (hence part of the executive branch) and is responsible for oversight of various aspects of bankruptcy cases. They have, for example, the responsibility for putting together the "panel" of trustees from which the bankruptcy court clerk's office will usually select the particular trustee for each individual case. They check to ensure that each such panel trustee is qualified for the position (has the appropriate experience, posts the applicable bond, etc.). The Office of the United States Trustee also reviews individual chapter 7 cases for instances of abuse, certified credit counselors and financial education providers, and selects auditors for individual cases. They also have standing to bring motions to dismiss cases which are an abuse of the system, and often comment on the progress of chapter 11 cases (for which they also have oversight responsibility). *See* Section 307. Finally, they review and may object to professionals' fees in any case.

Answer (A) is incorrect. As the debtor, Debbie has no standing to bring actions that affect the estate, although in some isolated instances, she may have standing to bring actions to the extent that they affect her exempt property.

Answer (D) is also incorrect. Commencement of a case under title 11 creates a bankruptcy estate with an estate representative. In a chapter 7 case, that estate representative is the chapter 7 case trustee. In a chapter 11 case, the estate representative is the debtor in possession so long as no chapter 11 trustee is sought or appointed. Creditors thus have no standing to take actions allocated to the estate representative, although in some cases (most notably in chapter 11 cases), creditors (or creditors' committees) may bring avoiding powers actions with prior court approval.

5.   In a chapter 11, the default management structure is for the prepetition debtor to stay in control as the "debtor in possession." *See* Section 1101. Disgruntled creditors can move to appoint a "chapter 11 trustee," who would displace the existing management and would control the debtor and run its business, pursuant to Section 1104(a). They may also seek the appointment of an "examiner," who would report on prepetition transactions while management of the debtor stays in place. In either case, the trustee or the examiner will be appointed by the Office of the United States trustee, subject to review by creditors in the case of the appointment of a trustee. These topics will be covered in more detail in chapter 20 of this book.

6.   **The correct answer is (C).** Under Federal Bankruptcy Rule of Procedure 7001, avoidance of a lien must be by an adversary proceeding, pursuant to which Reggie must file and serve a summons and complaint. In this proceeding, most of the rules of the Federal Rules of Civil Procedure will apply.

Answer (A) is incorrect because under Section 1107, a debtor in possession is given all the powers of a trustee, including the power to initiate avoiding powers actions.

Answer (B) is incorrect because no rule requires participation by a creditors' committee; indeed, in most chapter 11 cases, there are no active creditors' committees.

Answer (D) is incorrect because there is no linking requirement between exercising rights of avoidance and filing or confirming plans. When (and indeed whether) to file such actions in is the discretion of the debtor in possession.

7. **The correct answer is (D).** Under the Bankruptcy Code, the term "after notice and a hearing" is defined in Section 102(1). The definition is: "(1) 'after notice and a hearing' or a similar phrase —

(A) means after such notice as is appropriate in the particular circumstances, and such opportunity for a hearing as is appropriate in the particular circumstances; but (B) authorizes an act without an actual hearing if such notice is given properly and if — (i) such a hearing is not requested timely by a party in interest; or (ii) there is insufficient time for a hearing to be commenced before such act must be done, and the court authorizes such act."

Under this definition, it can be seen that **Answer (A) is incorrect**, since Section 102(1) explicitly provides for actions without a hearing in some circumstances.

As set forth in the statute, there are two circumstances in which a court can act "after notice and a hearing" without a hearing, and the existence of two grounds makes **Answer (B) similarly incorrect**. Although exigent or compelling circumstances are one of the reasons a hearing need not be held (*see* Section 102(1)(B)(ii)), it is not the *only* reason that a hearing need not be held.

Finally, **Answer (C) is incorrect** because nothing in Section 102(1) requires the party seeking the order arrange for a hearing date. Section 102(1)(B)(i) only requires that "notice [be] given properly," not that the movant set everything up in case an objection is raised.

The structure of Section 102(1) has given rise to the often quoted motto of bankruptcy: "scream or die." In many cases, if a properly noticed party does not object to a proposed order or motion, the court will take such lack of a response as consent, or waiver, and will issue the requested order. As a consequence, parties must be diligent and raise their objections in a timely manner, or they will lose their right to complain.

8.   **Answer (B) is incorrect**, since the jurisdictional requirements of Section 109 do not include citizenship. A bankruptcy case may be commenced so long as the person "resides or has a domicile, a place of business, or property in the United States," pursuant to Section 109(a). **Answer (D) is likewise incorrect**, as nothing in the involuntary statute requires an "exhaustion" of nonbankruptcy remedies.

    The issue thus comes down to whether Hal's status as a farmer matters. It does. Under Section 303(a), a farmer may not be subject to an involuntary proceeding (although a farmer may voluntarily commence a bankruptcy). As a consequence, **Answer (A) is incorrect**, and **Answer (C) is correct**

9.   **The correct answer is (A).** The requirement of credit counseling is a new requirement under the Code, first imposed by the 2005 Act. Section 109(h)(1) requires as a condition of eligibility that all individuals (that is, human beings) receive approved credit counseling within 180 days of filing. A certificate attesting to such counseling must be filed in the debtor's case, pursuant to Section 521(b)(1)(A).

    The counseling also permits some form of budget analysis. Section 109(h)(1), however, permits the counseling to be in a "group" session or even over the Internet. Not much information, therefore, is required to perform a budget analysis, **making (C) incorrect.**

    The inability to get an individual in to see a credit counselor is only excused if you can show that there was no availability for the seven days prior to the date of filing. If Redfern cannot show that all credit counselors were booked for the previous seven days, she is out of luck, **making (B) an incorrect answer.**

    Finally, a court has the power to excuse the credit counseling requirement, but only if the debtor states that he or she attempted to obtain credit counseling for seven days and exigent circumstances have prevented the person from obtaining credit counseling. Failure to get to a lawyer on time to explain this requirement will likely not be an exigent circumstance (and in any event the seven-day requirement is separate from exigency), thus **(D) is incorrect.** That leaves **(A) as the correct answer.**

10.   James is an individual filing for bankruptcy. Although the cost and time required for a chapter 11 lead few consumers to file under chapter 11, there is no bar against it. *See Toibb v. Radloff*, 501 U.S. 157 (1991). Accordingly, **Answer (A) is incorrect.**

    There is also no requirement that a debtor be insolvent in order to file a case under any chapter. *In re Marshall*, 300 B.R. 507 (Bankr. C.D. Cal. 2003). Accordingly, **Answer (B) is incorrect.**

    Under Section 305, a court may dismiss or abstain from a case otherwise properly filed if "the interests of creditors and the debtor would be better served by such dismissal or suspension." Some courts have used Section 305 (and sometimes Section 1112(b)) to abstain from or dismiss cases which are essentially two-party disputes, reserving bankruptcy court jurisdiction for cases in which a true collective action problem is presented. Because Answer (C) describes this situation, **Answer (C) is the most likely result. Answer (D), while incorrect**, is not out of the question, especially if the facts are changed to show that James has more than one debt which is due and unpaid.

11.   **Answer (D) is correct.** When a debtor has more than eleven creditors (that is, at least twelve), then an involuntary petition must be brought by "three or more entities, each of which is . . . a holder of a claim against such person that is not contingent as to liability or the subject of a bona fide dispute, . . . if such claims aggregate at least $14,425 more than the value of any lien on property of the debtor securing such claims held by the holders of such claims," pursuant to Section 303(b)(1).

The key here is that the claims must be unsecured claims that are "not contingent as to liability or the subject of a bona fide dispute." Cathy's claim is on a guaranty; it is contingent (the contingency is that Edward's son might pay and Edward would not be asked to pay anything on the guaranty). Debbie's claim is disputed, and currently in litigation. Thus, neither of them qualify as a petitioning creditor. That leaves $11,000 in qualifying claims, which does not meet the jurisdictional requirement. Thus **Answer (B) is incorrect**, since there are not $14,425 in qualifying claims.

Answer (C) is likewise incorrect. Because Cathy's and Debbie's claims do not qualify, it is immaterial that Alice and Ben may not have accelerated the maturity date of their debts. Even if they did, there would not be sufficient amount of qualifying debt.

Finally, the requirement regarding the number of creditors and the claims they hold is jurisdictional; that is, without the requisite number of creditors holding the specific types of claims, the merits of the petition will never be reached. Because **Answer (A)** goes to the merits (whether or not Edward was paying his debts as they become due), it is thus incorrect.

Authors' Note: Section 104 of the Bankruptcy Code adjusts various monetary amounts used in the Bankruptcy Code every three years. The last adjustment was made as of April 1, 2010. The $14,425 number will thus change again on April 1, 2013, so if you are reading this text after that date, the number will have been revised.

12.   **The correct answer is now (A).** When the state court entered a judgment against Edward, the disputed claim became resolved, especially since Edward did not move to stay the judgment or appeal the ruling. *See In re Cohn-Phillips, Ltd.*, 193 B.R. 757 (Bankr. E.D. Va. 1996); *In re Raymark Indus., Inc.*, 99 B.R. 298 (Bankr. E.D. Pa. 1989). That fact brings the number of qualifying petitioning creditors to three, and the amount of debt held between them to over $14,425. The court would then reach the substantive standard for entering relief on an involuntary petition, that is, whether "the debtor is generally not paying such debtor's debts as such debts become due," which in this case is a given fact.

Answer (B), while true, is incorrect, because the amount of claims is only part of the requirements. There also has to be a showing that "the debtor is generally not paying such debtor's debts as such debts become due." **Answer (C) is also incorrect**, since the requirement of Section 303(b)(1) is only that there be at least $14,425 in unsecured claims among the petitioning creditors, and Debbie's $50,000 judgment more than takes care of that amount. Thus, Alice and Ben can count for the number of creditors requirement while contributing nothing to the amount at issue requirement.

Answer (D) is incorrect because, as set forth above, Debbie's claims now qualify her as a petitioning creditor.

13. Again, **Answer (A) is incorrect** because it assumes that the jurisdictional requirements regarding number of creditors and amount of claims has been met. With Debbie's claim now being a secured claim, and Cathy's claims still being contingent, it appears that the jurisdictional requirements have not been met.

Similarly, although (B) is factually correct, **Answer (B) is an incorrect answer** because the relevant question is not how much debt Edward has, but how much unsecured debt Edward has (the statute requires the three petitioning creditors' claim to be "at least $14,425 more than the value of any lien on the property of the debtor securing such claims held by the holders of such claims.") *See* Section 303(b)(1).

The reasoning thus comes down to either (C) or (D). **Answer (C) is correct**, as case law allows the secured creditor to waive all or a portion of its secured claim to qualify as a petitioning creditor. *See In re Mechanical Inc. v. BCD 56 LLC*, 330 F.3d 111, 122 (2d Cir. 2003) (requiring actual waiver as of time of petition, or of joining petition). Since **Answer (D)** does not acknowledge the ability to waive a portion of the secured claim, it is incorrect.

14. **The correct answer is (D).** Under Section 303(c), "a creditor holding an unsecured claim that is not contingent" may "join in the petition with the same effect as if such joining creditor were a petitioning creditor" at any time "[a]fter the filing of a petition under this section but before the case is dismissed or relief is ordered." Thus, Frank's joinder, occurring before the trial started, is timely, and thus **Answer (A) is incorrect.**

Moreover, the only triable issue upon an involuntary petition is whether the petitioners qualify as such, and whether the debtor is not generally paying its debts as they become due. Thus, a court could not decide the validity of Frank's claim; it could only determine what type of claim it was (disputed). **Accordingly, Answer (C) is incorrect.**

Answer (B) is also incorrect but to understand why, you have to read Section 303(c). It is not parallel to Section 303(b)(1); it precludes creditors holding contingent claims from joining an involuntary petition, but does not preclude creditors holding disputed claims. Thus, **Answer (B) is incorrect.** As a consequence, Frank's debt and status as a creditor will count, and along with Alice and Ben, the jurisdictional requirements of Section 303(b) are met, making **Answer (D) the correct answer.**

15. The creditor may resume collection efforts. Under Section 521(a)(1), every debtor must file a schedule of assets and liabilities, a schedule of current income and expenditures, and a statement of the debtor's financial affairs. If such filings are not made within 45 days of the filing of the case, the case is "automatically dismissed effective on the 46th day after the date of the filing of the petition," pursuant to Section 521(i)(1). Because Harriette did not file the required documents, her case was dismissed as of the 46th day, and the creditor could resume collection efforts.

16. **The correct answer is (C).** Under Section 521(e)(2), an individual debtor under chapter 7 or chapter 13 must provide . . . not later than 7 days before the date first set for the first meeting of creditors to the trustee a copy of the Federal income tax return required under

applicable law . . . for the most recent tax year ending immediately before the commencement of the case and for which a Federal income tax return was filed. . . ."

Section 315(c) of the 2005 Act requires the development and implementation of procedures designed to keep private a debtor's tax return information. Thus, Congress was aware of such privacy concerns but still required provision of the information. Thus, **Answer (B) is incorrect.**

Answer (A) is incorrect because there are limits to what the trustee may request. A debtor is required to "cooperate with the trustee as necessary to enable the trustee to perform the trustee's duties under this title." That general duty, combined with the specific information provisions in the Code such as Section 521(e), means that the debtor has to produce substantial amounts of information, but not all — the cooperation extends only to the extent necessary for the trustee to perform his or her duty.

The existence of this general duty to cooperate thus points out why **Answer (D) is incorrect.** It is very likely that tax information will be relevant to the administration of the debtor's case, and three years' worth of tax returns will assist the trustee in distributions because taxes incurred during that period and not paid may very well be priority claims under Section 507(a)(8), as opposed to general unsecured claims.

17. The meeting is what is generally known as the first meeting of creditors. It is held under the authority of Section 341(a) of the Bankruptcy Code. It is an administrative meeting at which the trustee and creditors may ask the debtor questions about his or her financial affairs, and the debtor has to answer under oath. In most districts, it is the only hearing or meeting that the debtor need attend after filing in order to receive a discharge.

18. **The correct answer is (B).** First note that Megacorp has ceased paying its debts as they become due; that is the essence of any moratorium-based workout. Thus, it would have little defense to the involuntary petition, and it is quite likely that the court will have to grant the petition and enter the order for relief. Because of the likelihood of the entry of the order for relief, **Answer (A) is incorrect.**

Answer (C) is incorrect. Bankruptcy is an all-or-nothing proposition; you cannot file against some but not all creditors.

The choice thus resolves itself between (D), which would lead to a full blown case (and an avoidance of the general grant of a security interest (*see* Section 547(b)), and (B) which keeps the case in place, but stays all activity.

Section 305 of the Code allows for dismissal or a suspension of all proceedings in any case in which "the interests of creditors and the debtor would be better served by . . . dismissal or suspension. . . ." Here, with the overwhelming majority of creditors, a court is likely to enter the order for relief (thus preserving any preference action against the general grant of the security interest), but then immediately suspend all activity in the case to see if the negotiated workout could bring about rehabilitation. Since it would also be supported by the debtor, such a result means that allowing the case to be commenced but staying all activity is the best result, and that consequence is captured by **the correct response, Answer (B).**

Answer (D) might have been the correct answer had the debtor not agreed, or had the percentage of supportive creditors been less. **Answer (D) is incorrect.**

19. **The correct answer is (D).** Under Section 541(a) of the Bankruptcy Code, property of the estate is an expansive concept. It includes "all legal or equitable interests of the debtor in property as of the commencement of the case."

Here, Jeb has several property interests. The first is the copyright. The second is his contract rights under the royalty agreement; contract rights are property rights, and thus all of his rights in the contract come into the estate. As a consequence, **Answer (A) is incorrect**, since it excludes Jeb's rights under the contract.

Answer (C) is incorrect as to the need to apportion Jeb's interest; the whole contract comes in. Jeb may only get a 20% payment, but that is a function of the contract as a whole, and not because Jeb is somehow a part owner of the contract.

Jeb may or may not have rights against Raylene for her statements about the song. That issue will be decided in the court case mentioned. But the claim for such rights is another property right, albeit one that is contingent upon the outcome of the lawsuit. Accordingly, **(D) is correct**, and **Answer (B) is incorrect**, since it does not mention the rights that are subject to the lawsuit.

20. **The correct answer is (A).** Under Section 541(a) of the Bankruptcy Code, all of the debtor's legal and equitable interests in property held at the filing become property of the estate. As a consequence, the $25,000 in other property Fran held when she filed is property of the estate.

Working from the least inclusive to the most inclusive, the difference between Answer (C) and Answer (D) turns on whether the business post-filing profit is property of the estate. Under Section 541(a)(6), however, property of the estate includes "[p]roceeds, product, offspring, rents, or profits of or from property of the estate," and under Section 541(a)(7) property of the estate includes "[a]ny interest in property that the estate acquires after the commencement of the case." The profit from operations clearly fits either of these provisions (the difference between the two might be if there was a post-filing loan or gift from outside sources). As a consequence, **Answer (D) is incorrect** in that it does not include the post-filing profit.

Answer (C) is also incorrect since it does not include proceeds from the preference recovery action, which would be property of the estate under Section 541(a)(3).

We already know that Answer (A) is presumptively correct since all three elements it states have been found above to be property of the estate. Since the salary had to come from results from the store's operations, one might initially think that it too would be property of the estate. When an individual is a debtor in chapter 7, however, Section 541(a)(6) provides an exception for "earnings from services performed by an individual debtor after the commencement of the case." Thus the salary stays out of the estate. Accordingly, **Answer (B) is incorrect**, since it includes the earnings that Section 541(a)(6) excludes, making

Answer (A) correct because each of its three elements can be property of the estate.

21.   **The correct answer is now (B).** Under changes made to chapter 11 in 2005, an individual's earnings from services are property of the estate, pursuant to Section 1115 (The same result is obtained in chapter 13 under Section 1306). This facilitates the plans individuals must propose and confirm in cases under those chapters.

As a consequence, **Answer (B) is now correct**, because it has the three items of property already identified as property of the estate, and adds the income that Section 1115 brings into the estate. Since (A) excludes that income, **Answer (A) is not correct.**

Answers (D) and (C) are not correct for the same reasons as stated in the last problem.

22.   **The correct answer is (B).** This problem looks at the exclusions to property of the estate. Starting from the least inclusive, Answer (D), we need to know whether property, such as the house, in which the debtor has a community property interest (a title system prevalent in the Southwestern United States and California). Section 541(a)(2) is explicit here; property in which the debtor has a community property interest (and for which the debtor has joint control or which is liable for a claim against the debtor) is property of the estate. As a consequence, **Answer (D) is incorrect.**

The next task is the inheritance. It became Sally's property *after* filing, so there might be a natural inclination not to include it in the debtor's bankruptcy estate. But Section 541(a)(5) brings post-commencement receipt of inheritances (as well as post-commencement receipt of life insurance proceeds and post-commencement property settlements in divorce cases) received within 180 days of filing. Since Sally's inheritance was received 30 days after filing, the inheritance comes into the bankruptcy estate. Since the inheritance is estate property, **Answer (C) in incorrect.**

The difference between **Answer (A)** and **Answer (B)** is the status of Sally's Section 401(k) plan. Are retirement assets property of the estate and payable to creditors? The Supreme Court addressed part of this problem in 1992 in Patterson v. Shumate, 504 U.S. 753 (1992). In *Patterson*, the president of a small business filed bankruptcy. He sought to exclude his pension assets, which were valued at $250,000, from his bankruptcy estate under Section 541(c). These assets had been held by his company's pension plan, which qualified for favorable tax treatment under ERISA. In particular, the trust had an anti-alienation clause which satisfied 29 U.S.C. Section 1056(d)(1). The Court held that the anti-alienation provisions of ERISA were the type of provisions that meet the standards of Section 541(c)(2); that is, Section 1056(d) provided the type of "applicable nonbankruptcy law" restrictions recognized and respected by nonbankruptcy law. By extension, the Court held that Section 541(c)(2) thus precluded the assets from becoming part of Patterson's bankruptcy estate. The Court thus held that Patterson's trustee Shumate could not seize the pension funds in order to liquidate them for payment to creditors. Since 401(k) plans must, by definition, have an anti-alienation clause, many courts have held them to be property that does not become property of the estate. *See Carmichael v. Osherow*, 100 F.3d 375 (5th Cir. 1996); *In re Wingfield*, 284 B.R. 787 (E.D. Va. 2002).

Notwithstanding *Patterson v. Shumate*, retirement assets are not easy to categorize as property of the estate. Some courts have used a two-step inquiry to determine whether a plan is subject to ERISA. *See In re Orkin*, 170 B.R. 751, 753-54 (Bankr. D. Mass. 1994). Under the two-step inquiry, courts determine (1) whether the plan is "subject to" ERISA, and (2) whether the plan includes an anti-alienation clause that is enforceable under ERISA. *See In re Baker*, 114 F.3d 636, 638 (7th Cir. 1997); *In re Bennett*, 185 B.R. 4, 6 (Bankr. E.D.N.Y. 1995); *In re Hanes*, 162 B.R. 733, 740 (Bankr. E.D. Va. 1994). Other courts add a step; these courts insist that, in addition to the two steps set forth above, the court must determine whether the plan qualifies for tax exempt status under the Internal Revenue Code. *See In re Hall*, 151 B.R. 412, 418-19 (Bankr. W.D. Mich. 1993); *In re Sirois*, 144 B.R. 12, 14 (Bankr. D. Mass. 1992); *In re Witwer*, 148 B.R. 930, 934 (Bankr. C.D. Cal. 1992).

Still other courts simply phrase "[t]he relevant inquiry [as] whether, on the petition date, [the] debtor could have enforced under ERISA the Pension Plan's transfer restriction." *Lowenschuss v. Selnick*, 171 F.3d 673, 680 (9th Cir.), *cert. denied* 528 U.S. 877 (1999). These courts found that, even with a anti-alienation clause that facially meets the requirements of Section 541(c)(2), the pension assets are subject to claims of creditors because state law would not respect the clause. This typically occurs in plans for companies in which there is one employee and one owner, and they are the same individual and thus the plan is outside of the coverage of ERISA.

Regardless, the best answer here would not include the 401(k) plan as part of Sally's estate. Accordingly, **Answer (A) is incorrect**, and because it does not include the 401(k) plan but does include the house and the inheritance, **Answer (B) is correct.**

Authors' Note: The 2005 Act expressly made certain types of retirement assets exempt, pursuant to Section 522(b)(4), which is different than excluding them from the estate altogether. Exempt property still starts out as property of the estate, and then is excluded from it by the exemption process. With respect to the exemption for retirement assets, Congress exempted accounts set up under Sections 401 (such as 401(k) plans), 403, 408 (IRAs), 408A (Roth IRAs), and other similar accounts.

23.   **The correct answer is (A).** The automatic stay of Section 362(a) is very broad. It protects the debtor from "the commencement or continuation, including the issuance or employment of process, of a judicial, administrative, or other action or proceeding against the debtor that was or could have been commenced before the commencement of the case under this title, or to recover a claim against the debtor that arose before the commencement of the case under this title;" *See* Section 362(a)(1). The fraud cause of action is clearly something that "was or could have been commenced before" Jake's petition, and so it is presumptively stayed.

Moreover, it protects the debtor and his or her property without regard to actual notice (that's why it's "automatic"). Since notice is not required, **Answer (B) is incorrect.**

Recall also that the petition constitutes the order for relief in a voluntary case, pursuant to Section 301(b). Thus, a copy of the petition is the court order for purposes of the automatic stay. As a consequence, **Answer (D) is incorrect.**

Answer (C) is also incorrect. The stay is binding against "all entities," pursuant to Section 362(a), and thus it is irrelevant that the state court judge was not informed of the filing. When Francis' lawyer received a copy of the petition, it was incumbent on her to notify the state court that a bankruptcy had been filed, and to thereafter take no further action.

24.   **The correct answer is (C).** All courts hold that an action taken in violation of the stay, even if done without notice, can be reversed. Some courts hold that the action is voidable; other say that it is void. In either event, Dee or Dee's trustee will be able to "undo" or reverse the transaction. **Answer (A) is incorrect** since Chris may not retain ownership in the property to the extent that ownership was acquired in violation of the automatic stay.

Dee or Dee's trustee need not pay any money to reverse the transaction. It is considered in violation of a court order (the order for relief), and thus may be avoided without cost to the debtor or estate. Thus, **Answer (D) is incorrect.**

Answer (B) is tricky. What has fraudulent transfer law to do with this fact pattern? Not much. Before *BFP v. Resolution Trust Co.*, 511 U.S. 531 (1994), some courts had held that foreclosure sales qualified as constructive fraudulent transfers since the property was transferred (the foreclosure) for less than a reasonably equivalent value (here, 40% of fair market value), and at a time when the debtor was insolvent. But BFP adopted, as an interpretation of Section 548, the result under state law under the UFTA: regularly-conducted, non-collusive foreclosure sales cannot be fraudulent transfers. Accordingly, since this foreclosure was regularly conducted, with no hint of collusion, it cannot be set aside under Section 548, and thus **Answer (B) is incorrect.**

25.   **The correct answer is (C).** This problem raises the intertwined issues of postpetition debts

and property of the estate.

First, note that Macie's claim arose *after* the filing of Leonard's petition. As a consequence, Section 362(a)(1) will not apply; that paragraph is limited to actions or proceedings which arose and which could have been commenced (or were commenced) before the filing of the petition.

The remaining paragraphs of Section 362(a) require distinctions between actions against the debtor and actions against property of the estate. This distinction will arise in the normal chapter 7 case because, under Section 541(a)(6), postpetition earnings from services of an individual are **not** property of the estate. Since the problem here deals with such postpetition earnings, none of the paragraphs that deal exclusively with property of the estate apply. This will eliminate paragraphs (3) (actions to obtain possession of property of the estate, or obtain property of the estate from the estate or the exercise of control over such property of the estate); and (4) (the creation, perfection or enforcement of a lien against property of the estate).

The remaining paragraphs do not apply. Paragraph (2) relates to the enforcement of a prepetition judgment against the debtor; here, however, the default judgment arises postpetition. Paragraph (5) relates to the creation, perfection or enforcement of a lien against the debtor, but again only to the extent that the claim secured by the lien arose prepetition. Paragraph (6) prohibiting acts to collect, assess or recover claims applies only to prepetition claims, and paragraph (7), prohibiting setoff, also extends only to the setoff against prepetition claims. And paragraph (8) only applies to tax court proceedings.

Thus, the enforcement of a postpetition judgment against non-estate property is not stayed, making **Answer (C) correct**, and any answer in which Leonard wins (**Answers (A) and (B)**) **incorrect**.

Answer (D) is also incorrect. Since the stay does not apply, there is no need to inquire what Macie knew and why she did what she did. The answer is a reference to damages under Section 362(k) (formerly Section 362(h) before 2005), which may be awarded for "any willful violation of the stay provided by" Section 362.

26.   **The correct answer is (D).** The difference here is that a debtor's wages are property of the estate in a chapter 13 case under Section 1306 (and in an individual's chapter 11 case under Section 1115). Although the practice in some districts is to revest such wages back in the debtor (thus treating them as something other than property of the estate), the facts indicate that the plan does not try to revest Leonard's wages.

Thus, paragraphs (3) and (4) apply. Paragraph (3) prevents any act to obtain possession of property of the estate — here, Leonard's wages. Paragraph (4) prevents any enforcement of a lien against property of the estate — here, the lien of the garnishment. Note that both paragraph (3) and paragraph (4) apply regardless of when the claim that lies behind such actions arose. They thus can and do apply to actions related to postpetition claims.

As a consequence, **Answer (C) is incorrect**, because the stay does apply and Macie will have to find some way around it. **Answer (B) is also incorrect**, because it focuses on the obtaining the garnishment, rather than its enforcement. Although paragraph (5) extends the stay to the creation of a lien against property of the estate — and hence to the act of obtaining the garnishment — the damages did not arise from the fact of the garnishment, but from its enforcement.

With respect to enforcement, the analysis comes down to whether Leonard wins outright (Answer (A)), or whether Macie has a defense of lack of wilfulness. Here, Section 362(k) applies, which conditions damages on a wilful violation of the stay. The inclusion of this contingency makes (D) the better and more complete answer, leaving **Answer (A) as less complete, and hence incorrect.**

27. The collection manager may not set off any amounts JP Lawnmower owes to Harrison against Harrison's debt to JP Lawnmower without getting court permission first. Under Section 362(a)(7), "the setoff of any debt owing to the debtor that arose before the commencement of the case . . . against any claim against the debtor" is a violation of the automatic stay.

28. **The correct answer is (D).** The exceptions listed in each of the paragraphs of Section 362(b) are independent of each other; that is, they are each sufficient exceptions to the automatic stay without reference to any other paragraph. Thus, although the order is not criminal, that is not fatal. While Section 362(b)(1) does exempt criminal actions or proceedings against the debtor, there are many other grounds for exemption as well. Thus, since each paragraph is non-exclusive in this manner, **Answer (A) is incorrect.**

Answer (B) turns on the status of the administrative agency as a state, rather than a federal, agency. This does not matter, however, for the main governmental powers exception found in Section 362(b)(4). It grants an exception for a "governmental unit's" actions taken pursuant to "police and regulatory powers." "Governmental unit," in turn, is defined in Section 101(27) as any federal, state or foreign government or agency thereof. As state governmental agencies are thus covered, **Answer (B) is incorrect.**

Answer (C) is also incorrect. The description of police and regulatory powers in Section 362(b)(5) indicates that such powers "includ[e] the enforcement of a judgment other than a monetary judgment," but recall that the use of "includes" is not limiting — it just introduces an example without confining that which is defined to examples of that type. *See* Section 102(3). So the language of Section 362(b)(5) does not exclude enforcement of monetary judgments.

But in any event, that is not what is at issue here. PuffCo has not complied with a valid administrative order. Its lack of compliance thus exposes it to those remedies the administrative agency would invoke in the normal course of enforcing the regulation, which here includes shutting down of the plant. As this method of enforcement is in the ordinary course, there can be no doubt that the agency is acting pursuant to law, and thus it will be permitted to enforce its shut-down order without any permission from the bankruptcy court, making **Answer (D) correct.**

29. **The correct answer is (D).** Section 362(b)(2) exempts a broad range of orders and actions that relate to domestic support obligations (a term defined in Section 101(14A)). In particular, Section 362(b)(2)(A)(ii) exempts any action "for the establishment or modification of a order for domestic support obligations." Since temporary support obligations qualify as domestic support obligations (they are "owed to . . . a spouse . . . [and are in] the nature of alimony, maintenance or support . . . of such spouse . . . [and were] established . . . before the date of the order for relief . . . by reason of applicable provisions of . . . an order of a court of record . . . and not assigned to a non-governmental entity. . . ." — Section

101(14A)(A)-(D)), **this rules out Answer (A) as a correct response.**

Similarly, actions "for the establishment of paternity" are also exempted by virtue of Section 362(b)(2)(A)(i). Thus, **Answer (B) is incorrect**, as paternity actions are exempted.

Finally, the 2005 Amendments also exempted "the withholding, suspension or restriction of a driver's license, *a professional or occupational license* . . . under State law, as specified in section 466(a)(16) of the Social Security Act." Section 362(b)(2)(C). **This makes Answer (C) incorrect**, since the facts state the order was obtained in accordance with applicable state and federal law.

30.   **The correct answer is (A)**, although it takes a while to get there. The applicable sections needed to answer this question are Sections 362(b)(22) and 362(b)(23), added by the 2005 legislation. To make matters worse, Section 362(b)(22) is subject to Section 362(*l*), and Section 362(b)(23) is subject to Section 362(m), also added by the 2005 legislation.

Initially, Section 362(b)(22) applies to the continuation of any state court eviction or unlawful detainer action under which a landlord has obtained a prepetition judgment of possession. That would seem to be the case here, as Joan has obtained an order in state court. As indicated above, however, Section 362(b)(22) is subject to Section 362(*l*). Subsection (*l*) attempts to take into account various state laws that allow a tenant to reclaim property for which the landlord has obtained a judgment of possession by paying the amount of delinquent rent; that is, by curing the default.

To invoke this procedure, the debtor has to file a certification that the default can be cured, and must check the box on the petition that states: "Debtor claims that under applicable nonbankruptcy law, there are circumstances under which the debtor would be permitted to cure the entire monetary default that gave rise to the judgment for possession, after the judgment for possession was entered." If the debtor does this correctly, and he or she pays the next 30 days' of rent to the court, then he or she will get 30 days to provide the cure (or put another way, Section 362(*l*) suspends the exemption provided in Section 362(b)(22) for 30 days to allow for a cure of delinquent rent, *see* Section 362(*l*)(1)-(3)).

Harry did not check this box on the petition (it is located right under the box he did check indicating that Joan had obtained a prepetition judgment for possession). Section 362(*l*)(4) states that if the debtor indicates that there is a judgment for possession (as Harry did), but the debtor does not provide the required certifications (which Harry has not), then "Section 362(b)(22) shall apply immediately upon failure to file such certification, and relief from the stay proved under subsection (a)(3) shall not be required to enable the lessor to complete the process to recover full possession of the property." *See* Section 362(*l*)(4)(A). **This makes Answer (A) correct.** Had Harry checked the correct box and provided a certification, the soonest Joan could have continued the eviction would have been 30 days after the petition, but the absence of a certification **eliminates Answer (C) as a correct answer.**

Section 362(b)(23) may also apply. Under that paragraph, a landlord may also continue an eviction of the debtor, and is thus exempt from subsection (a)(3), if the breach of the lease giving rise to the eviction was "based on endangerment of such property of the illegal use of controlled substances on such property . . ." The landlord, however, has to file a certification regarding the endangerment or certify that the debtor "illegally used or allowed to be used a controlled substance on the property."

Section 362(b)(23) is, as stated above, subject to Section 362(m). That subsection imposes a

15-day waiting period after the certification is filed, 11 U.S.C. Section 362(m)(1). The debtor has the opportunity to contest the certification, in which case the court will hold expedited hearings on the veracity of the landlord's certification.

Harry's use of pot is certainly an illegal use of a controlled substance. Unlike Section 362(*l*) discussed above, however, Section 362(m) does not have any provision allowing a landlord to act any sooner than 15 days. Because of the immediate exemption provided in Section 362(b)(22)/Section 362(*l*)(4), Joan will not have to wait 15 days, **making Answer (C) incorrect.** In addition, because under any of the scenarios above, Joan will be able to continue the eviction action under the facts stated, **Answer (D) is also incorrect.**

31.   **The correct answer is (D)**, although Answer (C) has much to commend it. Under Section 362(c)(3), the automatic stay lasts only 30 days against property of the debtor if the debtor has had a bankruptcy case dismissed within the year preceding the current filing. Here, Henry had dismissed his prior chapter 13 case in April of 2007, eleven months prior to the current case. Thus, unless Henry moves to extend the stay, it will expire 30 day after filing.

Answer (A) is true, but irrelevant. Because Henry received a chapter 7 discharge within eight years of his current filing (he received a discharge in 2002, and it is now 2007), he is ineligible to receive another chapter 7 discharge, pursuant to Section 727(a)(8) (the 2005 legislation extended this to eight years from six). The inability to receive a discharge, however, is irrelevant to whether the stay applies. As a result, **Answer (A) is incorrect.**

Answer (B) is incorrect because the section it is most like, Section 362(c)(4), requires that there be two dismissals within the year preceding the current filing. If there had been two dismissals (Henry has only one), then the stay does not apply at all. Because the 2001 filing does not count under Section 362(c)(4), Answer (B) is incorrect.

Answer (C) assumes that none of the facts regarding Henry's prior filings make a difference as to the stay. And that is generally correct; Sections 362(c)(3) & (4) refer only to filings within the year preceding the current filing — filings before that time are irrelevant to the operation of the automatic stay. Since Henry did have the case dismissed with the year preceding his present case, **Answer (C) would appear to be incorrect.**

32.   **The correct answer is (A).** Under Section 362(d)(1), relief from stay can be granted for "cause." Under the statute, cause includes "the lack of adequate protection of an interest in property of" the party seeking relief from stay. From the perspective of movant First Bank, its interest in the property — its lien of $5 million — is adequately protected on these facts. Most courts would say yes, since First Bank's $5 million loan is protected by $5 million in equity — that is, it has a lien of $5 million against a property worth $10 million.

This $5 million equity cushion provides sufficient adequate protection that AI could successfully defend against a relief from stay action seeking to establish cause under Section 362(d)(1).

Section 362(d)(2), which would seem to be embodied in **Answer (B)**, is not available on these facts. While true that AI has no equity in the property (the $10 million in lien free value is exceed by the total amount of debt — $12 million — encumbering the property), Section 362(d)(2) also requires that the property not be necessary for an effective reorganization. Here, the facts are that the plant is AI's "most profitable," which likely equates into it being necessary for an effective reorganization. As a result, although Answer (B) is true — AI has no equity in the property — that fact alone is insufficient to grant relief from stay. Thus,

Answer (B) is incorrect.

Answer (C) is incorrect largely because it is irrelevant. Whether AI was in default or not when it filed, First Bank could move for relief from stay. The relevance of prepetition defaults typically arises only when calculating whether there is any equity cushion in the property — the larger the prepetition payments, the larger the claim in bankruptcy, and thus the more value the encumbered property has to have in order to provide adequate protection. Thus, **Answer (C) is incorrect.**

Answer (D) is also incorrect, but for a different reason. Section 361(3) explicitly excludes giving a claim administrative expense priority from the range of acts that can constitute adequate protection.

33.   With changed facts, we surprisingly do not get a changed answer. **Answer (A) is still the correct answer.** The movant is now a lienholder in second position. That means that adequate protection can no longer be provided by the existence of an equity cushion; here, Second Bank's lien of $7 million is only partially covered by the value of the property.

But under the rules for calculating secured and unsecured debts, Second Bank has a secured claim for $5 million and an unsecured claim for $2 million. Holders of unsecured claims typically do not have standing to seek relief from stay since, as unsecured creditors, they have no interest in property to protect. But Second Bank also holds a secured claim for $5 million. Adequate protection here arises from the fact that the collateral's value is stable. Second Bank will get its $5 million regardless of when the property is sold or liquidated (and that is all it is entitled to on its secured claim since for undersecured claims (ones for which the value of the collateral is less than the total amount of debt), there is no postpetition interest allowed, pursuant to Section 506(b). And since *United Savings Assn. of Texas v. Timbers of Inwood Forest Associates, Ltd* 484 U.S. 365 (1988), the expectancy of reinvesting the proceeds of defaulted loans is not recognized as an interest to be adequately protected. This means that the stability of the property's value thus ensures that Second Bank will receive as much in the future as it would today, so the secured claim is adequately protected. **Answer (C) is thus incorrect.**

Answers (B) and (D) continue to be incorrect for the reasons stated in the prior problem.

34.   **The correct answer is now (B).** Although Second Bank's interest is adequately protected under the analysis of the previous problem, that analysis is only relevant for the "cause" analysis set forth in Section 362(d)(1).

Section 362(d)(2) and 362(d)(1), however, are independent bases for seeking relief from stay. Under the revised facts, AI has now filed a chapter 7 liquidation case. In such a case, there is no prospect for the reorganization of the debtor, so that prong of Section 362(d)(2) will always be met. The issue is thus whether there is equity in the property for the debtor, and here there isn't. Thus, **Answer (B) is correct, and Answer (A) is incorrect** because the adequate protection of a interest under Section 362(d)(1) is irrelevant if grounds for relief from stay are present, as they are here under Seciton 362(d)(2).

Answers (C) and (D) are incorrect.

35.   The answer does not change. Although First Bank's interest is adequately protected under Section 362(d)(1), First Bank can similarly show that there is a lack of equity for the estate — $12 million in liens against $10 million in value, and the fact that AI filed a chapter 7

shows that the property is not necessary for an effective reorganization. Since Section 362(d)(2) is independent from Section 362(d)(1), First Bank can establish relief from stay on the same grounds as Second Bank did in the prior problem.

36. **The correct answer is (C).** You would need to know whether the judgment gave the state a monetary or a non-monetary right in order to properly advise the state. A non-monetary right such as an injunction that only bars Acme from engaging in future polluting activities without any provision for a monetary remedy does not create a right to payment. Therefore, it does not create a claim under Section 101(5).

    Answer (A) is incorrect because the source of the judgment (state or federal law) is irrelevant for purposes of determining whether or not the state has a claim under Section 101(5).

    Answer (B) is incorrect because the question of whether the judgment is rendered by a judge or a jury is also irrelevant for purposes of determining whether or not the state has a claim under Section 101(5).

    Answer (D) is incorrect because the question of whether the pollution resulted from negligent or reckless conduct is also irrelevant for purposes of determining whether or not the state has a claim under Section 101(5). Answers **(A), (B), and (D)** may be relevant for other legal purposes. However, they would not be relevant for purposes of determining whether or not the state has a claim under Section 101(5).

37. **The correct answer is (A).** Generally, a claim under Section 101(5) is dischargeable in bankruptcy and is paid in the liquidation process in chapter 7. Thus, **Answer (B) is incorrect.**

    Answer (C) is incorrect. The bankruptcy liquidation process can include both consensual (i.e., arising from the consent of the parties) and nonconsensual (i.e., involuntary) claims.

    Answer (D) is incorrect. Claims based on court judgments are subject to discharge in chapter 7 bankruptcy unless those claims fall under Sections 523 or 727 of the Code.

38. Yes. Although the maturity date for the bonds has not arrived, Section 101(5) includes both matured and unmatured obligations in the definition of a claim. Since the underlying bond debt is fixed and unconditional (i.e., the passage of ten years is a certain event), the mere fact that the debt has not matured does not mean it is not a claim.

39. **The correct answer is (D).** Since the obligation for future condominium fees arose under a prepetition contract, the condominium board has a right to payment under Section 101(5). The fact that the claim is contingent upon the board's actually incurring expenses for upkeep and repairs does not mean that it is not a claim.

    Answer (A) is incorrect because Section 101(5) applies to all chapters of the Code.

    Answer (B) is incorrect because the future condominium fees arose out of a prepetition contract. Since the fees arose out of a prepetition contract, the board's right to payment arose prior to the time of the filing. It is this right to payment that is determinative under

Section 101(5).

Answer (C) is incorrect because the board does not have to have a final judgment against Jones in order to have a claim. Section 101(5) includes rights to payment whether or not such rights are reduced to judgment.

40.   **The correct answer is (B).** At the time of the filing, Sarah's claim is unliquidated because its amount is not fixed. However, Section 101(5) expressly includes unliquidated claims.

Answer (A) is incorrect because the date on which she filed her lawsuit is not determinative of whether or not she has a claim in bankruptcy. Since the events that gave rise to the lawsuit happened prepetition, Sarah has a claim. The date on which she actually filed her lawsuit makes no difference for the purpose of determining whether or not she has a claim.

Answer (C) is incorrect because the uncertainty in the amount of her possible recovery does not mean that she does not have a claim for purposes of Section 101(5).

Answer (D) is incorrect because tort claims constitute claims under Section 101(5). As such, they are payable out of the estate and are dischargeable.

41.   **The correct answer is (A).** The salary due to the store manager for two weeks after the filing of the petition is usually considered an actual and necessary cost of preserving the estate. As such, it would be considered an administrative expense. It would be paid first under Sections 507(a)(2) and 503(b).

Answer (B) is incorrect. The store manager's portion of social security taxes which the debtor was required to withhold would not be paid first among these claims. The claim would have a lower priority pursuant to Section 507(a)(8)(C). Section 507(a)(8)(C) includes a number of different tax obligations. Some of provisions of Section 507(a)(8)(C) have time limitations that proscribe the limits of the priority. Section 507(a)(8)(C) does not have any such time limits.

Answer (C) is incorrect. The salary due to the store manager for three weeks prior to the filing of the petition also would not be paid first. Pursuant to Section 507(a)(4)(A), that claim would have a priority that is lower than the postpetition salary claim, but higher than the sales tax claim. It is important to note that the salary claim for the three weeks prior to the filing is limited to a certain time (i.e., earned within 180 days before the filing of the petition or the date of the cessation of the debtor's business). It is also limited in amount. To the extent that the store manager's claim exceeds the limit, it is a general unsecured claim.

Answer (D) is incorrect. The fees due to the attorney also would not be paid first. It does not fit into any of the priority categories of Section 507. It would be considered a general unsecured claim and, as such, falls under Section 726(a)(2)(A). The attorney would share pro rata with other general unsecured creditors in any funds remaining after the priority claims had been paid.

42.   No. The trustees fees and expenses associated with the sale of the home will be paid before the alimony and child support claims. In general, Section 507(a)(1) provides a first priority for the domestic support obligations. However, Section 507(a)(1)(C) also puts certain administrative expenses ahead of even domestic support obligations. Those administrative expenses must meet the criteria of that section and must be connected to the administration of assets that would otherwise be available for the payment of allowed unsecured claims for

domestic support obligations.

43. The tax claims for the years 2004, 2005, and 2006 would be entitled to priority under Section 507(a)(8)(A). This is because for those years-2004, 2005, and 2006-two conditions are met. First, the taxable year for each ends on or before February 1, 2008 (the date of the filing of the bankruptcy petition). Second, the tax return for each is due within three years before February 1, 2008. The tax claim for the year 2003 would fall outside of the priority because the tax return for that year is due on April 15, 2004 which is before February 1, 2005. The tax claim for the year 2007 would fall outside of the priority because the return for that year is not due within three years before the filing of the petition. The tax claim for the year 2008 would fall outside of the priority for two reasons: First, the taxable year for that tax claim ends after the date of the filing of the petition. Second, the return for that year is not due within three years before the date of the filing of the petition.

44. **The correct answer is (B).** Section 506(a)(1) provides that a claim is secured to the extent of the value of the collateral and unsecured to the extent of a deficiency. Here, the mortgage debt is $200,000. Since the townhouse is worth $175,000, the bank has a secured claim in that amount. The deficiency ($200,000-$175,000) is $25,000. Thus, the bank has an unsecured claim in that amount.

Answer (A) is incorrect because Section 506(a)(1) specifically provides that the amount of the secured claim is dictated by the value of the collateral, not the amount of the total debt.

Answer (C) is incorrect because the depreciation in the value of the townhouse does not leave the bank completely unsecured. The townhouse is still worth $175,000 and Section 506(a)(1) provides that the bank has a secured claim for that amount.

Answer (D) is incorrect because the original purchase price has no direct bearing on the determination of the secured claim under Section 506(a)(1).

45. **The correct answer is (B).** Section 506(a)(2) governs valuation of personal property (i.e., the van) that is collateral for a secured claim in an individual chapter 7 or 13 case. That section provides that the value of the property in an individual chapter 7 case is dictated by the replacement value of the property at the time of the filing without any deduction for the costs of sale or marketing.

Answer (A) is incorrect because although Myra is an individual in a chapter 7 case, the van is not a consumer good because it is not being used for personal, family, or household use. The van is being used solely for business purposes.

Answer (C) is incorrect because Section 506(a)(2) trumps a general theory of valuation that links the valuation standard to the type of insolvency proceeding under which the debtor files.

Answer (D) is incorrect because Section 506(a)(1) does not apply to valuation of personal property in a case such as Myra's. Section 506(a)(1) provides that collateral must be valued in light of the purpose of the valuation and the proposed use of the property. However, Section 506(a)(2) trumps Section 506(a)(1) in Myra's case because she is an individual in chapter 7 and her case involves personal property.

46. Yes. Section 506(a)(1) provides that a creditor who holds a valid right of setoff is treated as a secured claim holder to the extent of the right of setoff. Section 553 of the Code recognizes

setoff rights in bankruptcy and allows setoff to occur when four requirements are met. First, the creditor must hold a prepetition claim against the debtor. That is the case here because GoGo has a claim for $20,000 and that claim is prepetition. Second, the creditor must owe a prepetition debt to the debtor. That applies here because GoGo owes Tiptop $10,000 and that claim is also prepetition. Third, the claim and the debt must be mutual. This applies because the claim and the debt exist between the same parties. Finally, the claim and the debt each must be valid and enforceable as is the case in the problem. The practical effect of GoGo's being treated as the holder of a secured claim means that GoGo has a secured claim for $10,000 (the amount it owes TipTop) and an unsecured claim for $10,000 (the difference between the total debt of $20,000 and TipTop's debt of $10,000). GoGo is also entitled to the other protections of the Code for secured creditors to the extent of the secured claim.

47.   No. The CEO is a creditor of TipTop and this gives rise to a claim in TipTop's bankruptcy. However, the CEO does not owe a debt or obligation of any kind to Tiptop. In order for Section 553 to apply, the creditor must hold a prepetition claim against the debtor and the creditor must also owe a prepetition debt to the debtor. Here, the CEO has a claim against TipTop so he is a creditor with a prepetition claim against the debtor. However, the CEO does not owe a debt to TipTop, so he does not qualify as a creditor owing a debt to the debtor. The CEO cannot claim setoff rights under Section 553 and thus cannot be treated as the holder of a secured claim in Tiptop's bankruptcy case.

48.   **The correct answer is (D).** Section 552(a) provides that after-acquired property of the estate or the debtor is not subject to a prepetition security interest. This invalidates the after-acquired property clause with respect to the cars acquired by the dealer after the filing of the petition. This means that the cars are free and clear of First Bank's security interest and can be used (so long as they are not property of the estate) by the debtor in the ordinary course of business.

Answer (A) is incorrect because after-acquired property clauses are enforceable under the Uniform Commercial Code.

Answer (B) is incorrect because Section 552(a) invalidates the after-acquired property clause without regard to the creation and perfection of the security interest.

Answer (C) is incorrect because the mention of after-acquired property in the security agreement does not change the result.

49.   **The correct answer is (D).** The cash generated from prepetition inventory would be considered proceeds under the Uniform Commercial Code. Under the U.C.C., a security interest in proceeds is automatic and need not be specifically mentioned by the parties. Although Section 552(a) of the Code invalidates the postpetition effectiveness of a prepetition security interest in some cases (see the previous question, for example), Section 552(b)(1) contains a specific exception for the proceeds of prepetition collateral under a prepetition security agreement. Section 552(b)(1) specifically indicates that proceeds generated by prepetition collateral are subject to a prepetition security interest even if those proceeds are acquired after the date of the filing of the petition.

Answer (A) is incorrect because the immediacy of the deposit into a bank account has no direct bearing on whether the security interest in proceeds survives Dealer's chapter 7 filing. It might be relevant for the purposes of analyzing other issues under the Code or under state law. However, it is not directly relevant under the question and answer provided here.

Answer (B) is incorrect because under the U.C.C. the continuing effectiveness of a security interest in proceeds is automatic and need not be specifically mentioned in a security agreement.

Answer (C) is incorrect because the location of the deposit is not relevant to the issue of whether or not the security interest continues in proceeds. It might be relevant for purposes of analyzing other issues under the Code or under state law. However, it is not directly relevant under the question and answer provided here.

50. **The correct answer is (C).** Under Section 502(a), a proof of claim filed under Section 501 is deemed allowed unless a party in interest objects.

Answer (A) is incorrect because no such motion is required as long as the claim is filed under Section 501 and no party in interest objects.

Answer (B) is incorrect because just the opposite is true. A proof of claim filed in accordance with Section 501 is prima facie evidence of the validity and amount of the claim.

Answer (D) is incorrect because Acme's status as a trade creditor has no bearing on whether or not the proof of claim is deemed allowed under the facts in this problem.

51. Yes. ThinkTank's motion would be supported by Section 502(e). Assuming it is properly filed under Section 501, the EPA's claim filed by ThinkTank is allowable. Moreover, the allowance of both claims, that of the EPA and of Spillwell's would constitute a double recovery against the estate and would thus be disallowed under Section 502(e).

52. **Answer (A) is correct.** Under Section 502(g), a claim arising from the breach of an executory contract is treated as a prepetition claim even if the contract is rejected postpetition.

Answer (B) is incorrect. The private nature of the contract has no bearing on the validity of MC's argument under the facts stated in this problem.

Answer (C) is incorrect. Section 502(g) specifically states that the claim arising from the breach of an executory contract is treated as a prepetition claim even though the actual breach occurred postpetition.

Answer (D) is incorrect. The cause of the fall in the wholesale market price of sugar is not relevant to the validity of MC's argument under the facts stated in the problem.

53. No. Section 502(b)(9) disallows claims that are not timely filed except to the extent tardily filed under Section 726. Certain tardily filed claims are governed by Section 726 and are not automatically disallowed in chapter 7. The problem for Marvin's creditor is that this is a chapter 13 case. Section 502(b)(9) provides for disallowance of untimely filed claims in chapters 11, 12, or 13.

54. **The correct answer is (B).** The legal theory that supports equitable subordination under Section 510(c) of the Code is that the interests of the other creditors has been harmed or that an unfair advantage has been conferred on the claimant. Under the facts in the problem, a good argument could be made that enforcement of Major's security interest would be unfair to the general unsecured creditors of AHS. There is no evidence that Major's sale

transaction with AHS provided any benefit to AHS. It appears to be a sale negotiated between a closely-held corporation and a major stockholder and officer. Thus, the inherent fairness of the transaction could be questioned and would likely form the basis for an equitable subordination challenge under Section 510(c). Some cases suggest that it takes truly egregious conduct to get equitable subordination under Section 510(c). Under this standard, facts supporting such conduct would have to be more extensively developed for the equitable subordination claim to prevail.

Answer (A) is incorrect because there is no evidence that Major's claim has no basis in law. The claim results from a legally valid transaction. If the claim were unenforceable, it would be disallowed under Section 502, not subordinated under Section 510(c).

Answer (C) is incorrect because there is no evidence that Major's claim was obtained under duress. The sale transaction was not fraudulent nor is there evidence that it was conducted in anticipation of AHS's bankruptcy. If the transaction were fraudulent or if it was conducted in anticipation of bankruptcy, the claim would be disallowed under Section 502, not subordinated under Section 510(c).

Answer (D) is incorrect because there is no evidence that Major's actions violated federal antitrust laws. If there were such evidence, the proper course of action is not disallowance or subordination. Instead, AHS might be entitled to damages against Major under federal antitrust laws.

55. **The correct answer is (C).** If Major's claim is subordinated, that means that the claim will be postponed in rank until the claims of the other creditors are paid.

Answer (A) is incorrect because it confuses subordination with disallowance. Subordination means that the order of payment of the claim rather than the existence of the claim is at issue.

Answer (B) is incorrect because subordination does not mean that the debtor will receive damages for the creditor's conduct. AHS may well be entitled to such damages, but that would have to be established elsewhere.

Answer (D) is incorrect because subordination does not mean that Major is no longer a creditor of AHS. Major remains a creditor with a valid claim.

56. **The correct answer is (A).** Section 726 is the general distribution section for liquidation cases, both in the case of consumer and corporate cases. Section 726(a) would provide for payment in the following order in this case: 1)the priority claim under Section 507; 2)the allowed unsecured claim tardily filed where the creditor did not have notice of the case in time for timely filing; 3)the allowed unsecured claim tardily filed where the creditor had such notice of the case; 4)the prepetition tax penalty to the extent that it is not compensation for actual pecuniary loss. The Code sections that cover each of these claims are Sections 726(a)(1), (a)(2), (a)(3), and (a)(4), respectively. **All of the other answers are incorrect.**

57. Yes. Section 726(a)(2)(A) provides for a second priority payment for allowed unsecured claims, proof of which are timely filed under subsection 501(a), (b), or (c). Section 501(b) allows a guarantor such as Baumer to file a proof of claim on behalf of the Bank to which Baumer is also liable if the Bank does not timely file a proof of claim.

58. **The correct answer is (C).** Under Section 726(b), administrative expenses incurred under

chapter 7 after conversion from a chapter 11, 12, or 13 case have priority over administrative expenses incurred under any other bankruptcy chapters or even under chapter 7 before the conversion. The idea behind this section is to make sure that funds will be available in the chapter 7 case in order to encourage lawyers and other professionals to contribute to a successful wind-up of the debtor. **All of the other answers are incorrect.**

59.   **The correct answer is (D).** The basic damage claim is payable under Section 726(a)(2) because that section covers prepetition, timely filed, allowed unsecured claims that are not entitled to priority repayment under Section 507. The basic damage claim would fit that category. On the other hand, the treble damage claim would be considered an unsecured claim that is not compensation for actual pecuniary loss to AmCon. For that reason, the claim is payable under Section 726(a)(4).

Answer (A) is incorrect for the reasons stated above.

Answer (B) is incorrect. Section 726 would provide for repayment of the damage claim in BioMed's liquidation.

Answer (C) is incorrect for the reasons stated above.

60.   **The correct answer is (D).** There is no statutory authority that specifically authorizes substantive consolidation. The authority of a bankruptcy court to order substantive consolidation is found in the general discretionary equitable powers codified in Section 105 of the Code. **All of the other answers are incorrect.**

61.   **The correct answer is (A).** The majority view is that substantive consolidation is proper only where either (1) creditors dealt with the entities as a single economic unit, or (2) the affairs of the debtors are so entangled that consolidation will benefit all creditors. The purpose of substantive consolidation is to ensure the equitable treatment of creditors.

Answer (B) is incorrect because merely saving time and money is not sufficient justification for a court to order substantive consolidation.

Answer (C) is incorrect because mere commingling of assets does not lead to substantive consolidation. Most courts will order substantive consolidation only where it is impossible to untangle the assets and debts of the debtors without huge practical difficulty or prohibitive expense.

Answer (D) is incorrect because substantive consolidation is not justified simply because it would make it easier to confirm a plan.

62.   **The correct answer is (C).** The legal effect of substantive consolidation is to combine the assets and liabilities of related entities into a single pool. Liabilities are then satisfied from the common fund and inter-company claims are typically eliminated. The creditors are also combined for purposes of voting on a reorganization plan.

Answer (A) is incorrect because substantive consolidation does not result in automatic confirmation for the debtors' respective chapter 11 plans.

Answer (B) is incorrect because substantive consolidation does not necessarily result in the appointment of a trustee in a chapter 7 case.

Answer (D) is incorrect because substantive consolidation does not result in the voiding of otherwise valid liens held by creditors.

63.   **The correct answer is (B).** Section 363(b)(1) authorizes the trustee or a debtor in possession to use, sell or lease property of the estate outside the ordinary course of business. However, the trustee or debtor in possession must first provide notice and a hearing before the property may be used, sold, or leased other than in the ordinary course of business. This requirement applies when the proposed action with respect to the property is not in the ordinary course of business. In this example, Mariners' proposed use is arguably outside the ordinary course of business because Mariners is in the business of selling boats, not arranging travel tours. Moreover, Mariners' creditors would likely argue that such a transaction is not within the range of risks reasonably expected for a business of this type.

     Answer (A) is incorrect because Section 363 applies in both chapter 7 and chapter 11 cases.

     Answer (C) is incorrect because the use of the boats offered for sale (i.e., residential or commercial) is not determinative of whether Section 363 applies. Section 363 applies to virtually all transactions involving the use, sale, or lease of property of the estate other than in the ordinary course of business.

     Answer (D) is incorrect because it would be difficult to argue that the proposed use of the boats in this case is within the ordinary course of business of Mariners. It would seem unusual for a boat selling business to also be in the business of providing a full-scale travel service. Allowing the boats to be used in this way exposes creditors to risks beyond those which might be reasonably expected.

64.   **The correct answer is (A).** Section 363(c) authorizes the debtor in possession in a chapter 11 case to use, sell or lease property of the estate in the ordinary course of business without the need for a notice or a hearing. A lease of the type described in the problem would be normal for a large casino and is probably of a type that the casino entered into prepetition. The fact that the small casino is an acquisition target would probably not change this result.

     Answer (B) is incorrect for the reasons stated above.

     Answer (C) is incorrect for the reasons stated above.

     Answer (D) is incorrect because Section 363(c) specifically authorizes the use, sale or lease of property of the estate despite the bankruptcy filing.

65.   No. Section 363(c)(2) makes it clear that the casino cannot use, sell or lease cash collateral without either the consent of First Bank or court approval. The checks and their proceeds would qualify as "cash collateral" under Section 363(a). First Bank might consent to this use of cash collateral since it will help keep the business running and presumably increase First Bank's economic position. If First Bank does not consent, the debtor must get the approval of the court. Court approval will likely be conditioned on First Bank receiving adequate protection of its interest in the cash collateral.

66.   **The correct answer is (D).** Section 363(f) allows a sale of property free and clear of an interest in property, including a lien as long as certain requirements are met. Miller's inventory is subject to two liens held by the two banks mentioned. Several of the requirements in Section 363(f)(1) are met in the problem. However, even if only one of them were met, a sale free and clear of the liens can occur because Section 363(f)(1) is written in the disjunctive. **For these reasons, all of the other answers are incorrect.**

67.   **The correct answer is (C).** Sections 541(c) and 363 (l) work together to invalidate any contractual provisions such as the one in the problem that provide for the forfeiture of the debtor's property or that attempt to restrict the transfer of such property. These clauses are sometimes called "ipso facto" clauses. The practical effect of this is that if a trustee seeks to use, sell, or lease property pursuant to Section 363, such a clause cannot block that action.

       Answer (A) is incorrect because the clarity of the language, although possibly relevant to some other legal question, is not relevant to the question of whether the clause is enforceable in bankruptcy.

       Answer (B) is incorrect because the corporate officers' comprehension of the clause, although possibly relevant to some other legal question, is not relevant to the question of whether the clause is enforceable in bankruptcy.

       Answer (D) is incorrect because the legal enforceability of the clause is not dependent on state law. It is a bankruptcy law question.

68.   **The correct answer is (C).** Section 363(b)(1) restricts the use, sale, or lease of personally identifiable information about individuals to a person not affiliated with the debtor unless such sale, use, or lease meets certain requirements. The debtor must have disclosed a policy prohibiting the transfer of such information and the sale must be consistent with that policy or the debtor must seek court approval of the sale under certain conditions specified in Section 363(b)(1).

       Answer (A) is incorrect because the policy on the website does not trump bankruptcy law.

       Answer (B) is incorrect because the individual customers would likely not have a per se right to intervene in the bankruptcy case. That is one of the reasons why Section 363(b)(1) was deemed necessary. The idea is that since individual customers cannot intervene in the case, there should be some statutory safeguard to protect their privacy interest in the personally identifiable information.

       Answer (D) is incorrect because the trustee cannot sell the customer list without first determining whether such a sale is consistent with the debtor's policy and if it is not consistent, it must comply with Section 363(b)(1)(B).

69.   No, at least as a legal matter. Section 364(a) of the Code gives an administrative priority to persons who extend credit in the ordinary course of business. Since this transaction is a normal part of the golf cart business and this supplier has a long-standing relationship with the debtor, such a priority would be available to the supplier. No notice or hearing is required. Of course, there is no guarantee of repayment. If estate assets are insufficient to pay all claims, then the supplier might not actually receive payment.

70.   **The correct answer is (A).** Section 364(b) allows the trustee or debtor in possession to obtain unsecured credit outside the ordinary course of business. Notice and a hearing is

required. Section 102 defines "notice and a hearing" as requiring notice, but not necessarily an actual hearing. When seeking unsecured credit under the circumstances in the problem, the trustee would have to give notice, but an actual hearing would not be mandated unless a party in interest requested one.

Answer (B) is incorrect for the reasons stated above. Notice and hearing (as defined in Section 102) is required even without an objection by a creditor.

Answer (C) is incorrect because notice and hearing (as defined in Section 102) is required even if a creditors' committee has not been appointed.

Answer (D) is incorrect for the reasons stated above.

71. **The correct answer is (A).** Subject to court approval and after notice and a hearing, the debtor in possession can grant a junior lien on already encumbered property notwithstanding such a provision in the loan documents.

Answer (B) is incorrect for the reasons stated above.

Answer (C) is incorrect because the timing of the signing of the loan documents is not relevant for purposes of determining whether the senior lienholder could prevail.

Answer (D) is incorrect because there is no requirement that the debtor in possession seek and fail to obtain credit under the superpriority provisions prior to seeking credit in the form of a junior lien. A trustee or a debtor in possession can pursue any form of credit authorized under any of the provisions of Section 364.

72. **The correct answer is (B).** Section 366(b) allows a utility to proceed as described in the proposal. However, it does require that the utility give the customer twenty (20) days from the date of the filing to provide the deposit.

Answer (A) is incorrect because Section 366(a) does not make the proposal illegal.

Answer (C) is incorrect because Section 366(b) does not make this proposal illegal.

Answer (D) is incorrect because while Section 366(b) allows a utility company to require a deposit as described in the proposal, there is nothing in that code section that says the deposit must not exceed 10% of the customer's outstanding bill.

73. **The correct answer is (D).** Section 366(c)(1)(B) specifically states that in chapter 11 cases, an administrative expense priority shall not constitute an assurance of payment under Section 366(b). This means that the although the utility could accept such a priority, it cannot be compelled to do so.

Answer (A) is incorrect because nothing in the language of Section 366 explicitly endorses this policy argument. Arguably, such an endorsement is implicit in Section 366(c)(1)(B), but it is certainly not explicit.

Answer (B) is incorrect because nothing in the language of Section 366 endorses this policy argument. In fact, the language of section 366(c)(1)(B) seems to implicitly reject it.

Answer (C) is incorrect because nothing in the language of Section 366 states that the extent of the priority is a relevant factor.

74. Yes. Section 366(c)(4) states as follows: "**Notwithstanding any other provision of law**

(emphasis added), with respect to a case subject to this subsection, a utility may recover or set off against a security deposit provided to the utility by the debtor before the date of the filing of the petition without notice or order of the court." This subsection appears to override all other law, including state law, that would attempt to preclude such set-offs.

75.   **The correct answer is (A).** If a party other than the trustee seeks abandonment, the request must be made by motion and abandonment can only occur pursuant to a court order. *See* Section 544(b). **All of the other answers are incorrect.**

76.   **The correct answer is (C).** Section 554(b) does not contain a time limit for a party in interest to request abandonment. The party in interest has a reasonable period of time. This is usually interpreted to mean a period that allows for a deliberative consideration of the circumstances of the case. **All of the other answers are incorrect.**

77.   **The correct answer is (C).** Property abandoned under Section 554 goes to the debtor if the debtor has rights in the property. In this case, the property is also subject to a lien. The lien stays with the property. If the lien is based on a prepetition claim, the creditor must get relief from the stay in order to enforce the lien in most cases.

    Answer (A) is incorrect because abandonment does not automatically mean that a sale of the property will occur. Sale can occur after abandonment, but sale and abandonment are not the same thing.

    Answer (B) is incorrect because abandonment does not mean that the property goes to the state. If the debtor has no rights in the property and the state does, the property could be abandoned to the state. However, that is not the case in this problem.

    Answer (D) is incorrect because in the problem, the debtor and the lienholder both have interests in the property that supersede any interest held by unsecured creditors. Once the property is abandoned, it goes back to the debtor. The estate is divested of any interest.

78.   **The correct answer is (A).** The estate has no interest in the property because after the satisfaction of the security interest and the exemption, there is no value in the property for the estate. **For this reason, all of the other answers are incorrect.**

79.   **The correct answer is (A).** Under the standard "Countryman" definition (named after Professor Vern Countryman), an executory contract includes contracts on which performance remains due, to some extent on both sides. Courts are generally looking for whether there are any unperformed obligations on either side and whether breach of those obligations would excuse the other party from performance. In this case, the policies were executory on the date of the petition because both parties had material obligations to perform. The movie studio had an obligation to pay the premiums to the insurance company. The insurance company had an obligation to provide coverage.

   Answer (B) is incorrect because insurance policy contracts, like all other contracts, can be executory if they fit the Countryman definition.

   Answer (C) is incorrect because the short postpetition "life" of the insurance policy contract does not mean that it cannot be executory.

   Answer (D) is incorrect because the meaning of the term "executory contract" would not change whether the studio filed chapter 7 or 11. Section 365(a) is generally applicable to both chapters.

80.   **The correct answer is (C).** In order to decide whether a contract is executory under the Countryman definition, courts will try to determine whether there are any unperformed obligations on either side and whether breach of those obligations would excuse the other party from performance. This is not an executory contract because the debtor's non-performance of its obligation is not a breach that would excuse the insurer of its obligation to perform. For this reason, **answers (A) and (D) are incorrect.**

   Answer (B) is incorrect because nothing in the Code says that a bankruptcy filing automatically voids an insurance policy.

81.   **The correct answer is (A).** When the trustee elects to maintain the contract, that is called an "assumption" of the contract. Once the trustee elects to assume the contract, the bankruptcy estate is liable for the obligation under it.

   Answer (B) is incorrect because Freshfruit is the other party to the contract. It has an obligation to pay for the cranberries, not to deliver them.

   Answer (C) is incorrect. The trustee is the legal actor who makes the decision to assume the contract, but his/her decision to do so does not mean that he/she is personally liable for the obligation.

   Answer (D) is incorrect. Since this is a chapter 7 case, there is no debtor in possession.

82.   **The correct answer is (B).** When a decision is made to assume an executory contract, the bankruptcy estate assumes the obligation to perform. Freshfruit acquires an administrative expense claim in the grower's bankruptcy.

All of the other answers are incorrect. First, nowhere in the facts is it suggested that Freshfruit has a secured claim, so Answer (A) is incorrect. Second, the mere assumption of the contract by the grower would not result in the voiding of Freshfruit's claim, so Answer (C) is incorrect. To the contrary, the Code states that Freshfruit's claim will be elevated in its priority status. Third, nowhere in the facts is it suggested that Freshfruit is an undersecured creditor (a creditor whose claim exceeds the value of the collateral), so Answer (D) is incorrect.

83.   **The correct answer is (C).** Generally, to assume an executory contract, the estate must cure the default, compensate the non-debtor party for the damage caused by the default, and give adequate assurance of future performance. Before 2005, some courts had held that the existence of non-monetary breaches that were impossible to cure rendered the contract from which such breaches arose non-assumable as a matter of law. As amended in 2005, however, Section 365(b)(2) excuses the estate from curing certain impossible-to-cure, non-monetary defenses. Letting insurance lapse is one of these; Corsine cannot go back in time and procure the required insurance. So long as Corsine compensates Snidely for any losses, and provides adequate assurance of future performance (probably in the form of a new insurance policy), it will be able to assume the lease.

       Answer (A) is incorrect because monetary damage can cure the losses occasioned by failure to provide insurance. But if there has been no damage or loss that would have been covered by insurance, then there is nothing to compensate.

       Answer (B) is also incorrect, for basically the same reason. After 2005, there is no real difference between monetary and non-monetary losses; each has to be compensated. But there is no hard commercial loss here because of the lapse in insurance; had an insurable loss occurred during the lapse, the compensation would presumably have been the repair or replacement of the item damaged.

       Answer (D) is incorrect. Nothing in the Code requires such damages.

84.   **The correct answer is (A).** Since this appears to be a standard contract, Spiffy would have a claim for damages for breach of contract under state law. For this reason, **Answer (B) is incorrect.**

       Answer (C) is incorrect because Spiffy does not have a secured claim.

       Answer (D) is incorrect because nothing in the Code supports a claim for treble damages.

85.   **The correct answer is (A).** Under the Code, the breach is considered to have taken place prior to the filing even though the contract was rejected postpetition. *See* Section 502(g). For this reason, **all of the other answers are incorrect.**

86.   **The correct answer is (A).** Under Section 362(f)(1) and (f)(2), the bankruptcy trustee can assign the contract, but only if he or she assumes the contract and provides adequate assurance of future performance by the assignee.

       Answer (B) is incorrect because assuming the contract would not be enough. The assumption must be followed by an assignment under the conditions specified in Section 365(f)(2).

       Answer (C) is incorrect because normally the trustee does not have to go to state court at all. Section 365(f) contemplates that all of the actions necessary to effectuate an assignment happen in the bankruptcy court.

Answer (D) is incorrect because an assignment will normally be preceded by an assumption of the contract, not a rejection of it. Section 365(f)(2)(A) specifically requires an assumption of the contract.

87. **The correct answer is (B).** Under Section 365(k), an assignment relieves the bankruptcy estate from liability for breaches that occur after the assignment. This is the main reason why the Code requires the assignee to provide adequate assurance of future performance. **Answer (A) is incorrect** because the auto parts manufacturer has no recourse against the estate if the assignee breaches.

Answer (C) is incorrect because under Section 365(k), the auto parts manufacturer would not have a cause of action regardless of where the manufacturer chose to file suit.

Answer (D) is incorrect because the auto parts manufacturer would have no grounds to obtain relief from stay.

88. **The correct answer is (D).** Section 365(f)(1) invalidates contractual anti-assignment clauses. So, the contract would be assignable notwithstanding the contract. Section 365(f)(1) also renders null and void certain non-bankruptcy laws that uphold contractual anti-assignment clauses.

Answers (A), (B) and (C) are incorrect for the reason mentioned above. The contractual provision will not override bankruptcy law and a judge cannot unilaterally ignore the specific mandate of Section 365(f)(1) either on his own authority or in reliance on Section 105.

89. **The correct answer is (C).** Section 365(d)(3) requires the trustee to timely perform all obligations of the debtor under any unexpired lease of nonresidential real property until such lease is assumed or rejected. This means that the trustee must pay the rent in 10 days unless she can get an extension under certain narrow provisions of Section 365(d)(3) ("The court may extend, for cause, the time for performance of any such obligation that arises within 60 days after the date of the order for relief, but the time for performance shall not be extended beyond such 60-day period."). Section 365(d) was designed to give lessors of nonresidential real property special protection in the event of a lessee's bankruptcy filing.

Answer (A) is incorrect because the bankruptcy filing does not invalidate the lease.

Answer (B) is incorrect because Section 365(d)(3) makes clear that the trustee must timely perform all obligations until such lease is assumed or rejected. Thus, the lack of a decision on assumption or rejection does not relieve the trustee of her obligation.

Answer (D) is incorrect because Section 365(d)(2) has no applicability to this situation. It applies only in chapters 9, 11, 12, or 13 of the Code.

90. **The correct answer is (C).** Section 365(d)(4)(A) states that an unexpired lease of nonresidential real property under which the debtor is the lessee shall be deemed rejected and the trustee shall immediately surrender the property if the trustee does not assume or reject the unexpired lease by the earlier of 120 days after the filing or the date of the entry of an order of a confirmed plan. Since this is a chapter 7 case, the earlier deadline applies. Since the trustee did not act within the deadline or request an extension, the lease is deemed rejected.

Answer (A) is incorrect because under Section 365(d)(4)(B), the trustee would have needed to request the extension within the 120 day period and that was not done. Therefore, the trustee cannot ask for such an extension. **Answer (B) is incorrect** for the same reason. The current trustee may have only recently discovered the problem, but the text of Section 365(d)(4) contains no exception for such a circumstance. From a policy standpoint, it seems correct that the lessor should not bear the burden of the uncertainty associated with the revolving door of trustees.

Answer (D) is incorrect because Section 365(d)(4)(A) specifically states that the lease is deemed rejected. It is not deemed assumed.

91.		**The correct answer is (B).** The licensee may, pursuant to Section 365(n), choose either to treat the contract as terminated by the rejection or to retain its rights under the contract. Section 365(n) contains several other requirements in the event that the licensee of intellectual property decides to retain its rights. The effect of 365(n) is to protect the contractual rights of the licensee under the theory that a licensee of intellectual property has substantial expectations which should not be significantly impaired by a licensor's decision to reject.

All of the other answers are incorrect. There are no facts in the problem that would support a claim of punitive damages or quasi-contract. Moreover, Section 365(n) does not support the claim that the licensee can block rejection altogether.

92.		**The correct answer is (A).** Section 365(n)(1)(B) specifically states that if the licensee chooses to retain its rights, such retention includes a right to enforce any exclusivity provision of the contract.

Answer (B) is incorrect because it states the opposite of what Section 365(n)(1)(B) provides. Section 365(n)(1)(B) states that the licensee can enforce the exclusivity provision but cannot enforce any other right to specific performance.

Answer (C) is incorrect because state law does not control. Bankruptcy law, specifically Section 365(n)(1)(B), controls.

Answer (D) is incorrect because an invention is included in the definition of intellectual property in Section 101 (35A) of the Code. Here, the debtor in possession is a licensor of a right to intellectual property (i.e., the weight-loss drink).

93.		**The correct answer is (B).** The definition of intellectual property in Section 101(35A) does not include trademarks. It does include: trade secret, invention, process, design, or plant protected under title 35, patent application, plant variety, work of authorship protected by title 17, or mask work protected under chapter 9 of title 17 to the extent protected by applicable nonbankruptcy law.

Answer (A) is incorrect for the reasons mentioned above.

Answer (C) is incorrect because Section 365(n) applies in both chapter 7 and chapter 11 cases.

Answer (D) is incorrect. Although the licensee of a trademark might have expectations that merit protection, Congress has not included trademarks in the definition of intellectual property. The actual text of the Code must control.

AVOIDING POWERS: TRUSTEE'S STRONG ARM POWERS UNDER SECTION 544(a)

94.   **The correct answer is (D).** Section 544(a)(1) allows the trustee to assume the status of a creditor with a judicial lien on all property on which a creditor could have obtained a judicial lien, whether or not such creditor actually exists. Section 544 is referred to as the "strong arm clause." Section 544(a)(1) gives the trustee (or the debtor in possession under Section 1107(a) in a chapter 11 case, as in this example) the ability to avoid unperfected security interests in personal property subject to Article 9 of the U.C.C. In the above example, there exists an unperfected security interest on the date of the bankruptcy filing and the debtor in possession can thus "step into the shoes" of a hypothetical judicial lien creditor and avoid the Bank's security interest. This means that the full value of the collateral (in this case, equipment) goes into the bankruptcy estate. The Bank becomes an unsecured creditor.

    Answer (A) is incorrect because the reason for the Bank's failure to file the financing statement is immaterial under Section 544(a)(1);

    Answer (B) is incorrect because the personal guarantee would have no effect on the operation of Section 544(a)(1). It might aid the Bank in its ultimate recovery, but its mere existence does not affect Section 544(a)(1).

    Answer (C) is incorrect because there is no indication that the transfer of the security interest was either actually or constructively fraudulent. If it were, then Section 544(b) and/ or Section 548 of the Code would apply.

95.   **The correct answer is (A).** The U.C.C. requires that a financing statement contain, among other things, an adequate description of the collateral in order to properly perfect a security interest in the collateral. Since this financing statement did not contain any description, it does not meet those requirements. The trustee can thus use Section 544(a)(1) to avoid AP's unperfected security interest in the law books. The value of the law books goes into the bankruptcy estate.

    Answer (B) is incorrect because under the U.C.C. and the weight of authority interpreting its provisions, the purchase order signed by both parties along with the clear intention that the books would secure the purchase price would be sufficient to create a security interest in the books. The issue is whether the interest was *perfected*, not whether a security interest was created.

    Answer (C) is incorrect because AP's failure to provide a description of the collateral was indeed a material omission since the U.C.C. requires an adequate description.

    Answer (D) is incorrect because there is no 90 day reach-back period in the language of Section 544(a)(1). There is a 90 day reach-back period under Section 547(b), but not in the text of Section 544(a)(1). Chapter 9 of this book covers the preference provisions of Section 547(b) in detail.

96.   **The correct answer is (B).** The trustee cannot avoid the computer store's security interest because this case would fall under an exception to the strong arm clause. Section 546(b) of the Code provides that the trustee's avoiding power under Section 544 is subject to a law that permits perfection of an interest in property to be effective against an entity that acquires rights in the property before the date of perfection. This means that the trustee's avoiding power is subject to Section 9-317(a) of the U.C.C. Under that section, a person who files a financing statement with respect to a purchase-money security interest before or within 20 days after the debtor receives delivery of collateral takes priority over the rights of a buyer or lien creditor which arise between the time the security interest attaches and the time of filing. In this example, since the computer store filed its financing statement within 20 days of the debtor taking delivery of the collateral, the perfection occurred within the grace period of 9-317(a) and thus Section 546(b) comes into play. A purchase money security interest arises here because the computer store items are sold on credit and a security interest is taken to secure the purchase price.

       Answer (A) is incorrect because although the security interest was unperfected on the date of bankruptcy, the case would be subject to the Section 546(b) exception. As explained above, since the security interest was perfected within 20 days after delivery (17 days to be exact), it would be safe from attack.

       Both (C) and (D) are incorrect because Section 544(a)(1) operates "without regard to any knowledge" the trustee or any creditor may have. Remember that the trustee is a *hypothetical* lien creditor, not a real one. Thus, any actual knowledge is irrelevant.

97.   **The correct answer is (A).** Under Section 544(a)(3), the trustee has the rights of a bona fide purchaser of real property if at the time of the filing a hypothetical buyer could have obtained bona fide purchaser status. The trustee can avoid any liens or conveyances that a BFP could avoid.

       Answer (B) is incorrect because that section does not apply to these facts. It applies only in situations where state law gives a creditor avoidance rights after an execution against a debtor that is returned unsatisfied.

       Answer (C) is incorrect because this example deals with real property. It does not involve personal property. Section 544(a)(3) applies only to real property.

       Answer (D) is incorrect. Section 544(a)(3)'s application does not depend on the existence of an actual BFP ("whether or not such a purchaser exists").

98.   **The correct answer is (C).** A trustee can avoid an unrecorded transfer of land in a situation analogous to this one, but not after having been put on constructive notice (or inquiry notice) of a prior claim. Actual knowledge is disregarded in determining BFP status, but constructive or inquiry notice will defeat the trustee's avoiding powers. *See* 5-544 *Collier on Bankruptcy-15th Edition Rev.* P. 544.08.

       Answer (A) is incorrect for the reasons stated above.

       Answer (B) is incorrect. Obviously, the Bank still needs to record for good reasons unrelated to the strong arm clause. However, since the trustee takes the rights of a BFP under state law and since state law usually penalizes a purchaser who has constructive notice of an unrecorded mortgage, the state law would not permit avoidance in this situation.

       Answer(D) is incorrect for the reasons stated above.

99.   **The correct answer is (A).** This is a common fact pattern for the application of Section 544(a)(3) (i.e., The debtor mortgages real property and there is no recordation.). The fact that a *debtor in possession* is seeking avoidance (rather than the trustee) does not change the result. A debtor in possession can pursue lien avoidance pursuant to Section 544(a)(3) and Section 1107.

Answer (B) is incorrect for the reasons mentioned above.

Answer (C) is incorrect because neither the trustee nor the debtor in possession's actual knowledge is relevant under Section 544(a). A debtor in possession assumes the same hypothetical status as the bankruptcy trustee without regard to any knowledge the trustee or creditor may have.

Answer (D) is incorrect because as a hypothetical BFP, the trustee under Section 544(a)(3) is deemed to have paid value for the property. There is no requirement that the debtor in possession actually pays such value.

100. **The correct answer is (A)**, although much could be said for (C). The question essentially resolves itself into how to view the transaction. First, note that there are at least two transfers. The first occurs when the sheriff levies execution on the car. It is a transfer because it deprives Jack of possession, and the statute, Section 101(54), simply requires any relinquishment of a right, here the right of possession. The statute also covers "voluntary or involuntary" transactions, so the involuntary nature of the levy is not material. The second occurs when the car is sold. At this point, unless state law were to provide a remedy to Jack, his right of redemption is lost. This is also a transfer, impliedly under pre-2005 law, and explicitly under post-2005 law, pursuant to Section 101(54)(C).

A preference requires a transfer of an interest of the debtor in property within the preference period (here, because there is no insider relationship, 90 days) to a creditor on account of an antecedent debtor while the debtor is insolvent and which causes the transferee to receive more than the transferee would receive in a chapter 7 case. Here, the transfer is within the 90 days, is to a creditor (Jack owed Geezer money) on account of an antecedent debt (not for any simultaneous exchange of value). We can presume that Jack was insolvent under Section 547(g) since the transfer was within 90 days of the commencement of the case, which was a given fact. Finally, the "chapter 7" test will likely be met if Jack is insolvent, since it will effect a dollar for dollar satisfaction of Geezer's debt, and in bankruptcy, with an insolvent estate, creditors will not receive a dollar for dollar payment (look at it this way: if Geezer does not disgorge the $50,000, and the chapter 7 distribution to creditors is 50%, Geezer will get another $25,000 from the bankruptcy estate, for a total of $75,000, which is more than he would have received if the transfer had not occurred and Geezer had just received a 50% distribution). It is thus a preference.

Is it a fraudulent transfer? Here, the transfer to be avoided will be the sale, in which the $100,000 car is sold for $50,000. This is also a transfer since it eliminates Jack's ability to redeem the car from the sheriff, and the elimination of the equity of redemption, as noted above, is a transfer. Jack is insolvent, and so that requirement of a constructively fraudulent transfer is present. But was less than reasonably equivalent value received? Under state law, the UFTA specifically provides that a "regularly conducted, non-collusive" foreclosure sale cannot be attacked for returning insufficient value. Under Section 548, the Supreme Court in *BFP v Resolution Trust Co*, 511 U.S. 531, 114 S. Ct. 1757, 128 L. Ed. 2d 556 (1994), read that requirement into the statute. Thus, it is likely that a court would not find the foreclosure sale a fraudulent transfer (and the levy would not be a fraudulent transfer either — although if a transfer, it was a transfer in satisfaction in some part of an antecedent debt, which is value under Section 548(d).)

The answer is thus that the transactions are avoidable under the preference statute, but not as a fraudulent transfer.

101. Yes. The key point here is to understand that the payment to FNB is a payment *to* a creditor

and it is also a payment *for the benefit* of a creditor. Acme's president is a creditor of Acme because it guaranteed payment of the loan. Acme's payment to FNB releases Acme's president from its obligations under the guarantee. So, the payment to FNB is an indirect preference to Acme's president. The payment takes place outside the 90 days, but within one year and it is payment to an insider, so 547(b)(4)(B) applies and the payment is recoverable by the trustee under Sections 547 and 550. This is a fairly straightforward example of a transfer recoverable against an insider. A more sophisticated example of this principle is presented later in this chapter.

For a time, there was some debate about whether Acme could also be subject to a preference action in this situation. Under Section 547(i) of the 2005 Act and a few earlier Congressional moves, it is clear that the answer to that question is "no."

102. **The correct answer is (D).** Section 547(c)(2), as amended in 2005, gives a defense to creditors whose debt was incurred in the ordinary course of business of both the debtor and the creditor, and either (1) the payment (the transfer) was made in the ordinary course of business of the debtor and the creditor; or (2) made according to ordinary business terms for the industry in which the debtor is engaged. This was a key change in 2005. Before the amendment, the creditor had the burden of showing both payment in ordinary course, and that the payment was made according to ordinary business terms.

Here, the check was the normal way in which payment was made, thereby satisfying Section 547(c)(2)(B). Since the debt was incurred in the ordinary course of business, the defense is complete.

Answer (A) is incorrect because, by keeping the payment, Crunchtime will do better than other creditors. It will receive 100% payment of the bill which is more than other creditors will receive, by definition (since Delay is either actually insolvent or presumed insolvent).

Answer (B) is incorrect because, while true (and thus ensuring that Crunchtime cannot satisfy Section 547(c)(2)(A)), Crunchtime only has to satisfy one of subparagraphs (A) and (B) of Section 547(c)(2) to make its defense, and as shown above, Delay's payment method satisfied Section 547(c)(2)(B).

Answer (C) is incorrect because it is irrelevant. A preference defendant need only prove one of the many defenses set forth in Section 547(c); it need not show all. And while the substantially contemporaneous defense of Section 547(c)(1) is a good defense, it is not present on these facts.

103. **The correct answer is (A).** This question illustrates the application of the subsequent advance rule in Section 547(c)(4). Under this rule, the creditor can reduce the trustee's recovery to the extent that, after the transfer, it has made a subsequent advance for new value. In this question, the creditor's preference payment is safe under Section 547(c)(4) to the extent that the creditor gives new value to the estate. In this example, that amount is $8,000 ($10,000 preference-$8,000 new value = $2,000 recoverable). **All of the other answers are incorrect.**

104. Yes. The subsequent advance for new value defense does not apply if the subsequent new value is fully secured by a security interest that is itself not avoidable. It only applies if the subsequent new value is unsecured or secured by an avoidable security interest. *See* Section

547(c)(4)(A). The subsequent new value must also remain unpaid. *See* Section 547(c)(4)(B). The facts in the problem state that the subsequent new value remained unpaid, so that would not be an issue.

105. **The correct answer is (A).** This questions illustrates the operation of the Section 527(c)(5) defense in preference law. If your bankruptcy course covers Section 547(c)(5), your professor will probably give you a *very* detailed explanation on the history, purpose, and workings of the exception. Thus, we are not going to delve into all of that. The point of including a Section 547(c)(5) question in this book is to give you further help in understanding how to apply Section 547(c)(5) if you encounter a Section 547(c)(5) question on your exam.

The upshot of this question is that the bank has a valid security interest except to the extent that the deficiency was reduced between 90 days prior to the filing and the day of the filing. Here, that amount was \$20,000. (\$110,000-\$70,000 = \$40,000) and (\$100,000-\$80,000 = \$20,000). So, the trustee can avoid the bank's security interest to that extent. This leaves the bank with a \$60,000 allowed secured claim and a \$40,000 general unsecured claim. Prior to lien avoidance, the bank would have had an \$80,000 allowed secured claim (i.e., the value of the collateral). **For this reason, Answer (B) is incorrect.**

Answer (C) is incorrect because under Section 547(e) and also pursuant to the after-acquired property clause, there was a transfer of property of the debtor (i.e., the accounts receivable) within 90 days of the filing. You will have more opportunities to review this concept in subtopic C of this chapter.

Answer (D) is incorrect because accounts receivable can be subject to preference actions.

106. **The correct answer is (D).** As a part of the 2005 Act, Congress enacted Section 547(h). The section provides that a transfer made as part of an alternative repayment schedule that was created by an approved nonprofit budgeting and credit counseling agency is not avoidable as preference. Since this agency is on the list of approved agencies and the payment to creditor 4 appears to meet the other criteria of Section 547(h), the payment would likely be covered by the exception. The payment to creditor 4 would be a preference under Section 547(b) and would not qualify for protection under the ordinary course exception (Do you see why?), but Section 547(h) would likely save it.

Notice that this defense does not contain any explicit reference to any of the other defenses, so presumably none of the conditions associated with those defenses (ordinary course, contemporareous exchange, domestic support obligation, small consumer claims etc.) have to be present. Consistent with the above analysis, **Answer (A) is incorrect.**

Answer (B) is incorrect because the ordinary course defense would not work here. The hasty payment made under duress does not look "ordinary."

Answer (C) is a policy argument that would probably not be persuasive. Two difficulties with Section 547(h) are that it potentially undermines the goal of creditor equality and that it could encourage, rather than prevent the proverbial "race to the courthouse." One way to counter those effects would be to adopt the policy argument in Answer (C). If courts applied the Section 547(h) defense as narrowly as possible, this could have the effect of encouraging creditors to enact more realistic and more equitable alternative payment schedules. However, Section 547(h) was drafted broadly and will thus likely be applied broadly to a wide range of situations, even situations such as this one that directly implicate traditional preference concerns.

107.　**The correct answer is (A).** Pursuant to Section 547(a)(1)(A) and (e)(2)(B), this transfer of real property occurred on August 1. Section 547(e) considers the transfer as having occurred on the date on which it became effective under nonbankruptcy law. In the above example, recordation is necessary to perfect the transfer. Therefore, under Section 547(e)(2)(B), the transfer occurred on the date of perfection. It is very important to note that Section 547(e)(2)(A) contains a grace period. Thus if the recordation occurs within 30 days of the transfer taking place, the transfer will occur at the time the transfer takes effect between the parties. Here, that would mean that the transfer occurred on April 1. Although Section 547(e) is complicated, the main thing to keep in mind is that it is designed to give creditors an incentive to promptly record or otherwise perfect their liens so that secret liens will be discouraged. On an exam, a Section 547(e) problem usually crops up when a creditor delays perfection. In that case, it is important to work through the section carefully to determine which section of Section 547 (e) applies to the facts.

Ultimately, the reason why this is important is that under Section 547(b), the timing of the transfer can determine, among other things, whether the date of the transfer falls within the preference period. If all of the other requirements of Section 547(b) are met and none of the exceptions of Section 547(c) apply, then the bank's mortgage on August 1 can be considered a preferential transfer and can be avoided by the trustee since it occurs within the 90 day preference period.

The timing of the transfer can also determine whether there is an antecedent debt. If the transfer occurs on April 1, for example, then there can be no antecedent debt under Section 547(b)(2) because the incurring of the debt and the transfer would have occurred simultaneously.

Finally, the timing of the transfer establishes August 1 as the date for determining the debtor's financial condition under Section 547(b)(3).

Answer (B) is incorrect because of the delay in recordation. If the recordation had occurred within 30 days of April 1, then under Section 547(e)(2)(A) the transfer would have taken place on April 1.

Answer (C) is incorrect for the reasons stated above.

108.　**The correct answer is (A).** There is no preferential transfer on September 15 because the transfer is deemed to have been made on the day that the cash changed hands. Section 547(e)(2) states that a transfer is made for preference purposes when it is perfected in accordance with the rules stated in Section 547(e)(1). That section provides that real property transfers (other than an interest in fixtures) are perfected when a hypothetical bona fide purchaser of the same property could not acquire a superior interest. Thus, a real property transferee has to do whatever is necessary under state law to protect himself against a hypothetical purchaser. (See the previous problem for another example.) If the jurisdiction recognizes possession by the transferee as a substitute for recording, then the transfer will be deemed to have been made on the date when such possession is established or on the date when such recording takes place, whichever occurs first. Since possession was established on July 1, the transfer occurred on July 1.

Answers (B) and (C) are incorrect for the reasons stated above.

Answer (D) is incorrect because the state of mind of the transferee is not relevant under modern preference law.

109. **The correct answer is (B).** The transfer is deemed to have been made on March 18. Section 547(e)(1)(B) provides that a transfer of a fixture or property other than real property is perfected when a creditor on a simple contract cannot acquire a judicial lien that is superior to the interest of the transferee. Under U.C.C. 9-317(2)(A), an unperfected security interest is subordinate to the claim of a person who becomes a lien creditor prior to the time when the security interest becomes perfected. Under Section 547(e)(2)(B), the transfer occurs on March 18 because that is when the transfer is perfected and the transfer was perfected after the 30 day grace period of Section 547(e)(2)(A).

Answer (A) is incorrect for the reasons stated above.

Answers (C) and (D) are both incorrect. Section 547(e) applies to "transfers" under the Code.

110. **The correct answer is (D).** As discussed earlier, Section 547(b)(4)(B) allows a trustee to avoid a transfer made during one year before the filing when the creditor to whom or for whose benefit the transfer was made is an "insider" at the time of the transfer. The term "insider" includes a person "in control of the debtor" if the debtor is a corporation as in this example. It also includes other persons and entities, so consult the definition in Section 101(31) for questions as to the scope of the term. Since this transfer to Harry takes place outside the 90-day period, it can be avoided under Section 547 only if it can be proven that Harry was an insider at the time of the transfer. A key issue would thus be whether Harry's status as a corporate advisor and "rainmaker" translated into actual management and/or meaningful control of the corporation's affairs (for example, authority to dispose of corporate assets or ability to prevail in decisions regarding the operation of the business). This speaks to the entire idea behind the one-year reach back period for insiders. The courts will scrutinize the closeness of the relationship between the debtor and alleged insider and whether the insider used that closeness to gain the preference which it received. Unless it can be shown that Harry had actual managerial or directorial control, this might be tough sledding for the trustee.

Answer (A) is incorrect because that issue would have no bearing on the preference issue under Section 547. It might have some relevance for other legal issues, but not on preference analysis.

Answer (B) is incorrect because there is no indication in these facts that the sale transaction was constructively fraudulent as to Corporation B. Since the purchase price was a fair reflection of the market price, there was a fair exchange of value in the transaction. Corporation B paid the sale price and Corporation B received A's assets. Thus, Corporation B received something of value which would have been subject to levy by its creditors. (Note that the transaction could have arguably been fraudulent as to Corporation A since the proceeds of the sale went directly to Harry rather than to Corporation A. Harry paid off all of the creditors of A which would help lower the risk of a fraudulent transfer challenge later on if Corporation A rather than Corporation B had ended up in bankruptcy. Even so, it probably would have been better to structure the deal so that Corporation A received some of the proceeds directly rather than indirectly. More on that in Chapter 10.)

Answer (C) is incorrect because that issue would have no bearing on the preference issue under Section 547. It might have some relevance for other legal issues, but not on preference analysis. It may well be the case from a subjective viewpoint that the transfer should not have been made, but preference analysis sticks to the economic effect of the transaction and if the technical elements of preference law have been met, the transfer is avoidable unless an exception applies.

111.   No. The presumption of insolvency will not apply with respect to the transfer because it occurred more than 90 days before the filing of the petition.

112.   Yes. You need to tell the partner that although Section 547(f) contains a presumption of insolvency on and during the 90 days immediately prior to the filing of the petition, the effect of this presumption is only to shift the burden of going forward with the evidence. It does not affect the burden of proof. That remains with the trustee. The presumption operates in accordance with Rule 301 of the Federal Rules of Civil Procedure. Thus, if the creditor submits a true and accurate financial statement or, in some jurisdictions, its own bankruptcy schedules and that statement or those schedules show a positive net worth under a fair valuation, the trustee must come forward with evidence to prove insolvency at the time of the transfer by a preponderance of the evidence.

113.   **The correct answer is (D).** The first point to notice is that under Section 547(g), the creditor or party in interest against whom the preference is being sought has the burden of proving the nonavoidability of a transfer under Section 547(c). Thus, **both answers (A) and (C) are incorrect.**

As between (B) and (D), **D is correct** because under Section 547(c)(2), if BOC can show that late payments (between 15 and 35 days late) were routinely accepted between these two parties or in this type of sale (i.e., from a trucking company to a gasoline supplier), then BOC could meet the Section 547(c)(2) "ordinary course" exception. BOC would not want to show that it always demanded prompt payments on the invoices because that would make these two late payments not routine. For this reason, **B is incorrect.**

114. **The correct answer is (B).** Unlike Section 544(a), the trustee's right under Section 544(b) to avoid a pre-bankruptcy transfer is *not* independent of the right of any particular creditor. Under Section 544(b), standing is possible for the trustee only if the trustee is asserting already existing rights belonging to an actual unsecured creditor with an allowable claim.

   Answer (A) is incorrect because the right to avoid a transfer under Section 544(b) may have its origins in either state *or* federal law. For this reason, **Answer (C) is also incorrect.**

   Answer (D) is incorrect because the trustee does not have to make an affirmative action to claim the right to challenge the August 1 transfer. In other words, the right to challenge the transfer passes to the creditor automatically upon the filing of the petition.

115. **The correct answer is (C).** The fact that the trustee cannot proceed under Section 548 does not prevent her from using Section 544(b). In fact, this might be just the type of case where Section 544(b) might be most usefully employed. The running of the two-year period prevents the trustee from using Section 548 because that section has a two-year limitation period. Not so for the state fraudulent conveyance law in the problem which has a four-year period. For this reason, **Answer (A) is incorrect.**

   Answer (B) is incorrect because there is no requirement that the trustee seek relief in state court in order to proceed under Section 544(b). State law would provide the doctrinal framework for the Section 544(b) action, but the bankruptcy court has jurisdiction to hear and decide the matter.

   Answer (D) is incorrect because the fact that there was actual fraud involved does not change the operation of the two-year limitation period in Section 548. The two-year limitation period of Section 548 applies to cases of actual fraud and constructive fraud. The two-year limitation period would prevent the trustee from using Section 548, but not Section 544(b).

116. **The correct answer is (B).** Under Section 544(b), the successful avoidance of the transfer is not simply for the benefit of the creditor who would have been able to set aside the transfer under state law. Instead, it is for the benefit of the estate. The effect of this is that, in an example such as the one above, the entire $2,000,000 transfer is avoidable by the trustee. The authority for this result goes back to the famous case of *Moore v. Bay*, 284 U.S. 4 (1931). It was later codified both in the Bankruptcy Act in Section 70e and in the Code in Sections 550(a), 544(b), and 541(a)(3). This is a rather remarkable point and it helps explain why a trustee could have a powerful incentive to pursue avoidance under Section 544(b) in a case where the two-year period has already run under Section 548 (as in the previous example).

   Answers (A), (C) and (D) are incorrect for the reasons stated above.

117. Yes. This is a classic fraudulent transfer under Section 548. The sale of the property and the depositing of the proceeds in an out-of-state bank account under the name of a subsidiary could be considered very strong evidence of an intent to hinder, delay, or defraud creditors (Why out-of-state? Why not use one of its own accounts?). Also, the transfer occurred within the 2-year limitation period.

118. **The correct answer is (A).** The remedy of the trustee is stated in Section 550(a)(1). The trustee can recover the property from the buyer since the buyer is the "initial transferee" of the transfer. There are some complications here that arise from the defense in Section 548(c) which we shall explore in the next problem.

      Answer (B) is incorrect because the appreciation of the property has no impact on the trustee's recovery right under Section 550(a)(1).

      Answer (C) is incorrect because there is nothing in these facts that would trigger such a legal duty on the part of the Buyer, at least when it comes to fraudulent transfer law under Section 548 and the question of the trustee's recovery under Section 550(a)(1).

      Answer (D) is incorrect because the original transfer was not constructively fraudulent. The Buyer paid the full market value for the property at the time. It was the debtor's willful actions after the sale that made the transfer fraudulent.

119. **The correct answer is (C).** Pursuant to Section 548(c), the Buyer (or "transferee") who takes for "value and in good faith has a lien on or may retain any interest transferred to the extent that the [Buyer] gave value to the debtor in exchange for the such transfer or obligation." *See* Section 548(c). Thus, the trustee's recovery in this problem would be limited to $20,000. If the trustee successfully uses Section 548, then one of two things will happen in a case such as the one above. Either the Buyer will retain the property and the trustee can demand payment of $20,000 for the appreciated value or the Trustee will pay the Buyer $700,000 to recover the property which is now worth $720,000. Effectively, what is happening here is that the innocent purchaser is being protected against any loss in value while at the same time being denied any profit in the transaction. For this reason, **answers (A) and (B) are incorrect.**

      Answer (D) is incorrect because Section 548(c) does not give complete protection to the good faith Buyer. A good faith buyer who gives value is only protected to the extent that the transferee gives value in exchange for the transfer. *See* Section 548(c).

120. **The correct answer is (B).** This transfer meets the requirements of Section 548(a)(1)(B). The debtor, within two years of the filing, voluntarily made a transfer of the house and the debtor received less than a reasonably equivalent value in exchange for the transfer. The facts suggest that she became insolvent as a result of the transfer which means that Section 548(a)(1)(B)(ii)(I) is met. This is the constructive fraud prong of Section 548. It is based on the theory that a debtor must pay his creditors before other obligations, including those to family. When the debtor decides to transfer the house, creditors are being deprived of an asset that would otherwise be there.

      Answer (A) is incorrect because Section 548(a)(1)(A) deals with actual fraud and there is little evidence of actual fraud here. The debtor arguably had a laudatory motive (i.e., to protect her son's welfare). Also, the deed was recorded, hardly the type of act one would take if one was trying to keep the transfer "top secret." Of course, with the embezzlement problem, one could argue for actual fraud, but the point is that because of the constructive fraud prong of Section 548, the trustee does not need to make actual fraud the main theory of the case.

Answer (C) is incorrect because Donna's sister's lack of status as a creditor is irrelevant for purposes of Section 548. If the trustee was trying to use Section 547 (preference law) as the vehicle to avoid the transfer, then that would matter ("to or for the benefit of a creditor"). However, Section 548 simply avoids a transfer that is constructively or actually fraudulent regardless of whether the property ends up in the hands of a particular creditor or not.

Answer (D) is incorrect because the debtor's motive is not a factor under the constructive fraud prong of Section 548. Under that analysis, what matters is the economic analysis. Are creditors being deprived of assets that would otherwise be there for payment of debts?

121. **The correct answer is (C).** The transfer could meet the requirement of Section 548(a)(1)(B)(i) because the trustee could argue plausibly that the debtor received less than a reasonably equivalent value in exchange for the transfer of Greenacre. The market price of the property was in the range of $320,000 to $340,000 and this property was sold for $280,000, $30,000 less than the advertised price. A court would have to examine all of the circumstances surrounding the transaction to determine whether a fair economic exchange occurred between the transferee (the buyer) and the transferor (the developer).

This problem provides another example of the constructive fraud theory of fraudulent transfers in Section 548. The key point to remember is that constructive fraud does not require any focus on the state of mind of the parties. The idea is that the transfer has the economic effect of unfairly placing assets outside the reach of creditors. It should be mentioned that the transfer must be in the context of insolvency, resulting insolvency, or an equivalent measure of financial distress. See Section 548(a)(1)(B)(ii). Moreover, the buyer might have a defense here under Section 548 (c) which was discussed in an earlier problem and will be mentioned again when we get to defenses to fraudulent transfers.

Answer (A) is incorrect because this situation does not raise the issue of actual fraud. There is no indication of a close relationship between the parties nor was there any attempt to hide the transfer.

Answers (B) and (D) are incorrect because neither answer raises issues that are relevant under Section 548. It may indeed not be the buyer's fault that the business was not managed properly, but that is not a defense to a fraudulent transfer action. Moreover, the cause of the appreciation in the value of the property is not relevant. The bottom line is that the transfer was arguably for less than a reasonably equivalent value when all of the facts are considered.

122. **The correct answer is (D).** The question under Section 548(a)(1)(B) would be whether Z received less than a reasonably equivalent value in exchange for Z's incurring the obligation to L under the guarantee. The loan proceeds went to Y, not to Z, so it is impossible for Z to argue that it received a direct benefit from the loan to Y. This might appear to sink the case for L. However, there exists legal authority for the argument that a loan to one corporate entity can benefit related entities. If L can demonstrate that Z benefitted indirectly from the loan to Y, L might be able to stave off a fraudulent transfer action from the bankruptcy trustee. The indirect benefit cannot be ephemeral. It has to be specific.

This problem is designed to show how a routine corporate transaction can raise Section 548 issues if the parties designing the transaction are not sufficiently sensitive to the possible bankruptcy implications. If a corporate debtor gives up a security interest, incurs an obligation, or makes a corporate dividend and does not receive adequate consideration in return (and the deal occurs in the context of significant financial distress or resulting financial distress), the deal could be subject to attack by the trustee under Section 548. Leveraged buyouts (in which the assets of a corporation are used as security for loans that finance stock acquisitions) are particularly vulnerable if the deal goes south and it was not properly structured.

Answer (A) is incorrect because the issue would not be whether L provided reasonably equivalent value to Y. Y is not the debtor. Z is the debtor. Clearly, L provided a reasonably equivalent value to Y because it gave Y a loan, but that is not the issue since Y is not the debtor.

Answer (B) is incorrect because the lawfulness of the guarantee is not an issue under Section 548. It might be an issue under general principles of corporate law, but not here.

Answer (C) is incorrect because Y's insolvency is not an issue. Again, Z is the debtor, not Y. The issue would be whether Z was insolvent on the date of that the obligation was incurred or became insolvent as a result of the obligation.

123. Section 550(a) provides for recovery against Y. Y does not have the building anymore. However, the trustee can recover the value of the building from Y. As explained previously, Section 548(c) provides partial protection for Y. It gives Y protection to the extent that it gave value because Y arguably took in good faith (i.e., It did not have actual knowledge of X's insolvency and it seemed to think that the stock had a higher value than it actually did.). Thus, Y could deduct from the $200,000 the $40,000 value of the stock. The trustee could recover $160,000.

124. Under Section 550(b)(1), Z has no liability since it took for value, in good faith, and without knowledge of the voidability of the transfer.

125. **The correct answer is (A).** Section 550(e) protects certain good faith transferees when they make improvements to property. Under that section, the installation of central air conditioning and the preservation would be considered improvements. Section 550(e) protects good faith transferees to the extent of the lesser of the cost of any improvement the transferee makes in the transferred property, or the increase in value of the property as a result of the improvement. This section is designed to prevent a windfall to the estate and limit disincentives to improve property. However, Y would arguably not be considered a good faith transferee because he had knowledge of X's cash flow problems and he had reason to suspect that the transaction was improper. He also had reason to know that the sale would hinder, delay, or defraud creditors of X. In this case, the trustee could recover the building from Y pursuant to Section 550(a)(1) and Y would likely not have the protection of Section 550(e).

Answers (B) and (C) are incorrect for the reasons stated above. Both statements are overly broad. As explained above, a transferee from whom the trustee may recover under Section 550(a) is protected to the extent noted above if the transferee is a good faith purchaser.

Answer (D) is incorrect because both the central air conditioning and the preservation would be considered "improvements" under Section 550(e)(2), as would repairs, tax payments, and discharged liens.

126. **The correct answer is (A).** This is the classic situation in which a debtor in possession (or trustee, depending on the chapter and circumstances) would request turnover under Section 542(a). Section 542(a) is typically used in a bankruptcy case to recover property of the estate after the property has been seized but not sold by a creditor. It allows the debtor in possession or trustee to recover certain property with certain exceptions (i.e., unless such property is of inconsequential value or benefit to the estate). In exchange, the Code provides secured creditors like the Bank various rights, including the right to adequate protection and these rights replace the right of possession.

Answer **(B) is incorrect** because Section 542 applies in chapters other than chapter 11. The fact that this is a chapter 11 case reinforces the argument that the planes would facilitate the debtor's reorganization. However, turnover can be ordered in other chapters of the Code when it would facilitate the policy goals of those chapters.

Answer **(C) is incorrect** because the Bank's repossession prior to filing does not prevent the operation of Section 542. Despite the repossession, the planes are still property of the estate and still subject to turnover.

Answer **(D) is incorrect** because there is no evidence that the planes are of inconsequential value or benefit to the estate. In the fact pattern, the planes are likely to be of benefit to the airline in its reorganization even if they have little economic value.

127. **The correct answer is (D).** Section 542(c) provides that a party is not required to turn over property of the estate or pay a debt owing to the debtor if the party had no actual notice or knowledge of the commencement of the case and if the property was transferred or the debt was paid in good faith to a party other than the trustee or the debtor in possession. Section 542(c) provides protection to the Bank by clarifying that it has no liability to the trustee for the value of the check paid to the creditor. The fact that the payment of the check occurred in the ordinary course of business supports the good faith prong of the statute. It is important to note that Section 542(c) protects only the Bank as the transferor or payor. It does not protect the creditor who received the payment. That creditor could have some liability under Section 549 which governs postpetition transactions. (This will be covered in later in this chapter.) There are two limitations on the reach of Section 542(c): ("Except as provided in Section 362(a)(7)") and ("other than in manner specified in Section 542(d)"), but neither of those limitations is presented in these facts.

Answer **(A) is incorrect** because, among other things, Section 547 covers only prepetition transfers and this is a postpetition transfer.

Answer **(B) is incorrect** because there is no time limitation in Section 542(c).

Answer **(C) is incorrect** because Section 542(c) specifically states that actual notice or actual knowledge of the commencement of the case is relevant and that if the entity has no such notice of knowledge and transfers the property in good faith, then the transferor has no liability to the trustee.

128. **The correct answer is (A).** Section 545(1) gives the trustee the power to avoid the fixing of a statutory lien if the lien first becomes effective upon the happening of one of the events listed in Subsection (1). One of those events is the commencement of a case in bankruptcy. In the fact pattern, the state tax provisions make it clear that a lien arises on personal property "by any . . . voluntary act in reduction of or satisfaction of indebtedness." The filing of a bankruptcy case is such a voluntary act and thus the lien arises upon the occurrence of that act. Section 545(1) is designed to strike down state-created bankruptcy priorities. Section 507 sets the priority scheme in bankruptcy for unsecured claims and Section 545(1)'s purpose is to make it difficult, if not impossible, for certain types of statutory liens to jump to the head of the line. It is important to recognize Section 545(1)'s limitations. Section 545(1) applies only to statutory liens (i.e., those created by statute) and not to consensual or judicial liens. It does not, however, apply to all statutory liens, but only to those that arise because of or due to the happening of one of the events listed in Section 545(1).

The trustee will have to consult two other Code sections: Section 546 and Section 550. Those sections dictate time limitations for the bringing of an action and specify what the trustee can recover and against whom. Those sections will be covered later in this chapter.

It important to distinguish between Section 545(1) and Section 545(2). Section 545(1) operates to avoid statutory liens in the situations described above. Section 545(2) operates more like the strong-arm clause that was covered extensively in chapter 10. It strikes down liens that are not recorded or otherwise perfected as of the filing of the bankruptcy case.

Answer (B) is incorrect because the state tax provision does not trump bankruptcy law for the reason stated above.

Answer (C) is incorrect for two reasons. First, the Bank is a secured creditor. Second, the Bank's status as a secured creditor is not relevant to the question being asked. The Bank's status as a secured creditor is important to the trustee in the ultimate disposition of the assets of the estate (i.e., the priority question), but it does not affect the question of whether the trustee can avoid the fixing of the tax lien (i.e., the lien avoidance question).

Answer (D) is incorrect because the tax lien is a statutory lien. It is not based on an agreement to give a lien, but it arises when and if the debtor suffers financial distress of the kind listed in Section 545(1).

129. **The correct answer is (D).** Section 503(b)(9), added in 2005, gives a priority to creditors whose debt arises from deliveries of goods within 20 days of the filing of a bankruptcy case. Here, Fragile filed 19 days after the delivery, so it qualifies for the priority. The addition of this section thus makes **(A) an incorrect answer.** It also **eliminates (B)**, which does not mention the priority.

As between answers **(C) and (D)**, **(C)** does not take into account the expanded right of reclamation in amended Section 546(c). Under that section as amended in 2005, a vendor/creditor has up to 45 days to request reclamation, and in any event 20 days after the filing. In addition, Section 546(c)(2) specifically permits stacking of these rights. **So, (D) is the correct answer.**

130. **The correct answer is (A).** The garnishment payment is an example of a postpetition

transaction that is voidable under Section 549(a). Section 549 allows the trustee to avoid certain postpetition transfers which deplete the estate. It applies to most postpetition transfers except those authorized by the bankruptcy code or the court. For this reason, **Answer (C) is incorrect.** It is important to note that many transactions that are vulnerable to attack under Section 549 are also in violation of the automatic stay. That would be the case here.

Answer (B) is incorrect because the legality of the garnishment payment does not insulate the transfer from attack by the bankruptcy trustee.

Answer (D) is incorrect because good faith on the part of the transferee is not relevant under Section 549(a).

131. **The correct answer is (C).** Since ISP is a transferee and not a transferor, the payment is voidable due to the interaction of Sections 542(c) and 549(a). Section 542(c) protects the Bank as the transferor of the payment, but it does not protect ISP as the transferee. Section 549 allows the trustee to avoid the payment since it falls within the language of that section as a postpetition transaction.

All of the other answers are incorrect because they raise issues that are not relevant under Section 542(c) or 549(a), at least with respect to ISP.

132. **The correct answer is (B).** There is a separate statute of limitations for the trustee's avoiding powers under Section 549. It is two years after the date of the transfer (the date of honor in the case of a check), or the time the bankruptcy case is closed or dismissed, whichever is earlier.

Answer (A) is incorrect because there is no 90-day time period limitation in Section 549.

Both answers (C) and (D) are incorrect because neither good faith by the transferee (except with respect to purchasers of real property) nor fraud by the debtor are relevant under Section 549.

133. **The correct answer is (B).** Section 549(c) protects the transfer from avoidance by the trustee. Section 549(c) protects postpetition transfers of real property. Such a postpetition transfer will be safe if the transfer occurs and is properly recorded before a copy or notice of the bankruptcy petition is filed and if the transferee buys for fair equivalent value without knowledge of the petition. So, this postbankruptcy transfer of real estate is protected.

Answer (A) is incorrect because the preceding analysis makes it clear that Section 549(c) does not authorize such avoidance.

Answer (C) is incorrect because Section 545(2) applies to the fixing of a statutory lien. This problem does not involve any statutory liens.

Answer (D) is incorrect because the facts do not say anything about court approval of the transfer. Court approval of postpetition transfers routinely takes place in chapter 11 business cases under Section 363 of the Code, but the case in the fact pattern is a chapter 7 case involving an individual.

134. First, $40,000 would be paid to the Section 507(a)(1)-507(a)(7) priority claimants under Section 724(b)(2). Second, $10,000 would be paid to the tax lien claimant under Section 724(b)(5). Since the sales proceeds are now exhausted, the general unsecured claims remain

unsatisfied at least for now.

The explanation for this result can be found in Section 724(b)(1)-(5). Section 724(b) provides a scheme by which certain tax liens (i.e., those not avoidable and those securing an allowed claim for a tax) are subordinated to the payment of certain priority claims (i.e., Section 507(a)(1)-507(a)(7)). The scheme can be quite complicated to apply, depending on the facts of the case. The examples in this book are sufficient for an introductory bankruptcy course.

The purpose of Section 724(b) is to lessen the impact of non-bankruptcy provisions that grant favored status to tax claimants. When such provisions are enacted, tax claimants can move to the front of the line ahead of the Code's favored groups (in this case, priority claimants under Section 507(a)) and frustrate the Code's distribution scheme. Section 724(b) moves the Section 507(a)(1)-507(a)(7) priority claimants back to the front. It applies only in chapter 7 cases and the trustee has to first comply with Section 724(f).

135.   First, $40,000 would be paid to the senior security interest under Section 724(b)(1). Second, the remaining $10,000 would be paid to the Section 507(a)(1)-507(a)(7) priority claimants under Section 724(b)(2). Since the sales proceeds are now exhausted, the remaining balance of the claims remain unsatisfied and would be a general claim against the estate. The priority of those claims continues to be governed by other sections of the Code. Typically, tax claims are entitled to priority under Section 507(a)(8). Notice that Section 724(b) does not affect liens that are senior (or junior) to a tax lien. It only affects distributions between the priority claimants and the tax lien.

136.   No. Section 724(b) does not apply if the lien securing the claim for taxes is avoidable under another Section of the Code ("and that is subject to a lien that is not avoidable under this title. . . .").

137.   **The correct answer is (C).** Section 553(b) allows the trustee to recover $50,000 of the $70,000 that the bank setoff on March 30. Section 553(b) requires several calculations. First, Section 553(b) requires the court to compare the amount owed by the Debtor ($110,000-the Bank's claim against the Debtor) on the 90th day before the date of the filing of the petition with the amount owed to the debtor ($50,000-the Bank's debt to the Debtor) on the 90th day. On that date, the "insufficiency" (i.e., the amount by which the Bank's claim exceeds the Bank's debt) is $60,000 ($110,000-$50,000=$60,000). Next, Section 553(b) requires the court to compare the same amounts on the date of setoff. In the fact pattern, the insufficiency on the date of setoff is $10,000 ($80,000-$70,000=$10,000). This analysis reveals that the setoff allowed the Bank to improve its position to the extent of $50,000 ($60,000-$10,000=$50,000). Thus, the trustee can recover $50,000. If there is no improvement in position between the 90th day and the date of setoff, then the trustee cannot recover any amount under Section 553(b). If there is no insufficiency on the 90th day, Section 553(b) requires the court to determine whether there was an insufficiency on any day after the initial 90-day point, but before the date of filing.

The purpose of Section 553(b) is to discourage precipitous prepetition setoffs that might accelerate a Debtor's plunge into immediate financial distress. It does not apply to postpetition setoffs. A postpetition setoff is stayed by Section 362(a)(7).

Answers (B) and (D) are incorrect for the reasons stated above.

Answer (A) is incorrect because while bankruptcy law generally respects state law setoff rights, Section 553(b) is a limitation on that principle.

138.   No, Section 553(b) does not apply because no setoff has occurred at either Bank #1 or Bank #2 within the 90-day period. It is unlikely that Bank #1 can do anything about this. Bank #1 loses, but all other creditors gain if the money is in an account that is non-exempt. The money becomes available for distribution to all other creditors. Fraudulent transfer law and related doctrines might apply if the Debtor takes the money from Bank #1 and then transfers it to an exempt account, tries to hide it, or transfers it to family and friends. There could also be a denial of discharge if the money is taken out of the Bank #1 account and transferred to Bank #2 with intent to hinder, delay or defraud the court or creditors. Since none of those facts are presented here, it is unlikely that Bank #1 would have a remedy.

139.   **The correct answer is (B).** Section 553(b) requires a comparison of the amount owed by the Debtor ($120,000-the Bank's claim against the Debtor) on the 90th day before the date of the filing of the petition with the amount owed to the Debtor ($70,000-the Bank's debt to the Debtor) on that same date. On that date, the "insufficiency" (i.e., the amount by which the Bank's claim exceeds the Bank's debt) is $50,000 ($120,000-$70,000=$50,000). Next, Section 553(b) requires the court to compare the same amounts on the date of setoff. In the fact pattern, the insufficiency on the date of setoff (i.e., the amount by which the Bank's claim exceeds the Bank's debt) is also $50,000 ($100,000-$50,000=$50,000). This analysis reveals that the setoff did not allow the Bank to improve its position because the amount of the insufficiency stayed the same on the two relevant dates.

Answer (A) is incorrect because the Bank's motives (good or bad)are not relevant under Section 553(b).

Answer (C) is incorrect because the fact that everything happened prepetition does not save the setoff. In fact, Section 553(b) specifically applies to prepetition setoffs. What saves the setoff here is the mathematical operation of Section 553(b) as applied to these particular facts.

Answer (D) is incorrect for the reasons stated above.

140.   **The correct answer is (A).** Section 550(a) allows the trustee to recover Greenacre from Adelaide. Section 550(a) allows a trustee to recover property for the benefit of the bankruptcy estate to the extent that a transfer has been avoided under Sections 544, 545, 547, 548, 549, 553(b), or 724(a). The trustee may recover the property itself or on court order, the value of the property. For this reason, **Answer (D) is incorrect.**

Answer (B) is incorrect because real property is recoverable under Section 550(a).

Answer (C) is incorrect because Dan's pure motives are irrelevant under these facts. They do not provide Adelaide with a defense to the trustee's recovery action.

Answer (D) is incorrect because the trustee does not have to prove that Adelaide knew that the transfer was fraudulent. In fact, as the initial transferee, Adelaide does not have a defense to the Section 550(a) recovery action.

141.   **The correct answer is (A).** Section 550(a) allows the trustee to recover the property itself or on court order, the value of the property. The fact that the sketches were destroyed in the fire does not mean that the estate is without a remedy. The trustee can recover damages from Adelaide if a court orders her to pay such damages to the estate.

Answer (B) is incorrect because Section 550(a) allows the trustee to recover the value of the property "if the court so orders." The trustee is not required to show that the defendant was negligent in order to get this relief. The court may consider certain factors in deciding whether to order recovery of the property or its value, but the defendant's lack of care in protecting the property is not usually among those factors and the trustee is not legally required to make this showing.

Answer (C) is incorrect because it would probably not be difficult to determine the value of the sketches. This type of property is routinely auctioned and a value could be determined from auction prices. There may be instances in which it may be extremely difficult to determine the value of certain property. In those instances, a court may be reluctant to order that the value of the property be recovered. However, this is probably not one of those instances.

Answer (D) is incorrect because Adelaide's actions with regard to the property are not relevant under Section 550(a). If a court orders Adelaide to pay damages to the estate, she will have to do so. The trustee does not have to prove that she tried to hide the property. Nor can she bolster her case by showing that she did not hide it. She does not have a defense under Section 550.

142.   **The correct answer is (C).** B is liable under Section 550(a)(2) because B is the immediate transferee. However, the Section 550(b)(1) defense is available to B. The reason is that B gave value in good faith and without knowledge of the voidability of the transfer. If B can prove these elements (and the burden is on B), then it can use the defense.

Answer (A) is incorrect because it only tells part of the story. B is liable under Section 550(a)(2) as the immediate transferee of the initial transferee (A, in this example). However, as explained above, the Section 550(b)(1) defense will probably save B from ultimate liability.

Answer (B) is incorrect because B is not the initial transferee under Section 550(a)(1). A is the initial transferee under Section 550(a)(1).

Answer (D) is incorrect because the fact that the cars are now in C's possession would not be relevant for determining B's liability. Since Section 550 allows the trustee to recover the value of the property in certain instances instead of the property itself, all the trustee has to do is establish that B is liable under Section 550. If the trustee can so prove, then B is liable regardless of who has possession of the property.

143.   **The correct answer is (B).** Since B is protected by Section 550(b)(1), then C is protected by Section 550(b)(2). Additionally, since C provided value and acted in good faith and without knowledge of the voidability of the transfer, C is also entitled to the protection of Section 550(b)(1) in its own right.

Answer (A) is incorrect because it only tells part of the story. C is liable under Section 550(a)(2) as the mediate transferee of the initial transferee (A, in this example). However, as explained above, both Sections 550(b)(1) and Sections 550(b)(2) will save C from ultimate liability.

Answer (C) is incorrect because, again, it only tells part of the story. C can use the Section 550(b)(2) defense, but he would also be entitled to the Section 550(b)(1) defense in this example.

Answer (D) is incorrect because C's remoteness from the initial transfer is not, in and of itself, enough to protect it. As has been shown, Section 550 specifically contemplates liability for remote transferees. The trustee must apply the provisions of Section 550(a) and (b) to each transferee to determine the extent of each transferee's liability.

144. **The correct answer is (A).** If Section 550(b)(1) insulates B from liability (as the facts here so indicate), then C would be protected by Section 550(b)(2), but only if C took in good faith ("any immediate or mediate good faith transferee of such transferee"). Also, Section 550(b)(1) does not help C here because C cannot establish good faith.

   Answer (B) is incorrect because although the chain of title question may be relevant for purposes of some state law question, it is not relevant for purposes of determining C's liability under Section 550. For much the same reason, **Answer (C) is incorrect.** C's lack of good faith might be relevant for the purposes of determining certain state law questions, but it is not relevant for purposes of Section 550.

   Answer (D) is incorrect because the transferee who is asserting the Section 550 defense has the burden of proof.

145. No. The trustee can certainly recover from any combination of transferees mentioned in Section 550 (i.e., initial, immediate, or mediate transferees). However, Section 550(d) specifically states that "the trustee is entitled to only a single satisfaction under Section 550(a)."

146. **The correct answer is (C).** Usually, the party who receives a transfer of property directly from the debtor is the initial transferee. However, courts have found that a party acting merely as a conduit who facilitates the transfer from a debtor to a third party is not a transferee. If that party is not a transferee, then it cannot be an "initial transferee." Courts that have adopted the "conduit theory" hold that in order for a party to be a transferee, that party must have dominion over money or other property, or the right to use the money or property for its own purposes. In this example, both of the banks would be considered conduits. Bank 1 transferred the funds immediately and Bank 2 is merely holding the funds for deposit. Both banks are conduits acting for X, so X is viewed as the initial transferee under Section 550(a). **For these reasons, all of the other answers are incorrect.**

147. **The correct answer is (B).** The conduit exception is probably unavailable to the accountant because she retained a portion the payment as her fee. As such, she is free to do what she wants with the $12,000 and thus has an interest of her own in the property. The accountant is thus not ignored in the chain of transferees and is acknowledged as the initial transferee. The accountant cannot use the Section 550(b) defense.

   Answer (A) is incorrect because the payment was not made directly to Z. It was made to the accountant. It is important to note that Z could still be liable under Section 550(a) because it is possible to argue that Z is "the entity for whose benefit the transfer was made." Under this theory, Z cannot use the Section 550(b) defense either.

   Answer (C) is incorrect because good faith does not insulate either Z or the accountant from liability under Section 550(a).

   Answer (D) is incorrect because (B) is the right answer.

148. **The correct answer is (A).** Z is liable under Section 550(a)(2) because Z is the immediate transferee of X. However, Z can use the Section 550(b)(1) defense because Z takes for value,

in good faith and without knowledge of the voidability of the transfer.

Answer (B) is incorrect because X is liable under Section 550(a)(1). X is the initial transferee. As such, X cannot use the Section 550(b)(1) defense.

Answer (C) is incorrect because Y is liable under Section 550(a)(1). Y is "the entity for whose benefit the transfer was made." As such, Y cannot use the Section 550(b)(1) defense.

Answer (D) is incorrect because, as explained above, Z can use the Section 550(b)(1) defense. X cannot use it for the reason explained above.

149. **The correct answer is (C).** Section 551 of the Code allows the state tax lien, avoided under Section 545, to be preserved for the benefit of the bankruptcy estate. What this means in practical terms is that the trustee inherits the same position held by the state tax lien and may assert that priority as against other claimants, such as the Bank in this example. The trustee's rights are derivative, but important. Notice that because the Bank timely and properly perfected its security interest, the trustee would not be able to void its security interest under Section 544 or any other section that would allow an unperfected security interest to be voided. However, pursuant to Section 551, the trustee can trump the Bank's security interest indirectly by use of the derivative rights bestowed by Section 551.

      Answer (A) is incorrect because Section 551 specifically says that preservation under that section is for the benefit of the estate. This means that the property interest subject to the avoided transfer automatically becomes property of the estate.

      Answer (B) is incorrect because Section 551 has no effect on whether the Bank's security interest becomes unperfected or not. Perfection under Article 9 is governed by Article 9, not Section 551.

      Answer (D) is incorrect because Section 551 does not allow the trustee to assume secondary rights held by the state tax lien claimant. For example, the trustee would not be allowed to invoke rights under an inter-creditor subordination agreement and thus elevate its rights ahead of other creditors pursuant to such an agreement. Section 551 merely gives the trustee the right to step into the shoes of the trustee to assert only the avoided lien. No other interests are bestowed.

150. **The correct answer is (C).** When the trustee avoids a prepetition security interest because the secured party has not properly perfected it, the avoided lien is still subject to the same state law defect as before. The lien is not magically cured of whatever ailed it. As such, if the interest would be subordinate under state law, it is also going to be subordinate under Section 551. The trustee's derivative rights under Section 551 do not affect the validity of superior claims to the property. For this reason, **all of the other answers are incorrect.**

151. **The correct answer is (E).** (A), (B), and (C) are correct. Each statement tells you something about the basic operation of the discharge under Section 524. Section 524 applies in all bankruptcy chapters. The discharge voids the debtor's personal liability for the debt. It does not affect the lien unless that lien is otherwise avoided. Since this lien was not avoided, it will survive the filing and this means that AFC can continue to enforce it. In this case, the debt exceeds the value of the collateral by the amount of $5,000. The discharge prevents AFC from acting to collect the deficiency. **Since (A), (B), and (C) are all correct, Answer (D) is incorrect.**

152. **The correct answer is (B).** As noted in the previous problem, AFC's claim against the debtor was discharged to the extent of the debtor's personal liability on the debt. Here, that amount is $5,000. Thus, if AFC sues the debtor in state court in the amount of $40,000, the debtor should respond with proof of its bankruptcy discharge and assert that as a defense to the state court action.

Answer (A) is incorrect because the discharge means that AFC is enjoined from acting to collect the $40,000. Since AFC is so enjoined, there is little reason for the debtor to pay the entire $40,000. The debtor has a defense to the extent of $5,000. AFC can enforce its lien to the extent of $35,000.

Answer (C) is incorrect because the debtor cannot force AFC to appear in bankruptcy court to pursue its claim. The state court where AFC brought the action is the court that will settle the matter.

Answer (D) is incorrect because there is no "ordinary course of business" exception to dischargeability under Section 524 or Section 523.

153. No. Section 524(a) applies only to prepetition debts (i.e., debts that arose before the debtor filed the petition).

154. No. Section 524(e) provides that the "discharge of a debt of the debtor does not affect the liability of any other entity on, or the property of any other entity for, such debt." This means that a bankruptcy discharge for Business Partner #1 does not affect Business Partner #2's liability.

155. No. Section 727(a) provides that the court shall grant the debtor a discharge unless the debtor is not an individual or the creditor can prove that the debtor fits into one of the other eleven exceptions in 727(a). Frannie is an individual and the facts give no indication that she fits into one of the exceptions. If the creditor believed that it had grounds for asking the bankruptcy court to deny Frannie her discharge, then it would have had to object to her overall discharge under Section 727 or to a discharge of its particular debt under Section 523. The creditor did not do either here. We will cover the specific grounds for denial of

discharge under both sections in later chapters.

156. **The correct answer is (A).** The point of this problem is to make sure that you understand the difference between Section 727 and Section 523. If an individual debtor files for chapter 7 and none of his creditors assert any of the Section 727(a) exceptions, then he receives a Section 727 discharge which affects all of his prepetition debts. Conversely, if any one creditor successfully establishes grounds for objection to discharge under Section 727(a), then that objection affects all debts. Contrast this with Section 523. Proof of an exception to discharge under Section 523 affects only the particular debt at issue (here, the credit card debt). So, in this case, the other eleven debts are discharged because of the interaction of Section 727 and 524. The specific credit card debt is not discharged because of Section 523(a)(2) (which, again, will be covered in later chapters).

All of the other answers are incorrect for the reasons explained above.

157. **The correct answer is (D).** Section 727(b) limits the chapter 7 discharge to debts that "arose before" the date of the bankruptcy petition. This debt arose after the petition was filed.

Answer (A) is incorrect because it is the fact that the debt was incurred postpetition that drives the analysis here. What the debtor told the trustee about its postpetition intentions may be relevant for some other purpose, but it is not relevant under Section 727(b).

Answer (B) is incorrect because the creditor would not have to object in this situation in order to have the debt be unaffected by the discharge. It is automatic.

Answer (C) is incorrect because the amount of the debt is not relevant under Section 727(b). It is the timing of the debt, not the amount, that matters.

158. **The correct answer is (A).** Except as provided elsewhere in the Code, the confirmation of a chapter 11 plan operates as a bankruptcy discharge. Discharge is the primary effect of plan confirmation. Section 1141(a) tells you who is affected by plan confirmation. (Hint: It is just about everyone and it affects them whether or not they accepted the plan.) Section 1141(d)(1)(A) has the effect of providing a broad, general discharge to most chapter 11 corporate debtors who are so eligible.

Answer (B) is incorrect because while the debtor in possession's recovery of fraudulent transfers is important for the estate and for creditors generally, it is not the event that operates as a bankruptcy discharge.

Answer (C) is incorrect because while the lifting of the automatic stay on the office furniture allows that creditor to recover its property, it is not the event that operates as a bankruptcy discharge.

Answer (D) is incorrect because the closing of a bankruptcy case does not effectuate discharge in chapter 11.

159. **The correct answer is (B).** Section 1141(d)(3) provides that confirmation of the plan does not discharge the debtor if the plan provides for the liquidation of all or substantially all of the debtor's estate, the debtor does not engage in business after consummation of the plan, and the debtor would have been denied a discharge under Section 727 if the case were in chapter 7. All of those conditions are met here, including the last one. Since Acme is a corporation, discharge would be prevented under Section 727(a)(1). The basic idea to

remember here is that since Acme is being liquidated and will not remain in business, the Code dictates that Acme be treated no differently than a corporate debtor in chapter 7 would be treated. Hence, Acme will not be entitled to a discharge. We will see what happens to individual chapter 11 debtors in the next set of problems.

Answer (A) is incorrect because Acme's decision to stay in chapter 11 has no effect on discharge in this case. It might have had such an effect under a fact pattern different than the one here.

Answer (C) is incorrect because, as explained above, Section 1141(d)(3) means the Acme is not eligible for a chapter 11 discharge.

Answer (D) is incorrect. The outcome of the SEC investigation could have powerful consequences. However, without more facts, it is impossible to know the consequences and what impact they might have, if any, on bankruptcy or on any other matter related to the company. Such an inquiry is beyond the scope of this book.

160. No. Section 1141(d)(2) provides that "a discharge under chapter 11 does not discharge a debtor **who is an individual** (emphasis added) from any debt excepted from discharge under Section 523 of this title." Since Acme is not an individual, it is not subject to the exceptions to discharge.

161. **The correct answer is (D).** In the 2005 Act, Congress added Section 1141(d)(5). This section delays the discharge of an individual debtor until completion of all payments under the plan unless the court orders otherwise for cause after notice and hearing. Prior law rendered the individual discharge more like the corporate discharge in chapter 11, but no more. It is important to note that Section 1141(d)(5) does allow for an earlier discharge for cause and after notice and a hearing. **All of the other answers are incorrect.**

162. You need to tell him that the shredding of the documents was a bad idea if he wants to emerge from his chapter 11 case with a bankruptcy discharge. In individual chapter 11 cases, the grounds for denial of a discharge under Section 727 apply. By ordering the shredding, MMNeatK may give creditors grounds to object to his discharge under Section 727(a)(3) (i.e., destroying financial and business records). Chapter 15 of this book will cover Section 727 in detail.

163. **The correct answer is (A).** Pursuant to Section 1141(d)(2), a discharge under chapter 11 does not discharge a debtor who is an individual from any debt excepted from discharge under section 523. So, exceptions to an individual debtor's discharge will be the same regardless of whether the individual files in chapter 7 or in chapter 11. It is possible that the judgment could end up being nondischargeable under Section 523(a)(6) as a debt for willful and malicious injury. For this reason, **Answer (B) is incorrect.**

Answer (C) is incorrect because it is not the best answer. At the civil trial, the possibility of punitive damages might have played a role in the way the case was litigated and it might play a role in determining whether the debt was for willful and malicious injury, but those are questions that will be addressed down the road. What you need to tell MMNeatK right now is that the plaintiff has a judgment against MMNeatK that could be considered nondischargeable under Section 523(a)(6). This means that what MMNeatK heard on the television commercial was not entirely accurate.

Answer (D) is incorrect because debtor knowledge does not play a role in the analysis.

164.   No. Section 1328(a) tells us that the chapter 13 discharge includes all debts provided for by the plan or disallowed under Section 502 of the Code. However, "provided for" does not mean what the creditor's attorney thinks it means. "Provided for" simply means that the debt is addressed in the plan. It does not mean that total payment must be made. In fact, a debt can still be "provided for" in a chapter 13 plan even if the plan proposes that no payment be made. Since this debt is addressed in the plan, it is "provided for."

165.   **The correct answer is (C).** As in individual chapter 11 cases, the chapter 13 discharge does not take effect until the debtor has completed all payments under the plan. This is different from a corporate chapter 11 case where the discharge takes effect upon plan confirmation. Since Leona is in chapter 13, the chapter 13 rule applies.

   Answer (A) is incorrect. It has no bearing on the question.

   Answer (B) is incorrect because chapter 7 does not provide an exact date for discharge. This makes it unlike chapters 11, 12, and 13. Since answer B is incorrect, **Answer (D) is also incorrect.**

166.   No. Section 1328(a) requires Harry to certify that he has paid all of his domestic support obligations due at the time of the discharge, including pre and postpetition obligations (to the extent that the prepetition obligations are provided for in the plan). This change was a part of the 2005 Act. For the definition of "domestic support obligation," see Section 101 of the Code. The child support claims would meet that broad definition. Domestic support obligations are extremely difficult for individuals to discharge in chapter 7 and in chapter 11 cases as well. These subjects will be explored in more detail in chapter 17 of this book.

167.   **The correct answer is (C).** Section 1328(a)(2) specifies that certain debts (including, but not limited to, those specified in Section 523 (a) (2), (3), (4), (5), (8) or (9)) are not dischargeable in chapter 13. This debt could fall under either Section 523(a)(2) (certain fraud or false pretenses debts) or (a)(4) (certain fiduciary fraud debts or embezzlement or larceny debts). The debt would also fall under Section 1328(a)(3) as an obligation arising from a criminal prosecution and conviction where Kyle was ordered to pay restitution.

   Answer (A) is incorrect. It has no bearing on the question.

   Answer (B) is incorrect. It has no bearing on the question.

   Answer (D) is incorrect for the reason stated above.

168.   **The correct answer is (C).** Section 1328(a) provides for an exclusion from a chapter 13 discharge for any debt provided for under Section 1322(b)(5). Section 1322(b)(5) debts are long-term debts such as the computer loan debt in the example that are paid beyond the period of the plan. The idea is that these debts will continue to be enforceable after the plan period, so logic dictates that they not be dischargeable.

   Answer (A) is incorrect because no provision of Section 1328 makes this factor relevant to a determination of whether the computer loan would be dischargeable.

   Answer (B) is incorrect because no provision of Section 1328 makes this factor relevant to a determination of whether the computer loan would be dischargeable.

Answer (D) is incorrect because even if Samantha was able to obtain the so-called "hardship discharge" under Section 1328(b), such a discharge would not apply to the computer loan. ("A discharge granted under subsection (b) of this section discharges the debtor from all unsecured debts provided for by the plan or disallowed under Section 502 of this title, except any debt-(1) provided for under section 1322(b)(5) of this title.") Section 1328(b).

169. **The correct answer is (B).** The grounds for objecting to discharge in Section 727 do not apply in chapter 12 cases. They also do not apply in chapter 13 cases. A creditor seeking to have a chapter 12 debtor penalized for fraud or misbehavior must use Section 1225 (good faith) or Section 1208 (dismissal or conversion). Similar provisions exist in chapter 13 and they should be consulted by creditors if creditors suspect bad behavior in chapter 13 case. For another point of contrast with individual debtors in chapter 11, note that Section 727 does apply to them.

Answer (A) is incorrect for the reasons stated above.

Answer (C) is not the best answer. While the intent of Janey and her family may be relevant under Section 1225, an inquiry into intent will not help determine whether or not Section 727 applies to chapter 12 cases. The nonapplicability of 727 to chapter 12 is a question of law, not of fact.

Answer (D) is incorrect for the reasons stated above.

170. **The correct answer is (D). Answer (A) is incorrect** because Section 1328(f)(1), as amended in 2005, provides that Rachel cannot receive a discharge under chapter 13 if she received a discharge under any other chapter (other than chapter 13) during the four years preceding her chapter 13 filing. (The gap between the new chapter 13 case and her chapter 7 discharge is only two years).

Rachel's May 2005 discharge under chapter 7 (which incidentally discharged the guaranty debt) thus precludes a discharge after completing payments under her proposed current plan.

Answer (B) is similarly flawed. Rachel was able to discharge her guaranty debt in 2005, and so that debt does not count for purposes of chapter 13 eligibility. As a consequence, she is well within the current chapter 13 eligibility requirements found in Section 109(e) (and which, in 2005, were $307,675 in unsecured debt and $922,975 in secured debt). Answer (C) confuses the ability to obtain a discharge with the ability to confirm a plan. Rachel could very well pay the arrearages in her chapter 13 plan and exit chapter 13 without the discharge (and after the cure, without any mortgage default). **Thus, Answer (C) is also incorrect.**

171. **The correct answer is (C).** Discharge hearings are not mandatory; the language of Section 524(d) only requires a hearing if the court so orders. Very few courts, if any, regularly hold discharge hearings. **Thus, Answer (A) is incorrect.**

Answer (B) is incorrect. Even if Harry omitted some creditors from his filing, that would not stop the discharge. The clerk's office performs no check on the completeness or accuracy of filings. Individual creditors who are omitted may have grounds for nondischargeability under Section 523(a)(3), but that would not affect the general discharge. Also, starting eighteen months after the date of enactment of the 2005 amendments (October 2006), the

Office of the United States Trustee may hire auditors to audit cases, and may bring actions to revoke the discharge if the audit uncovers any material misstatement of income, expenses or assets in the case. Omission of a creditor is not among the grounds, and it applies only to revocation, not the initial discharge.

Answer (D) is incorrect. There is no requirement that a debtor "promise" not to file again; indeed, there are cases that such a promise is unenforceable as against public policy, at least with respect to those who have not filed before. *Huang v. Bank of China*, 275 F.3d 1173 (9th Cir. 2002). There is a provision that limits a debtor's right to receive a discharge to no more than one every eight years, but that provision simply blocks issuance of a discharge if the debtor had filed previously; it does not act prospectively as in the problem.

That leaves financial education. One of the innovations of the 2005 Act was a requirement that the debtor in a chapter 7 or 13 case receive a course of approved financial education before receiving a discharge. *See* Section 727(a)(11) and Section 1328(g). Until Harry files evidence that he has completed this course (which the Office of the United States Trustee indicates is a minimum two-hour course), the clerk will not issue a discharge, **making (C) the correct answer.**

172. **The correct answer is (C).** To claim exemptions, the debtor is required to file a list of exemptions pursuant to Section 522(l). The debtor completes an official form that contains a description of the property, the law providing for each exemption, the value of each claimed exemption, and the current value of the property without deducting the exemption.

   Answer (A) is incorrect. Pursuant to Bankruptcy Rules 1007 and 4003(a), the schedule listing claimed exemptions must be filed with the petition or within 15 days thereafter.

   Answer (B) is incorrect. There is no requirement that the debtor contact the chapter 7 trustee or ask him/her to inventory the property;

   Answer (D) is incorrect for the reasons stated above.

173. **The correct answer is (A).** Section 522(l) provides that if the debtor fails to file a list of exempt property, then "a dependent of the debtor may file such a list." Sarah's minor children would meet the definition of "dependent" and could thus could claim the exemptions as long as they do so within the required time frame. (Bankruptcy Rule 4003 states, "If the debtor fails to claim exemptions or file the schedule within the time specified in Rule 1007, a dependent of the debtor may file the list within 30 days thereafter.")

   Answer (B) is possible, but it is not the best answer because it is not clear that Sarah will lose her exemptions. If her dependents claim them in a timely fashion, then they can be preserved.

   Answer (C) is incorrect. There is no "good cause" exception to the requirement in Section 522(l) that the debtor or the debtor's dependents list the property claimed exempt.

   Answer (D) is incorrect. Sarah's employees are not her "dependents" and are thus not entitled to file an exemption claim.

174. **The correct answer is (C).** Under Bankruptcy Rule 4003(b)(1), an objection to a debtor's claim of an exemption must be made within thirty (30) days of the creditor's meeting. The time can be extended in cases where the debtor amends the schedules or "for cause" (provided a party in interest asks for an extension before the time to object expires). **All of the other answers are incorrect.**

175. **The correct answer is (C).** Section 522(l) provides that unless a party in interest objects, the property claimed as exempt on . . . [the debtor's list] is exempt. The United States Supreme Court in *Taylor v. Freeland & Kronz*, 503 U.S. 638 (1992) held that if property is not covered by applicable exemption law and the trustee or creditors do not timely object, the property can still be exempt. This can be so even if the debtor has no colorable basis for the claimed exemption.

   Answer (A) is incorrect for the reason stated above.

Answer (B) is incorrect because Section 522 and Bankruptcy Rule 4003(b) do not distinguish between trustees and creditors. The provisions refer to "party in interest" which could mean a trustee, a creditor, or others.

Answer (D) is incorrect. The bankruptcy judge will not intervene. The fact that the exemption has no colorable basis will not make a difference.

176.   No. Spouses in individual cases which are being jointly administered must both elect either the applicable state exemptions or the federal exemptions. They cannot mix and match with one selecting state and the other selecting federal. The same rule holds true for husbands and wives in joint cases pursuant to Section 302.

177.   **The correct answer is (D)**, although (C) could be correct as well. Under the 2005 Act, Section 522(b)(3)(A) requires a person to be resident in a state for at least 730 days (approximately two years, depending on leap years) in order to claim the benefit of that state's exemption laws. Frank has not met that standard, so he may not claim exemptions under South Dakota's exemption laws. That means that **Answer (A), total exemption, is incorrect.**

   Answer (B) is incorrect. Section 522(a)(3)(A) goes on to indicate that if the person has not resided in a state for 730 days, then the state where the debtor resided for the majority of the 180-day period preceding the move supplies the exemption. That would be Indiana, but Indiana law requires that Frank be a resident in Indiana in order to claim the exemption, and the property he wishes to exempt — his new home in South Dakota — doesn't fit this bill. **That eliminates Answer (B)** — the answer that adopts Indiana law — as an answer.

   That leaves (C) and (D). The end of Section 522(a)(3) states that "[i]f the effect of the domiciliary requirement under subparagraph (A) is to render the debtor ineligible for any exemption, the debtor may elect to exempt property that is specified under subsection (d)." That might indicate that (D) is correct; Frank gets the federal list of exemptions under Section 522(d) (which is about $21,625). But what if only Indiana's homestead is linked to residency? Say for example Indiana's motor vehicle exemption had no location requirement, and thus Frank could take advantage of it. Does that mean that he was not "render[ed] ineligible for *any* exemption"? Depending on how courts read this provision, Frank may get no homestead exemption, making (C) a plausible Answer (albeit a tough answer) as well.

178.   **The correct answer is (B).** Although Jan has been in Nevada more than 730 days (which would have occurred in January of 2008), and thus can claim Nevada's exemptions under Section 522(b)(3)(A), she still has to worry about Section 522(p). Under Section 522(p), her homestead exemption is limited to $146,450 until she has been a resident in her new state for 1215 days, which she has not (that time period would elapse on April 29, 2009). So **Answer (A) is incorrect.** She does not get the full value of the Nevada exemption.

   So does she get $146,450? Probably. There are no domicile or other restrictions on Jan, so she will get some exemption, **making (D) an incorrect answer.** But what about Answer (C)? Under Section 522(o), the homestead exemption is reduced dollar-for-dollar for each dollar of non-exempt assets converted into exempt assets (as with Jan's sale of non-exempt assets and purchase of an exempt homestead), but only if the transfer was made with the intent to hinder, delay or defraud creditors, a concept that comes straight from fraudulent transfer law (see Section 548(a)(1)(A)). Here, however, the facts state that Jan held no intent to defraud, and thus the transfer will not act to reduce her homestead from the already limited $146,450. **Therefore, Answer (C) is incorrect, and B is the correct answer.**

179.   **The correct answer is (C).** Section 522(o) of the 2005 Act reduces the debtor's homestead exemption under state law to the extent that the value of the debtor's interest in the homestead is linked to the disposition, with fraudulent intent, of non-exempt property in the ten years before the petition. Thus, the most important issue is whether the debtor showed the requisite fraudulent intent to hinder, delay or defraud creditors. There are facts in this problem that suggest fraudulent intent ("I'm not losing any sleep over whether my creditors lose anything . . ."), but there are also facts that suggest that the debtor might have been motivated by other desires (i.e., to take advantage of the market in home prices and to save money on leisure activities).

Answer (A) is incorrect because states can have a generous homestead exemption. It is precisely this fact that motivated Congress to take action to regulate the use of homestead exemptions in bankruptcy. Section 522(o) is a good example of this type of regulation.

Answer (B) is incorrect because Section 522(o) has a ten year reach-back period. Since the debtor filed on April 8, 2010, the transactions in 2003 and 2005 fit within that period (April 8, 2000 to April 8, 2010).

Answer (D) is incorrect. Prudent lending is desirable. However, whether the creditors acted prudently in extending credit to the debtor is not relevant under Section 522(o).

180. **The correct answer is (C).** Section 726 applies in all liquidation cases, both those involving individual debtors and those involving corporations or other business entities. **All other answers are incorrect.**

It is important to keep in mind that a hypothetical chapter 7 distribution determines the minimum amount a creditor can receive in a chapter 11, 12, or 13 plan. Section 726 is not used to make an actual distribution in those chapters as it in a chapter 7 liquidation case.

181. **The correct answer is (A).** Pursuant to Section 725, lienholders holding valid liens must be paid first, before unsecured and general claimants are paid. **All other answers are incorrect.**

182. **The correct answer is (D).** If Turner's claim is subordinated, that means that the claim will be postponed in rank until the claims of the other creditors are paid. Section 726(a) states, "Except as provided in section 510 of this title. . . ."). **All other answers are incorrect.**

183. **The correct answer is (B).** The order of distribution for claims in a chapter 7 cases is as follows: 1) Section 507 priorities; 2) Allowed unsecured claims timely filed or filed late by a creditor without notice or actual knowledge of the bankruptcy; 3) Allowed unsecured claims filed late by a creditor with notice or actual knowledge of the bankruptcy; 4) Fines and punitive damages; 5) Postpetition interest on prepetition claims; 6) The debtor.

So, Creditor B will be paid first. Creditor C will be paid second. Creditor D will be paid third. Creditor A will be paid fourth. Each claim must be paid in full before any subsequent claim receives any payment. Within each category, the claimants share pro rata (assuming the proceeds are insufficient for full payment within that category, which is usually the case). **All other answers are incorrect.**

184. **The correct answer is (A).** To qualify as an administrative expense, the claim must arise after the petition is filed. This claim arose before the filing. Even though it was only three days before, the claim does not qualify for an administrative expense.

Answer (B) is incorrect because if this qualified as an administrative expense claim, it would do so in a chapter 7 case or a chapter 11 case. Administrative expenses tend to be less of an issue in chapter 7 cases since the goal of a chapter 7 case is not to reorganize a continuing business. However, administrative expenses are incurred and approved in chapter 7 cases.

Answers (C) and (D) are incorrect because neither the nature of the goods nor the nature of the creditor is likely to change the result. If the expense had occurred after the filing, then (C) and (D) might be relevant in deciding whether the expense was an actual and necessary cost of preserving the estate.

185. **The correct answer is (C).** When an executory contract is assumed by the trustee, this results in an administrative expense for the other party to the contract. This claim will thus be assigned priority status under Sections 726(a) and 507(a). Neither section states this result directly, but it has nonetheless become a matter of black letter law in bankruptcy. **All other answers are incorrect.**

186. **The correct answer is (A).** This is a claim that arises postpetition. So, **Answer (B) is clearly incorrect.** The issue is not whether the claim arose prepetition or postpetition. The issue is whether the removal of the power lines and transformer boxes are likely to benefit the estate and thus, AGE's creditors. Is the benefit of the removal too speculative to justify an administrative expense claim? The state might argue that removing the lines and boxes would benefit AGE's estate by removing a potential source of future tort liability. That seems like a plausible argument, but the issue would be whether that removal would have a direct and immediate impact rather than an indirect and speculative one. If the impact was considered merely indirect and speculative, then the claim would likely be denied because it would not be considered an actual and necessary cost of preserving the estate.

Answer (C) is incorrect. Whether AGE intended to abandon the power lines could be relevant to some other issues, particularly some issues of nonbankruptcy law (Would, for example, AGE intend to abandon any legally valid easements over which the lines were running? Would this result in the termination of any such easements?). However, these issues would not be relevant to the matter at hand in bankruptcy law.

Answer (D) is incorrect. There is no such special priority in Sections 507 or 503.

187. **The correct answer is (D).** Under Section 726(b), administrative expenses incurred under chapter 7 after conversion from a chapter 11, 12, or 13 case have priority over administrative expenses incurred under any other bankruptcy chapters or even under chapter 7 before the conversion. The idea behind this section is to make sure that funds are available in the chapter 7 case in order to encourage lawyers and other professionals to contribute to the successful wind-up of the debtor. **All other answers are incorrect.**

188. **Employee A:** All of employee A's claim qualifies under Section 507(a)(4). Section 507(a)(4) provides a priority for employee A's claim because that section covers, among other things, salary unpaid at the time of bankruptcy. There is an $11,725 (set to adjust again on April 1, 2013) limit on each claim and the salary must have been earned within 180 days of the filing or within 180 days of the debtor having closed the business, if applicable. Since employee A's claim is for salary, fits within the time limit, and is under the statutory ceiling, the claim would get the Section 507(a)(4) priority.

Employee B: Part of employee B's claim qualifies. Section 507(a)(4) also covers severance pay. Since the contract was signed within the 180 day time period, it meets the time period limitation. Notice that the priority would not cover the entire claim. The difference between $18,000 and $11,725 ($6275) would be a general unsecured claim.

Employee C: Employee C's claim would not qualify for the priority because it was earned postpetition. It would also probably not qualify for administrative expense treatment unless it was approved by the court and incurred in the ordinary course of business pursuant to Sections 364(a) and 507(a)(2).

Employee D: Employee D's claim would also not qualify for the priority because it is a postpetition claim.

189. **The correct answer is (A).** The property tax claim would be entitled to priority under Section 507(a)(8)(B). That section covers property taxes "incurred before the commencement of the case and last payable without penalty after one year before the date of the filing of the petition."

Pursuant to the state statute, this tax was assessed (and thus incurred) before the petition. (The date of assessment was November 1, 2008 and the date of filing was June 1, 2009.). Also pursuant to the state statute, it is last payable without penalty on December 31, 2008 since this is the last day of the calendar year in which the tax claim was assessed. Since this is after June 1, 2008 (one year before the date of the filing of the petition), the property tax claim is entitled to priority.

Answer (B) is incorrect because there is no dollar limit in Section 507(a)(8)(B).

Answers (C) and (D) are incorrect because neither factor is relevant under the priority analysis in Section 507(a)(8)(B).

190. **The correct answer is (C).** Claim 1 is entitled to priority under Section 507(a)(8(C). That section accords priority to "a tax required to be collected or withheld and for which the debtor is liable in any capacity." That would cover a social security withholding tax such as the one in this case where Tony, the employer, is liable.

The priority status of claim 2 would depend on whether the claim met the timing criteria of Section 507(a)(8)(E). That section covers certain employment taxes as long as those taxes are of the type covered in Section 507(a)(4) and as long as the returns for those taxes were due after three years before the date of the filing of the petition. We would need to know more facts. **All other answers are incorrect.**

191. **The correct answer is (C),** although that is not without some question.

Answer (D) is wrong because it treats Sally as a general unsecured creditor, and she is a priority creditor, entitled to be paid in full before unsecured creditors see a dime. 11 U.S.C. Section 507(a)(1)(A). It also doesn't take into account the trustee's ability to recover his or her administrative expenses from the money thus far recovered. *See* Section 507(a)(1)(C).

The ability of the trustee to recover his or her expenses found in **Section 507(a)(1)(C) makes both answers (A) and (B) incorrect.** As written, the trustee gets a priority administrative expense, with priority over support payments under subparagraph (A), by virtue of the language found in subparagraph (C).

Thus, the only answer left is (C), which adds that Sally can force the sale of Harry's house — this may be possible under Section 522(c)(1) which contains an exception to the defensive effect of exemptions for claims under Section 523(a)(5) — which include domestic support obligations of which Sally's claims are an example. Indeed, Section 522(c)(1) goes so far as to add a parenthetical to the following effect: "notwithstanding any provision of applicable nonbankruptcy law to the contrary, such property [that is, the exempt property] shall be liable for a debt of a kind specified in section 523(a)(5)." This certainly looks like preemption for trustees to pursue otherwise exempt property such as Harry's homestead.

192.   **The correct answer is (B)**, although there is something to be said for (C) as well.

Initially, the question picks up that the 2005 Act created a new exemption from the automatic stay. Section 362(b)(2)(D) provides an exemption for any act "(D) of the withholding, suspension, or restriction of a driver's license, a professional or occupational license, or a recreational license, under State law, as specified in section 466(a)(16) of the Social Security Act." Thus, **Answer (D) is clearly wrong.**

Answer (A) is clearly not wrong. Answer (B) recognizes that courts have held that Section 362(b) simply contains a list of activities that are immune from the automatic stay of Section 362(a); it does not contain a list of sacrosanct activities that can never be the subject of an injunction. Thus, if Zack shows the traditional grounds for an injunction (irreparable damage, likely success on the merits, a balance of the equities in favor of his continuing to work and no violation of public policy), he might prevail. Collection of support payments, however, is recognized as quite important. Thus a court would likely also want to know that such injunctions were anticipated to preempt a scheme that federal law (through the Social Security Act provisions mentioned in the exception) mandates states to create and enforce. Thus **(B) is probably better than (A).**

That leaves the question open as to whether Zack can enjoin enforcement consistent with the scheme, thus bringing into the question federal preemption. **If federal preemption is not thought to be part of the problem, then Answer (C) is the best answer**, since Zack cannot pay any creditor — including Debra — unless he works, and he can't work if his driver's license is suspended. That would seem to tip the balance of equities in Zach's direction.

193.   **The correct answer is (D).** The most likely theory underlying Bill's objection to Larry's discharge would be that the transfer on August 1, 2007 (i.e., the deed to trust in favor of Acme) was a fraudulent transfer of property of the debtor within one year of the filing of the petition with actual intent to hinder, delay, or defraud creditors. All of the technicalities (i.e., a transfer, within one year, property of the debtor) would be met here.

So, the issue would be whether Larry had the requisite intent. That analysis would turn on the "badges of fraud" analysis that courts typically use when trying to infer fraudulent intent from the actions of the transferor. To whom was the transfer made? Here, the transfer was made to someone with whom it is not clear there was an actual debt. Was the transfer concealed? There is not a lot of evidence here, but Larry's non-cooperation with Bill's discovery efforts looks suspicious. In a real case, more facts could be developed that could help determine the debtor's state of mind.

Answer (A) is incorrect because the transfer on August 1, 2007 could not be considered a transfer of property of the estate. The bankruptcy case had not yet been filed, so there was no bankruptcy estate at that time.

Answer (B) is not the best answer. As is noted above, these technicalities are clearly met. So, these are issues in a Section 727(a)(2) action, but they would not be contentious issues in this particular case.

Answer (C) is not the best answer either, for much the same reason.

194.   **The correct answer is (A).** The Code defines "transfer" broadly in Section 101(54). It refers to every mode of disposing of or parting with an interest in property. It would include a situation such as this one where the debtor created with Y a tenancy-in-common in fee simple absolute in Blackacre. When the debtor creates the tenancy-in-common, he is relinquishing sole ownership in fee simple absolute in favor of concurrent ownership in fee simple absolute As such, he is parting with an interest in property and thus, a transfer has occurred. **For this reason, Answer (B) is incorrect.**

Answer (C) is incorrect because the Code does define transfer. It would not have to be determined with reference to state law. As stated above, the conversion from sole ownership to concurrent ownership would be considered a transfer.

Answer (D) is incorrect because Y's status as a non-relative would not matter for purposes of determining whether a transfer occurred. A conversion from sole ownership in fee simple absolute to tenancy-in-common in fee simple absolute would be considered a transfer regardless of whether that conversion involved a relative or not. A transfer to a relative might, of course, be relevant to the question of whether the debtor intended to hinder, delay, or defraud creditors.

195.   **The correct answer is (A).** Section 727(a)(8) bars a chapter 7 debtor from receiving a

discharge if the debtor has been granted a discharge in a chapter 7 commenced within 8 years before the date of the filing of the petition. The date of the second filing was June 15, 2008. The debtor in this case would not be barred because he was granted a discharge in a case that was commenced on January 10, 2000. This was not within 8 years before the date of the filing.

Answers (B) and (D) are incorrect because they both incorrectly assume that the date of discharge is the relevant date for purposes of calculating the eight-year restriction.

Answer (C) is incorrect because Section 727(a)(8) does not contain a prohibition or limitation on *filing* for chapter 7. It says that if a debtor *has received a discharge* in a chapter 7 case filed in the past eight years, the debtor will be denied another discharge.

196. No. The creditor's ability to file a chapter 7 involuntary petition is unaffected by Section 727(a)(8).

197. **The correct answer is (C).** Insolvency alone is not a defense to an obligation to keep financial records. Creditors need to be able to verify that statements made by debtors in bankruptcy schedules are accurate, so debtors need to keep and preserve financial documents and records. If a debtor fails to keep such records, the debtor should face a penalty. Denial of discharge is a powerful penalty. If the debtor's financial condition can be used as a basis for excusing the debtor from that statutory obligation, then the incentive effect of Section 727(a)(3) would be diminished. For this reason, **Answer (A) is incorrect**.

Answer (B) contains a correct statement. In keeping with Congressional intent to provide debtors with a fresh start, Section 727 is supposed to be construed strictly against the creditor and liberally in favor of the debtor. However, that sentiment probably would not help the debtor in this case. There is a strong indication that the Tom was inattentive to record keeping and to corporate form.

Answer (D) is incorrect because Section 727(a)(3) says that the failure to keep and preserve sufficient records from which financial condition might be ascertained prevents discharge "unless such act or failure to act was justified under all of the circumstances of the case." So, the debtor can offer an justification. If the court finds that the justification convincing, that could save the debtor from a discharge denial under the section.

198. **The correct answer is (A).** Section 727(a)(12) was added with the 2005 Act. Under this provision, Sally is not supposed to be granted a discharge in chapter 7 if the court finds, after notice and the opportunity for a hearing, that there is reasonable cause to believe that Section 522(q)(1) is applicable, or that there is any proceeding pending in which Sally may be found guilty of a felony of the kind described in Section 522(q)(l)(A), or liable for as a debt of the kind described in Section 522(q)(1)(B). In this case, Section 522(q)(1) is applicable because Sally has elected a homestead exemption which exceeds the amount listed in Section 522(q)(1) (Here, the homestead exemption is unlimited and, as of this writing, the exemption amount in the statute is $146,450, so Sally's exemption necessarily exceeds the amount listed. As with dollar amounts listed elsewhere in the Code, that amount changes every three years.) and because Sally is liable for a debt of the kind described in Section 522(q)(1)(B)(i.e., a debt arising from a violation of federal and state securities laws). Section 727(a)(12) is a part of recent Congressional efforts to make it difficult for individuals who have engaged in corporate fraud or other egregious misconduct (even if they have not necessarily been convicted yet) to move to states with generous exemption laws on the eve of bankruptcy to

escape their creditors.

Answer (B) is incorrect. Although Sally did nothing illegal or improper once her bankruptcy case started, that does not mean she will be able to receive a Section 727 discharge.

Answer (C) is partly incorrect and partly correct. The "probably yes" part is incorrect for the reasons stated above. The second part of the answer is probably correct because the specific debts to the fraud victims might indeed be nondischargeable under relevant provisions in Section 523.

Answer (D) is incorrect because of the above mentioned interplay between Section 522(q)(1) and Section 727(a)(12).

199. **The correct answer is (A).** Section 727(c)(1) provides that the trustee, a creditor, or the U.S. Trustee may object to the debtor's discharge. There are no facts here which suggest that Lumber Merchants is Sam's "creditor" as that term is defined in Section 101 ("an entity that has a claim against the debtor that arose at the time of or before the order for relief").

The Code does allow a "party in interest" to request the court to order the trustee to examine the acts and conduct of the debtor to determine whether there are grounds for denial of discharge. "Party in interest" is not defined in the Code, so it is unclear whether Lumber Merchants would qualify. Even if it did, that would merely entitle it to ask the court to order an examination. It would not give Lumber Merchants standing to object.

Answer (B) is incorrect because Lumber Merchants' legal ability to object to discharge is not a matter of having or not having direct proof. It is a matter of whether Lumber Merchants has standing.

Answers (C) and (D) are incorrect. Sam's default may have a ripple effect on George's creditors, including Lumber Merchants. However, that possibility (or even probability) is not sufficient to grant Lumber Merchants' standing to object to Sam's bankruptcy discharge under Section 727. If George's store filed for chapter 7 bankruptcy, then Lumber Merchants would probably have standing in that case because it is likely that Lumber Merchants is a creditor.

200. **The correct answer is (C).** A creditor who seeks to object to discharge under Section 727 must file a complaint objecting to discharge and the complaint must be filed not later than sixty (60) days after the first date set for the meeting of creditors. If no creditors object in a timely manner, the debtor receives an overall Section 727 discharge. (Although it is still possible for specific debts to be nondischargeable under Section 523.). **All of the other answers are incorrect.**

201. **The correct answer is (B).** Chapter 7 does not provide a specific point during the bankruptcy case when the debtor receives a discharge. If there are no objections, the discharge is usually granted as soon as possible after the expiration of the 60 day period referred to above. **All of the other answers are incorrect.**

202. **The correct answer is (C).** Section 727(d)(4) applies to this situation. That section, added with the *2005* Act, provides that the failure to explain misstatements or the failure to provide materials in a bankruptcy audit under 28 U.S.C. Section 586(f) can form the basis for creditors, the trustee, or the U.S. Trustee to request revocation of the debtor's discharge.

However, the debtor's material misstatement in the example does not automatically result in revocation of a discharge, even if the requesting party can prove that the debtor made a material misstatement. In other words, Section 727(d)(4) is not a strict liability provision. It is the *failure to satisfactorily explain* the misstatement or the *failure to satisfactorily explain* not making certain items available that provides grounds for revocation. If the debtor in the example can satisfactorily explain the misstatement, revocation is not authorized. For this reason, **Answer (A) is incorrect.**

Answer (B) is incorrect. The fact that the U.S. Trustee conducted the audit makes no difference in the answer.

Answer (D) is incorrect because the fact that there were no misstatements in the debtor's petitions, schedules, and statements is not relevant to the revocation question. Section 727(d)(4) does not apply to misstatements in the petition, schedules or other papers.

203. **The correct answer is (B).** The facts tell you that the presumed abuse standard does not apply, since $95 a month would only repay about $5,700 over 60 months ($95 times 60 = $5,700). The floor is $7,025, pursuant to Section 707(b)(2)(A)(i)(I). As a consequence, **(A) is incorrect.**

But passing the presumptive abuse test set forth in Section 707(b)(2) is not the only hurdle a debtor has to face. Under Section 707(b)(1), the court and the Office of the United States Trustee (or bankruptcy administrator in Alabama and North Carolina) may still bring a motion to declare that the filing is an "abuse" (as opposed to the "substantial abuse" standard which was the law prior to October 17, 2005).

What is "abuse"? That is aided somewhat by the standards set forth in Section 707(b)(3) — which tend to codify the judicial interpretations of "substantial abuse" which evolved before 2005. Those include a lack of good faith, and whether "the totality of circumstances . . . of the debtor's financial situation demonstrates abuse." Here, with a stable new job, Fred can devote $500 a month to pay his creditors, and actually pay them off in less than five years ($500 times 60 months would be $30,000, and the facts indicate that his total unsecured debt is $25,000). Although it remains to be seen what courts will do, it is likely that Fred's case will be found abusive, and it will be dismissed or Fred will be allowed to convert to chapter 13.

The analysis above would indicate that **(C) is incorrect.**

As Fred's income is above the applicable state's median income, the Office of the United States Trustee (or bankruptcy administrator), or the court, *or any "party in interest" including a creditor*, can bring a motion to dismiss for presumed abuse under Section 707(b)(6). This assures that someone will likely bring up the point that Fred has the ability to pay off his creditors in a chapter 13 plan, which **eliminates Answer (D).**

204. **The correct answer is (D).** When a debtor's applicable income falls before the state's median, then no one may bring an action under Section 707(b)(2). *See* Section 707(b)(7). This eliminates answers (A) through (C), leaving (D) as the correct answer. In such cases, only the court or the Office of the United States Trustee may bring a motion, and then only under Section 707(b)(1) for non-presumptive "abuse" (which might very well prevail in this case, given the analysis in the last question).

205. **The correct answer is (A).** In order to redeem collateral, the secured creditor has to be paid the amount of the allowed claim secured by the lien (i.e., the value of the lienholder's collateral if the lienholder is undersecured, as in this case). In this case, that amount is $6,000. So, that is what Margaret has to pay in order to redeem the collateral. The purpose of Section 722 is to allow the debtor to keep certain encumbered property. Section 722 only applies if the debtor is an individual and it only applies to certain property. We'll explore the "certain property" part in later questions in this chapter. Margaret would have to pay the

$6,000 in full at the time of the redemption. Prior to the 2005 Act, there was some uncertainty regarding whether redemption could be accomplished on an installment basis. The 2005 Act added the words "in full at the time of redemption" to eliminate that uncertainty.

Answer (B) is incorrect for the reasons stated above. **All of the other answers are also incorrect.**

206.   **The correct answer is (C).** Section 722 would permit Charles to pay the secured creditor $3,575. In a situation such as this one where the property is worth more than the amount of the creditor's lien, the amount of $3,575 is the amount of the allowed claim secured by the lien. (If you are having difficulty with the concept of the "allowed secured claim," you should read Section 506 carefully.) **All of the other answers are incorrect.**

207.   **The correct answer is (A).** There could be some other problems with Virginia's attempt to redeem, but the most prominent problem at the moment is that the copyrights are not tangible property. Redemption covers only *tangible* personal property, so it would not cover the copyrights. **All of the other answers are either incorrect or not applicable to the facts in the problem.**

208.   Not very likely. Charlotte has two problems. First, it is not clear that the equipment is "intended primarily for personal, family, or household use." Charlotte will probably argue that because she owns the property in her own name and that because she is the only one using it, that this makes the property more like personal, family, or household property. The difficulty is that this is property is used in her business and with a profit motive in mind. Second, Charlotte purchased the equipment for the purpose of engaging in the practice of chiropractic medicine. Since this is her means of making a living, it would be difficult to argue that the debt secured by the equipment is a "consumer debt."

209.   There will have to be a new valuation. According to Section 348(f)(1)(B) of the Code, valuations in chapter 13 cases do not carry over to converted chapter 7 cases (". . . valuations of property and of allowed secured claims in the chapter 13 case shall apply only in a case converted to a case under chapter 11 or 12, but not in a case converted to a case under chapter 7."). This change was a part of the 2005 Act. Prior to 2005, the amount of the allowed secured claim remained the same in a case converted from chapter 13 to chapter 7. Whether this works to Barry's advantage or not depends on specific facts that we do not have here. If the property has depreciated in value (which is very likely the case with a car), then Barry will likely get the benefit of that depreciation.

210.   **The correct answer is (D).** Section 524(c) of the Code enforces the discharge by declaring void any contract for which the consideration is in whole or in part on a discharged debt. Here, that is exactly what the agreement Jay signed does — he agrees to pay any deficiency, which will be discharged in bankruptcy.

Answer (A) is incorrect because it is irrelevant that the claim was secured — what is at issue is not the secured debt, but the unsecured deficiency. Fran would have been able to repossess and sell the car, because that would constitute enforcement of Fran's secured claim (so long as the repossession was not married with some claim or demand for payment of the unsecured deficiency).

Answer (B) is incorrect — it does not matter where the claim is brought, although there is jurisdiction in the bankruptcy court. **As between (C) and (D), (D) is the better** answer because Fran's actions are just the type of creditor activity that the reaffirmation process is designed to prevent.

211. **The correct answer is (A).** The difference is court approval of the reaffirmation agreement. That process is designed to ensure that there is no undue hardship involved in agreeing to be bound by a debt that could have been discharged. The 2005 amendments added mandatory disclosures that have to be in every reaffirmation agreement and those are set forth in Section 524(k) as the answer indicates.

    Answer (B) is incorrect. There is no exclusive jurisdiction in bankruptcy court over court-approved reaffirmation agreements. Fran's action could be brought in state court.

    Answer (C) is incorrect, and so is (D), because the court approval under Section 524(c) strips the protection of the general discharge from the court-approved agreement, and allows Fran to pursue Jay.

212. **The correct answer is (B).** While most courts do not hold that making the suggestion of a reaffirmation agreement violates the automatic stay in Section 362, it is wise for creditors to be very careful about proposing reaffirmations to debtors like Jane. There are a couple of potential problems here in what the bank did. First, it did not contact Jane's attorney about the possibility of reaffirmation. Second, there is no indication that the creditor made a real effort, in writing or otherwise, to explain the nature of reaffirmation, its effects, or the advantages and disadvantages. The follow-up phone call could also be a problem if it appears to be part of an effort to coerce Jane, especially because there is no contemporaneous communication with her attorney. The bank should avoid anything that could appear to a bankruptcy judge to be intimidating or abusive.

    Answer (A) is not necessarily wrong. It is just not the best answer. The bank does want to strike a deal and the deal could be to Jane's benefit, so she should tell her bankruptcy lawyer about it. But, it is the possibility of a violation of the automatic stay that is most important at this point. If Jane feels pressured by the bank's communications, that could interfere with her ability to fully assess the costs and benefits of the deal.

    Answer (C) is incorrect. The rule is not that only the debtor can start a discussion about reaffirmation. In most jurisdictions, the creditor can start negotiations as long as the creditor is not coercive or deceptive about it.

    Answer (D) is not the best answer. There is nothing magical in distinguishing between the letter and the phone call when it comes to determining whether the bank violated the automatic stay. Either or both could be considered coercive or deceptive, depending on the nature of the communication.

213. **The correct answer is (D).** Although reaffirmation usually makes more economic sense in dealing with secured debt (because it is usually used as a means to keep property that would otherwise be liquidated), a debtor can reaffirm unsecured debt. Hope's reasons for wanting to reaffirm are not *per se* unreasonable or irrational. In fact, it might allow her to get credit from Dr. Roberts at a lower cost in the future when and if child #5 needs braces. When a debtor seeks reaffirmation of unsecured debt, it is important for the court to carefully scrutinize the debtor's motive and make sure that the procedural protections of Sections

524(c), (d), and (k) are followed.

Answers (A) and (B) are incorrect for the reasons noted above.

Answer (C) is incorrect because it confuses Section 524(f) with reaffirmation under Sections 524(c) and (d). Section 524(f) provides that "nothing contained in subsection (c) or (d) . . . prevents a debtor from voluntarily repaying a debt." Hope could proceed under this section and pay Dr. Roberts voluntarily even in the absence of a reaffirmation agreement. Dr. Roberts can accept the payment. What Section 524(f) does not do is give Dr. Roberts an enforceable agreement to extract further payment or make Hope legally bound to make such payments (Remember: Once Hope gets her discharge, she has no personal liability to Dr. Roberts on the debt). If he wants such an enforceable promise that will be binding in the future, he must proceed under Section 524(c) and (d).

214. **The correct answer is (B).** Section 523(a)(1) makes certain types of tax debts nondischargeable. The section includes, among other things, taxes that are entitled to priority under Section 507(a). See chapter 5 of this book for examples of this. Section 523(a)(1) also includes taxes for which a return was filed late ("after the date on which such return was last due under applicable law") and within 2 years before the bankruptcy ("after two years before the date of the filing of the petition"). This is why Wally's 2001 federal income tax debt is nondischargeable.

We made this point earlier in this book, but it bears repeating: Always keep in mind that Section 523 nondischargeability issues relate to whether or not a particular debt is dischargeable. Section 523 does not cover an overall denial of discharge. Overall denials in individual filings are governed by Section 727.

Answer (A) is incorrect because Section 523(a)(1) does not have a grace period.

Answer (C) is incorrect. All federal income taxes are not *per se* nondischargeable. Section 523(a)(1) is complex and must be consulted before determining which federal income taxes are nondischargeable and which ones are not.

Answer (D) is incorrect. A debtor's willful attempt to evade taxes could form the basis for an objection to discharge under Section 523(a)(1)(C). However, the debtor's lack of willfulness in the example does not save this particular tax debt from being nondischargeable.

215. **The correct answer is (A).** Section 523(a)(2)(A) provides for an exception to discharge for a debt for money, property, services or new or renewed credit to the extent that it was obtained by false pretenses, a false representation, or actual fraud. The section reaches all kinds of oral or written fraudulent misrepresentations by the debtor. However, one kind of fraudulent misrepresentation is excluded: "a statement respecting the debtor or an insider's financial condition." The reason for this exclusion is that fraudulent misrepresentations of this type are covered by Section 523(a)(2)(B). Since an oral misrepresentation that relates to a debtor's financial condition is not covered under Section 523(a)(2), debtors will sometimes concede that they made false misrepresentations that induced a creditor to lend them money, but they will argue that those misrepresentations relate to "the debtor's financial condition" and are thus excluded from the reach Section 523(a)(2) (making the debt dischargeable).

David might do that here. He might argue that his falsehoods related to his financial condition and thus that the debt is safe from attack as a nondischargeable debt. Chris, however, would argue that David's lies were about his ownership of assets and about his general ability to repay. He would argue that they were not related to his overall financial condition (i.e., how much money he has in the bank, what his other debts consisted of, his credit score, etc.) or his net worth (i.e., assets minus debts). Given the facts of this case and the case law in this area, Chris probably has the better argument. If so, Section 523(a)(2) applies and David loses. This analysis makes **(C) and (D) incorrect.**

Answer (B) is incorrect. The debtor's maliciousness or lack thereof is not relevant under Section 523(a)(2). A debt for willful and malicious injury can be nondischargeable under Section 523(a)(6). Section 523(a)(6) requires intentional behavior. David's conduct could be considered negligent, but probably not intentional, wrongful conduct.

216.   **The correct answer is (C).** Under Section 523(a)(2), First Bank *does* have to show that Shorty published or caused to be published written financial statements with an intent to deceive. **Answers (A), (B), and (D) are all true statements.** They relate to other elements of a cause of action under Section 523(a)(2)(B).

It is important to note that showing reasonable reliance might be a real problem for First Bank. The inventory reports were indeed false, but if you read the facts carefully, you will see that First Bank never actually formally required them. Also, the debtor will likely argue that First Bank should not have relied on an elderly debtor's handwritten "cattle count book" and should have done its own accounting, particularly given the nature of the land on which the debtor maintained the cattle.

217.   **The correct answer is (A).** Section 523(a)(5) makes domestic support obligations nondischargeable in bankruptcy. The term "domestic support obligation" is defined in the Code as "a debt that accrues before, on, or after the date of the order for relief . . . that is . . . owed to or recoverable by a spouse, former spouse, or child of the debtor . . . a governmental unit . . . or in the nature of alimony, maintenance, or support. . . ." While the definition of domestic support obligation is broad and Section 523(a)(5) covers a wide variety of domestic claimants, its reach is not limitless. The debt has to actually be for support. Thus, a debt arising out of some other kind of obligation is not covered, even if that obligation has been designated by the parties as support. What this means is that the wife's rent obligation is dischargeable (assuming no other provisions of Section 523 are applicable, of course). **All of the other answer are incorrect.**

218.   You need to explain that courts look at several factors in determining whether a debtor qualifies for the undue hardship exception of Section 523(a)(8). Among the factors are: 1) whether the debtor is making an effort to repay the loan, 2) whether the debtor is making an effort to find suitable employment, and 3) whether the debtor is making an effort to be more financially prudent. In the facts above, it does not appear that Barbara is doing any of these things consistently. The rejection of a job in her field because it is not with a "prestige school" could be viewed as evidence that she is not making an effort to find suitable employment. She hasn't made much effort to pay back the student loans and she does not appear to want to modify her research expeditions despite the fact that she is now in chapter 7. Given her current circumstances, it is unlikely that Barbara will be able to qualify for undue hardship.

219.   **The correct answer is (A).** Most of the discharge exceptions in Section 523(a) come into effect automatically as long as the debt meets the listed criteria. Some of them, however, require an affirmative objection by the creditor. Section 523(c)(1) requires creditors whose objections are based on Sections 523(a)(2), (4), or (6) to file a complaint objecting to discharge within 60 days of the first date set for the meeting of creditors. For more on this,

see Bankruptcy Rule 4007. Since the objection here would most likely be based on Section 523(a)(4) (i.e., a debt arising out of embezzlement), Second Bank needs to affirmatively object by filing a complaint, or requesting an extension to do so within the time period. Second Bank did not do that, so it loses the right to exclude the debt from discharge.

Answers (B) and (C) are incorrect because there is no dollar cap in Section 523(a)(4). Nor does the fact that the debt arose out of embezzlement excuse Second Bank from having to affirmatively object.

Answer (D) is incorrect. A careful reading of Section 523(a)(4) reveals that it covers debts arising from embezzlement or larceny even if the debtor is not a fiduciary. The point still remains that Second Bank has to affirmatively object to discharge or it loses the right to object.

220. **The correct answer is (D).** Pursuant to 28 U.S.C. Section 1334(b), dischargeability litigation can take place in either state court or bankruptcy court unless the issue is dischargeability under 523(a)(2), (a)(4) or (a)(6). Thus, the state court to which the creditor has sought relief can hear this matter. For this reason, **Answer (A) is incorrect.**

Answer (B) is incorrect because Section 523(a)(14) is one of the dischargeability sections that takes effect automatically if the debt meets the listed criteria (which is true here). Remember: Section 523(c)(1) says that only creditors whose debts qualify under Section 523 (2), (4), or (6) must affirmatively object. Moreover, it does not matter that the debt is owed to the credit union. Section 523(a)(14) makes it nondischargeable because the debtor borrowed the money to pay a nondischargeable tax. **This makes (C) incorrect.**

221. You need to tell her that a system of the type she describes could be a problem for the credit union in light of Section 523(d). That section provides that a court has discretion to award attorneys fees and costs to the debtor if it is determined that the creditor's objection to dischargeability was not substantially justified and if there exist no special circumstances that would render the award unjust. It applies to objections to discharge in consumer cases under Section 523(a)(2) (i.e., actual fraud cases, "consumer spending spree" cases, and the materially false financial statement cases). The point of this provision is to deter creditors from making frivolous objections that would give them undue leverage to extract payment. You should advise the credit union to object to discharge where appropriate, but to make a more individualized determination that the objection has a sound basis in fact and in law.

222.   No. Chapter 13 debtors must be individuals with regular income. This means that Marty's partnership cannot file chapter 13. However, Marty can file on his own behalf as long as he meets the other requirements of Section 109(e). Marty's *interest* in the partnership would be considered property of Marty's bankruptcy estate. The assets of the partnership would not be included.

223.   **The correct answer is (A).** Carl can file chapter 13 *today* because he is under the statutory debt limit of $360,475 for unsecured debt and $1,081,400 for secured debt. *See* Section 109(e). Remember that these amounts are adjusted for inflation every three years, so if you are doing this problem under new dollar amounts, you will have to account for the adjustments and such an accounting could impact the outcome of this question. The next adjustment will occur on April 1, 2013. The warranty claims total $15,000, but they are contingent claims. If none of the customers have problems with their cars in the next ten days, then Carl will have no liability on the warranties. If they do, then he will because the triggering event has occurred. Assume that Carl does not file today and that tomorrow all three customers present warranty claims. At that point, Carl's unsecured debt would total $340,000 ($325,000 + $15,000). Carl still remains eligible because $340,000 <$360,475. For these reasons, **answers (B) and (D) are incorrect.**

    Answer (C) is incorrect. Carl has "regular income" as that term is defined in the Code because he receives a pension and he has a business that provides him with income that is stable and sufficient to fund a chapter 13 plan.

224.   No. The general rule is that a debtor may not exclude a joint debt with the non-debtor spouse for which the debtor is fully liable from the debt limits under Section 109(e).

    It would also not help much for the wife to file chapter 13. This is because the debt limits are not doubled in a joint 13 filing. If husband and wife filed jointly, they'd still be over the statutory debt limit. One possible strategy could be to try to reclassify some of secured debt and shift it into unsecured status since there is room under that ceiling, but with $3,000,000 in secured debt, this seems unlikely to work either. The husband and wife will need to explore either a chapter 7 case (if they can qualify under the means test) or a chapter 11 case.

225.   First, you need to tell her that Section 727(a)(8) bars a debtor from receiving a discharge in a chapter 7 case if the debtor "has been granted a discharge" in a chapter 7 "case commenced within 8 years before the date of the filing of the petition." However, Section 727(a)(8) does not affect the debtor's right to file a chapter 7 petition. The restrictions apply only if the debtor received a discharge, not if the debtor merely filed. So, what Amanda

heard on the radio program was not accurate.

Second, you need to tell Amanda is that Section 727(a)(8)'s restrictions do not apply in chapter 13. What this means in practical terms is that Amanda can file for chapter 13 as long as she meets the other requirements (i.e., eligibility, good faith, and plan confirmation standards).

The 2005 Act amended Section 1328 to prevent a debtor from getting a chapter 13 discharge if the debtor received a discharge in a prior chapter 7 or chapter 12 case filed within the four year period before the date of the filing of the petition. This provision would not bar Amanda from receiving a discharge in a chapter 13 case. For example, if Amanda filed for chapter 13 bankruptcy on February 1, 2008, she would not have received a discharge in a case filed between February 1, 2004 and February 1, 2008. She received her discharge in a case filed on June 1, 2002 (i.e., not within the four year period before February 1, 2008). Section 1328 also applies if the debtor received a discharge in a prior chapter 13 case filed within the two year period before the petition. *See* 1328(f)(2).

226. **The correct answer is (C)** because that is the only statement that is false. The automatic stay that applies to Marietta does not apply to her father-in-law. The point here is to understand the operation and implications of Section 1301 of the Code. Under that section, the automatic stay in a chapter 13 case is extended to just about any individual who is a co-debtor of the debtor on a consumer debt. The problem for Marietta's father-in-law is that the debt in this case is probably not a consumer debt (i.e., a debt incurred primarily for personal, family, or household use). Generally, debts incurred with a profit motive are not consumer debts. This debt was incurred for the purpose of starting a business, albeit a small, home-based one.

All of the other statements are true and thus **answers (A), (B), and (D) are not correct answers to the question.**

227. **The correct answer is (C).** The co-debtor stay takes effect in this case because the debt is a consumer debt and Sam's parents are not incurring the debt in the ordinary course of business. However, it does not continue forever. One event that terminates the co-debtor stay is a conversion to chapter 7. That has happened in the example. **All of the other answers are incorrect.**

228. **The correct answer is (A).** Section 1301(c)(1) allows the court to grant relief from the co-debtor stay when the co-debtor received consideration for the claim held by the creditor. The rationale is that the creditor should be free to go after the party who actually received the benefit of the loan. **All of the other answers are incorrect.**

229. **The correct answer is (B).** Under Section 1306(a)(2), earnings from services performed by the debtor after the filing are property of the estate. If this were a chapter 7 case, the result would be different. Since chapter 13 involves the repayment of claims from future earnings or other income, it makes sense to include them in the estate. So, the rule in chapter 13 is that earnings from services performed during the chapter 13 case are considered property of the estate. **All of the other answers are incorrect.**

230. **The correct answer is (C).** Section 1306(a)(1) states that in chapter 13, property of the estate includes all property of the estate under Section 541. Since the insurance proceeds

would be property of the estate under Section 541(a)(6), they are included in the estate.

Answer (A) is partially correct. It is not the best answer, though, for the reasons stated above.

Answers (B) and (D) are incorrect.

231.   **The correct answer is (D).** Although (A) is tempting, Section 1325(b)(2) as redrafted by the 2005 Act indicates that disposable income is to be determined with respect to "current monthly income," a term now defined in Section 101(10A). Thus, Edgar is within his rights to seek confirmation with the lower number — which gives him a negative disposable income, and thus he meets the confirmation test found in Section 1325(b) (there is a question as to whether Edgar would meet the "good faith" requirement in Section 1325(a), but the counter argument is that it would be a perversion of good faith to indicate that a debtor could follow what the statute states and not be in good faith). This analysis leads to the conclusion that **(A) is incorrect.**

So Edgar can confirm his plan, but can he discharge the fraud debt? Under the law prior to the 2005 Act, Edgar could. The discharge of Section 1328(a) was called the "superdischarge" because it allowed discharge of some debts not dischargeable in chapter 7 such as debts based upon fraud. Not any more; as changed by the 2005 Act, fraud debts are not subject to the chapter 13 discharge.

But they are not automatically rendered nondischargeable. As in chapter 7, debts nondischargeable for fraud under Section 523(a)(2) must be determined to be nondischargeable by the bankruptcy court, and must be so declared in a lawsuit (called an adversary proceeding) begun in bankruptcy court no later than 60 days after the first date set for the meeting of creditors. Thus, Zoe will have to take affirmative action to have her debt declared nondischargeable, **thus making (D) the correct answer. Answer (B) is too categorical**; it does not take into account the need to file a nondischargeability action, and thus is wrong for that reason (although it is correct that no discharge in a chapter 13, except for hardship, issued before the completion of plan payments). Similarly, if Zoe sleeps on her rights, and does not file a nondischargeability action in time (or loses it, which is not likely given the claim and issue preclusive effect of a state fraud judgment), the fraud debt can be discharged, **making (C) an incorrect answer.**

232.   **The correct answer is (C).** Section 1325(a)(5)(C) provides, among other things, that a plan can be confirmed if the debtor surrenders property securing a claim to the holder. This means that Ben's move would be acceptable to a court and that Continental Bank would not have an issue in the plan confirmation. **All of the other answers are incorrect.**

233.   **The correct answer is (A).** A chapter 13 debtor like Clarence will have to make car payments with a present value of $20,000. Section 1325(a)(5)(B) mandates payment of the value of the secured claim as of the effective date of the plan. This is the present value of the claim and it is calculated by adding interest to the claim's face value. The interest is intended to compensate the finance company for the delay in payment.

Prior to the 2005 Act, it would have been possible for Clarence to retain the car in chapter 13 by paying the finance company the present value of $12,000, the replacement value of the car. The 2005 Act contains an unnumbered but still legally enforceable provision at the end of Section 1325(a)(9) that limits so-called "strip downs" for certain debts. If you read the section carefully, you will see that it applies to Clarence's loan (i.e., a purchase money loan on a motor vehicle incurred within 910 days of Clarence's filing for his personal use). **All of the other answers are incorrect.**

234.   Yes. Antonin's plan to cure the defaults is permitted under both Sections 1322(b)(3) ("the plan may provide for the curing or waiving of any default") and 1322(b)(5) (allows long-term debt to be paid off beyond the period of the plan). Moreover, Section 1322(c)(1) makes it clear that cure is allowed even in situations like Antonin's where the underlying debt (i.e., the home mortgage) cannot be modified.

235.   **The correct answer is (B).** There are two issues that are most important. First, Ally earns below the median income and her disposable income has been determined appropriately. The real issue is raised by the fact that Ally proposes to make payments over a period of two years and eight months. Section 1325 provides that Ally must apply all of her disposable income in the applicable commitment period to payment under the plan. If the debtor earns less than the median income, Section 1325 requires a three year period. So, Ally must pay the equivalent of at least three years of disposable income, not the two years and eight months that she has proposed.

The second issue is whether her plan is being proposed in good faith. The court must look at the case and decide whether, based on a totality of the circumstances, the debtor demonstrates lack of good faith. Good faith is not defined in the Code. What is relevant is the debtor's state of mind. There are some facts here which could suggest that Ally's chapter 13 plan might be in trouble on this issue. Her previous bankruptcy filing and her suggestion that she is filing in order to evade certain creditors might count against her. On the other hand, the choice of chapter 13 does not *per se* demonstrate a lack of good faith and she says that she is choosing chapter 13 in order to "do the right thing."

Answer (A) is incorrect because Ally's plan satisfies the best interests test. Her plan pays more than the present value of zero. The present value of zero is what unsecured creditors would get if this were a chapter 7 case.

Answer (C) is not the best answer because it mentions only one issue;

Answer (D) is incorrect because there is no provision that bars a debtor who has filed a chapter 7 case from *filing* a subsequent chapter 13 case. Section 1328(f) prevents the granting of a chapter 13 discharge if the debtor received a discharge in a chapter 7 or chapter 12 case filed within the four year period before the petition, but that section would not apply here because Ally received her discharge in a chapter 7 case filed six years ago.

236.   **The correct answer is (C).** The bankruptcy judge's refusal to confirm Ally's chapter 13 plan probably means that she needs to amend or revise the plan and then resubmit it. It usually does not result in a dismissal, a conversion, or a denial of discharge. If Ally repeatedly proposes unlawful and/or infeasible plans, the plan can then be dismissed (i.e., terminated) or converted under Section 1307. **All of the other answers are incorrect as applied to these facts.**

237.   **The correct answer is (C)** because that is the only statement that is false. Section 1305(a)(2) provides that a creditor can prove a claim for a *postpetition* consumer debt incurred by the

debtor for household or personal purposes. Proving the claim allows it to be dealt with in the course of the chapter 13 case. Moreover, if the debtor obtains prior approval from the trustee of the debt (or if prior approval is not practicable), any balance on the debt after the chapter 13 distribution has concluded is discharged. Since the hospital in this case elected to prove its claim in the chapter 13 case, it needs to file a proof of claim. All of the other statements are true and this makes **(A), (B) and (D) incorrect answers to the question asked.**

238. **The correct answer is (A).** Section 1328(b) gives a bankruptcy court discretion, after notice and hearing, to grant what is known as a "hardship discharge." This type of discharge can be granted to a debtor who has not completed payments under the plan. The hardship discharge depends on three conditions being satisfied: 1) The failure to complete payments is due to a situation that is beyond the debtor's control; 2) The distributions actually made to unsecured creditors must satisfy the best interests test; and 3) Modification of the plan would not be practical. All three of these factors seem to be present in Randy's case.

The second part of Answer (A) is also correct. If Randy is granted a hardship discharge, it does not apply to debts that are nondischargeable under Section 523(a). Since the debt to the former business partner could be considered a debt for willful and malicious personal injury under Section 523(a)(6), it is nondischargeable under that section. This analysis and the analysis in the preceding paragraph lead to the conclusion that **answers (B) and (D) are incorrect.**

Answer (C) is incorrect because it is unlikely that Randy will be ordered to modify his plan. The impact of the natural disaster and the likelihood of permanent disability probably make modification not practicable. Even if Randy is required to modify his plan, discharge of the debt to the business partner is not linked to such a modification.

239. **The correct answer is (B).** Since Liza was granted a discharge in a chapter 13 case under Section 1328(a) and since Stan's claim is one for willful and malicious damage *to property* (instead of personal injury), Stan's claim is dischargeable. By contrast, Stan's claim would be nondischargeable if Liza had filed for chapter 7. For these reasons, **Answer (A) is incorrect. Answers (C) and (D) are incorrect** because they raise issues that are not relevant to the question asked.

240. **The correct answer is (C).** Upon request of the debtor, the trustee, or the holder of an allowed unsecured claim, a chapter 13 plan may be modified, pursuant to Section 1329(a). In this case, the creditors would most likely be asking for modification to increase the amount of payments in the plan. This is a permissible reason for allowing modification. However, some courts hold that a confirmed chapter 13 plan constitutes res judicata when it comes to circumstances that existed or were foreseeable at the time of confirmation. Arguably, in Margaret's case, it was foreseeable to the creditors that she would receive a promotion in the near future. She told them about the possibility and gave them a chance to request an alteration of the plan before it was confirmed. They did not take action when they had the chance to do so. Courts adopting this approach hold that res judicata bars an increase in payments unless the creditors can show that Margaret's improved financial situation is due to an unanticipated and substantial change in her income.

Answer (A) is not the best answer. Unfairness to creditors is certainly one factor that courts use in deciding whether to modify a plan when the debtor experiences an unanticipated and substantial change income. However, that consideration alone would not justify granting modification in this case when the creditors had a chance to request a revised plan and they did nothing.

Answer (B) is incorrect because it is contradicted by the facts of the problem. Margaret's promotion was not a certainty, but it arguably was foreseeable.

Answer (D) is incorrect because the trustee is not the only party who has standing to request modification. The debtor can do so, as can the "holder of an allowed unsecured claim." *See* Section 1329(b).

241. Yes, it is possible under certain circumstances. Section 1329(a)(4) allows a plan to be modified to "reduce amounts to be paid under the plan by the actual amount expended by the debtor to purchase health insurance for the debtor" if the debtor provides documentation of the cost and if the debtor meets other conditions (i.e., the expenses have to be reasonable, the cost is not materially larger than what the debtor previously paid, or if the debtor did not have health insurance, the amount is not materially larger than the hypothetical cost of health insurance for a debtor in the debtor's situation, and the amount is not otherwise allowed for purposes of determining disposable income under section 1325(b)). The purchase also could cover the cost of health insurance for certain dependents. Section 1329(a)(4) was added as a part of the 2005 Act.

The provision seems well-intended, but it is unclear what practical impact it will have. Modifying a plan is time-consuming and expensive. It is unlikely that many chapter 13 debtors will have the resources to request modification and if they do, they always take the risk that a creditor will use the opportunity to modify the plan in ways the debtor would not find appealing. Many debtors in Karen's situation would likely end up with a conversion or a dismissal.

242. **The correct answer is (D).** Section 1328(e) allows a court, after notice and a hearing, to revoke a chapter 13 discharge on grounds of fraud. The substantive basis for the revocation clearly exists, according to the facts of the problem. The problem for the creditors, however, is that their request is not timely. Section 1328(e) requires such a request be made "before one year after a discharge . . . is granted." This means that the request must be made *within a year of the discharge.* Chad received his discharge on June 10, 2008. The creditors thus had until June 10, 2009 to bring their request. Their July 1, 2009 request was late.

The section also requires that the party in interest not know of the fraud until after the discharge was granted. The creditors would fit that requirement because they did not learn about the fraud until September of 2008, but that is not enough to save their request under the statute. The statute requires the creditors to have learned about the fraud after the discharge was granted, but it also requires them to request a revocation within a year of the discharge in order to preserve their rights. **All of the other answers are incorrect for the reasons provided above.**

243.   **The correct answer is (C).** The explanation is a bit tricky. It starts with 109(d) which provides, among other things, that chapter 11 is available to any person who could be a debtor under chapter 7. There are two exceptions to this basic rule, one for railroads and one for stockbrokers and commodity brokers. "Person" is defined in Section 101(41) to include an "individual, partnership, and corporation." Notice that the definition does not include sole proprietorships. The reason is that in a sole proprietorship, unlike a corporation, there is no legal separation between the individual and the business. If a sole proprietor wants to elect bankruptcy relief, he or she will have to file as an individual rather than as a sole proprietor. Such a filing could take place under chapter 7, 11, or 13. Much will depend on the unique situation and needs of the individual.

  Answer (A) is incorrect because entities that qualify as non-profit corporations under state law can usually file chapter 11. It is very important to consult state law and then to run the particular situation through Sections 109(d) and 101(41). A non-profit corporation that is not organized as a corporation under state law will usually not be eligible for chapter 11 relief. It is also important to note that pursuant to Section 303 of the Code, some non-profits are excluded from involuntary bankruptcies under either chapter 7 or chapter 11.

  Answers (B) and (D) are incorrect. Both limited liability corporations and S corporations are considered "corporations" within the meaning of 101(41). Thus, either type of corporation is eligible for chapter 11 relief.

244.   The business lawyer's advice is not very useful in light of the 2005 Act. The 2005 Act added Section 1123(a)(8). Under that provision, a plan proposed by an individual debtor must "provide for the payment to creditors under the plan of all or such portion of earnings from personal services performed by the debtor after the commencement of the case or other future income of the debtor as is necessary for the execution of the plan." *See* Section 1123(a)(8). This would prevent Billy from acting on the business lawyer's advice (Billy probably needs to go to a bankruptcy specialist). So, whether Billy's goal is to avoid the application of the means test or to avoid surrendering control of his estate to a chapter 7 trustee, Section 1123(a) prevents a chapter 11 filing for an individual debtor, followed by a liquidating plan.

245.   Probably. The requirement that a chapter 11 debtor propose a plan that directs future income to creditors applies only to individual debtors ("in a case in which the debtor is an individual, . . ."). It does not apply to corporate debtors. Thus, the strategy that was suggested by the business lawyer could work if TBTF filed instead of Billy. Of course, any filing in either 7 or 11 or any plan proposed in chapter 11 would be subject to other considerations such as good faith. Moreover, the corporate debtor would not be subject to Section 727(a).

246.   **The correct answer is (D).** Section 1104(a)(1) focuses on the *current management* of the

debtor (". . . for cause, including fraud, dishonesty, incompetence, or gross mismanagement of the affairs of the debtor by current management, . . ."). If the court is satisfied that Spiegel is free from any taint of Clinka, then the fact that Clinka grossly mismanaged the company is not sufficient grounds to appoint a trustee. It appears from the facts that Spiegel is exercising independent management authority pursuant to her duties to the corporation and her employment contract. Moreover, she is qualified for the job. The fact that Spiegel and Clinka have professional and social ties and the fact that Clinka chose Spiegel as his successor are not, taken alone, sufficient evidence to establish cause under Section 1104(a)(1). **All of the other answers are incorrect for the reasons stated above.**

247. **The correct answer is (A).** When it comes to mismanagement as a possible type of "cause" for the appointment of a trustee, Section 1104(a)(1) makes explicit reference to "gross mismanagement." Thus, a court is not supposed to order a trustee simply when current management makes bad decisions or engages in business mistakes. In this case, the restaurant chain obviously made some bad decisions, at least in hindsight. The expansion of locations appears overly aggressive and the menu additions were not a hit. However, the managers appear to have relied on plausible projections and advice. The downturn in the economy probably didn't help. In any event, this is probably not enough evidence to support meeting a standard of gross management. A court is more likely to give the managers an opportunity to rectify the situation before bringing in a trustee. One of the basic policy goals of chapter 11 is to give management an opportunity to move beyond business mistakes and get another chance to turn the company around. **The above analysis makes (C) and (D) are incorrect.** For an example of a case in which a court held that the standard of gross mismanagement was met, see *In re Evans*, 48 B.R. 46 (Bankr. W.D. Tex. 1985) (Debtor failed to file income tax returns for three years despite specific notice from the I.R.S., failed to pursue several potentially preferential transfers, and failed to collect a substantial debt, all of which met the standard of gross mismanagement).

   Answer (B) is not the best answer. There is no evidence that the managers have engaged in fraud, so the appointment of a trustee on the basis of fraud is not an issue.

248. Not likely. The trustee appointed by the court under Section 1104 must be a "disinterested person." The definition of "disinterested person" is in Section 101(14). Jane is not a disinterested person because she was an officer of LSI within two years before the filing. Section 101(14)(B) would be applicable here. Section 101(14) also concerns itself with making sure that creditors or those with interests materially adverse to the estate do not receive an appointment as a trustee. There is nothing in the fact pattern suggesting that Jane is a creditor or that she has an interest that is materially adverse to those of the estate, but her status as a former officer is enough to bring her under the coverage of those who would be disqualified pursuant to Section 101(14)(B).

249. **The correct answer is (D).** All of the above activities (pursuing litigation, working with secured lenders, cooperating with potential acquirers, etc.) would be legally permissible strategies for the creditors' committee to pursue. The goal of the unsecured creditors' committee is to maximize value for the general unsecured creditors. Different creditors might have different views on what constitutes maximum value. The committee will need to discuss and negotiate on an appropriate strategy, but all of the choices listed above are legally permissible under Section 1103 of the Code and under current case law. For these reasons, **Answer (E) is incorrect.**

250. **The correct answer is (C).** Prior to 2005, either (A) or (B) might have been the most likely responses from the non-member unsecured creditors and/or the committee. Participating committee members have fiduciary obligations that require access to and evaluation of a debtor's proprietary information and other confidential documents. This usually led committee members to deny a request for sensitive or privileged information and then to force the non-committee members to take their demands to court.

The 2005 Act has changed the dynamics in these situations. Section 1102(b)(3) requires committees to provide their non-member creditor constituents with "access to information," "solicit and receive comments," and "be subject to court order" compelling additional information. *See* Section 1102(b)(3). There is no definition of these terms (especially what "access to information" means) and the statute is still relatively new. However, there have been a few cases interpreting Section 1102(b)(3) and they tend to suggest that creditors' committees must be more proactive in providing information to non-members. *See In re Refco*, 336 B.R. 187 (Bankr. S.D.N.Y. 2006). In *Refco* and other cases, courts have approved protocols that, among other things, outline procedures for dealing with requests for confidential information. Answer (C) is thus probably the most likely outcome under the facts of the problem.

Answers (A) and (B) are not the best answers anymore, in light of the above analysis.

Answer (D) is not the best answer because Section 1102 does not provide for such an inspection and it is unlikely that a bankruptcy judge would immediately intervene in the case at this stage. Arguably, Section 105(a) provides the judge with the legal authority to do so, but the better practice would be for the judge not to intervene unless the parties themselves could not agree to a resolution.

251. **The correct answer is (D).** Second Bank will probably need to resign from the committee in order to seek to acquire assets or give an interview of the kind described. The reason for this is that members of a creditors' committee have a fiduciary duty to all creditors represented by the committee. This fiduciary duty requires the avoidance of any conflict of interest that would impair the duty of loyalty. Activities such as purchasing claims, buying assets of the debtor, or giving interviews in which sensitive information obtained from the debtor might be disclosed would raise conflict of interest problems. Since the correct answer is (D), both of the activities described in **answers (B) and (C)** are not permissible activities for Second Bank.

Answer (A) is incorrect because a committee member may decline to extend postpetition credit. There is no requirement that committee members extend postpetition credit to a chapter 11 debtor. Declining to extend such credit would not breach any fiduciary duties that Second Bank would have to the other committee members.

Answer (E) is incorrect for the reasons stated above.

252. **Answer (C) is the best answer,** although there are some interesting subtleties here. The role of the examiner is mostly investigative. The bankruptcy court may order the examiner to investigate any aspect of the case, business operations, or events and circumstances prior to the filing. The kinds of investigations conducted by an examiner can be similar to investigations conducted by a creditors' committee. In fact, where the debtor's conduct has been incompetent, but not egregiously so, a court may cite the existence of an active creditors' committee as a reason not to appoint an examiner. There are circumstances under

which the appointment of an examiner is mandatory (Section 1104(c)(2)), but if the appointment of an examiner is discretionary, the court might decline to appoint on the grounds that a creditors' committee can conduct an examination of the debtor, its conduct, or asset transfers.

Answer (A) is not correct because the role of the debtor in possession is to continue to operate the business during the pendency of the chapter 11 case. Additionally, the debtor in possession is expected to carry out the functions exercised by a trustee in other chapters of the Code. The debtor in possession may do some investigations prior to initiating, for example, preference litigation or fraudulent transfer actions. However, the debtor in possession is not expected to investigate its own competency and honesty.

Answer (B) is not correct because there are two basic differences between the trustee and the examiner. First, the trustee, if appointed, replaces the debtor in possession. An examiner does not. Second, the trustee, if appointed, runs the debtor's business and manages the chapter 11 case. The examiner does not. Of course, it is sometimes difficult to keep the roles completely separate in an actual case. It should also be said that examiners have sometimes done more than investigate debtor conduct, competence, and honesty. In some cases, they have been used to assist debtors in possession in the operation of the business and to advise courts on specialized topics.

Answer (D) is not correct because the United States Trustee's primary role is that of supervision and administrative oversight of the bankruptcy system. It has wide and extensive monitoring duties. However, the United States Trustee is not intended as a replacement for the trustee, the debtor in possession, the creditors' committee, or the examiner in an individual case.

253.   **The correct answer is (A).** Section 1121(b) provides that the debtor has the exclusive right to file a plan during the first 120 days of the case. If the debtor does so, no other plan can be filed during the first 180 days (180 days - 45 days = 135 days). The idea is to give the debtor sufficient time to obtain creditor acceptance without having to compete against other plans. If the plan is not accepted by all impaired classes within the extended period (and the debtor does not timely request an extension), the debtor's so-called "exclusivity period" terminates. Any party in interest may then propose a plan. **All of the other answers are incorrect.**

254.   **The correct answer is (B).** Section 1121 provides that the appointment of a trustee terminates the debtor's exclusive period for filing a plan. **All of the other answers are incorrect.**

255.   **The correct answer is (B).** Section 1121(d)(1) provides that upon request of a party in interest and after notice and hearing, a court may reduce the exclusivity period for cause. The determination of whether cause exists to reduce the time periods is fact-specific. All of the evidentiary points listed in the problem would be relevant to the question of whether cause existed. Answer (B) would be the most effective in helping the creditors establish cause to reduce the debtor's exclusivity period.

Other evidence might include whether the creditors possessed confidence in the debtor or whether the court had previously granted extensions of time that proved futile.

All of the other answers are incorrect because those pieces of evidence would help the debtor maintain exclusivity.

256.   **The correct answer is (E).** A secured creditor in Grant Bank's situation that makes the Section 1111(b) election will likely subject itself to all of the above consequences. Section 1111(b) is a complex provision, but it helps to understand it if you keep its policy goal in mind. The policy goal of Section 1111(b) is to balance debtor protection with creditor protection. When applied in conjunction with other code sections (most notably Sections 506 and 1129), it gives the debtor the ability to retain property subject to a lien so that the debtor can use the property to reorganize. At the same time, it gives the secured creditor the opportunity to blunt the potential unfairness that could result from a judicial valuation of its property and the possible resulting loss if the property appreciates (as it likely will in this case) and the debtor ends up defaulting.

Answers (A), (B), and (C) are correct because they all accurately describe the likely result of Grant Bank's election. Since Grant Bank is an undersecured creditor in its own class (which is typical) and since it has a non-recourse mortgage, it can make the Section 1111(b) election. Once it makes that election, it will lose its deficiency claim. It will also lose its voting rights as an unsecured creditor. In return, it will gain a secured claim for the full amount of the debt, $800,000. This means that the debtor has to pay, under the plan, at least the full face value of the secured claim and that Blackacre secures the payment of $800,000. The debtor's plan must so provide. (Read Section 1129(b) carefully to get this part of the analysis.) Grant Bank will also lose its right to receive a distribution on its unsecured claim. **Answer (D) is incorrect** because it only includes two of the consequences of the election.

Whether the above-described exchange makes sense for Grant Bank depends on several factors, including but not limited to the dollar amount of any possible deficiency, the amount of available assets to pay deficiency claims, and competing chapter 11 plans. In truth, the Section 1111(b) election plays a larger role in the negotiations over the plan than it actually has in terms of a real election. By making it possible for the secured creditor to maintain a lien on the collateral to secure the full value of the amount of its allowed claim irrespective of the value imposed by the court under Section 506(a), the secured creditor can use the threat of the election to force the debtor to negotiate a plan more favorable to the secured creditor.

Answer (D) is incorrect for the reasons stated above.

257.   **The correct answer is (C).** The mortgage provisions do not prevent Grant Bank from being affected by Section 1111(b). Section 1111(b) overrides both provisions. It also overrides such provisions under nonbankruptcy law. Therefore, the fact that the parties have contractually limited Grant Bank to non-recourse status and have attempted to restrict claim bifurcation is irrelevant to the operation of Section 1111(b). It is also not relevant that Grant Bank apparently calculated its interest rate differently than it would have if the if the mortgage was with recourse. **This analysis makes answers (A) and (B) incorrect.**

The point of this question is to get you to see that Section 1111(b) has an automatic character. It operates without regard to particular contractual provisions and without regard to nonbankruptcy law. In this example, Grant Bank ultimately decides to elect Section 1111(b) treatment and thus lose its deficiency claim. If it had not done so, Grant Bank would have had recourse status, be subject to claim bifurcation, and have a deficiency claim without regard to provision 1 or provision 2.

Answer (D) is also incorrect because there is no such deadline for an election under Section 1111(b). Bankruptcy Rule 3014 provides that such an election may be made at any time prior to the conclusion of the disclosure statement hearing or "within a later time as the court may fix." Bankruptcy Rule 3014 contains several other procedural rules that govern the election process.

258.   **The correct answer is (D).** The Section 1111(b) election converts the secured creditor's claim, including the unsecured deficiency claim of $500,000, into a secured claim. Pursuant to Section 1111(b) and Section 1129(b), the debtor's plan must provide that the secured creditor receive at least the full face value of the secured claim ($1 million). Section 1129(b) also requires that Greenacre secure the payment of $1 million.

Answer (B) is incorrect because if the secured creditor making the Section 1111(b) election were to receive only the value of Greenacre, that would run counter to the purpose of the section. Section 1111(b) is designed to protect an eligible secured creditor in chapter 11 cases from having its lien "stripped down" to the value of the collateral. Yet, this is exactly what would happen if the plan provided that the secured creditor would be paid only an amount equal to the value of Greenacre.

Answer (C) is incorrect because immediate liquidation of Greenacre would frustrate the debtor's ability to reorganize because it would not be able to retain property subject to a lien. In enacting Section 1111(b), Congress wanted to strike a balance between preserving a debtor's need to reorganize and protecting the legitimate expectations of non-recourse creditors.

Answer (A) is incorrect because Section 1111(b) contains no such provision.

259.   **The correct answer is (C).** The right of a chapter 11 debtor to voluntarily convert a case from chapter 11 to chapter 7 is probably not absolute. Section 1112(a) governs voluntary conversions. The language of Section 1112(a) restricts a chapter 11 debtor's ability to convert under specified circumstances. However, the language of the section contains the phrase, "The debtor may convert a case under this chapter to a case under chapter 7 of this title unless. . . .". This permissive language suggested to some that chapter 11 debtors had an absolute right to convert to chapter 7 unless their case fell into one of the specified exceptions in Section 1112(a), none of which involve an inquiry into the debtor's conduct. The United States Supreme Court ruled in *Marrama v. Citizens Bank*, 549 U.S. 365 (2007), that there does exist a "bad faith" exception to the conversion right created by Section 706(a) and that a chapter 7 debtor who was found to have acted in bad faith forfeited his right to convert his case to chapter 13. *Marrama* involved an attempted conversion from chapter 7 to chapter 13. *Marrama* did not directly address conversions from chapter 11 to chapter 7. However, the reasoning of the decision applies equally to attempted conversions from chapter 11 to chapter 7. There is ample evidence that Max engaged in bad faith conduct and he has so admitted. For all of these reasons, **Answer (C) is the best answer and Answer (B) is incorrect.**

Answer (A) is incorrect because Max's ability to meet the means test is not the only issue a court would have to consider in ruling on his conversion motion. Meeting the means test would make him eligible for chapter 7 under Section 707(b). However, evidence that Max is a bad faith debtor would likely render him ineligible for relief under the chapter to which he is seeking conversion, chapter 7.

Answer (D) is incorrect because a case can generally be converted from one chapter to another at any time during the course of the bankruptcy case. There are some limitations to this point, but none that would be relevant on these facts and at this stage of Max's case.

260. The main obstacle is that Sarah might have a difficult time establishing that she has a stable and regular income. Section 1112(d) permits Sarah to request a voluntary conversion from chapter 11 to chapter 13. However, it is not an absolute right. The most important point here is that Sarah must be eligible for chapter 13 relief before a court can convert her case from chapter 11 to chapter 13. Section 1112(f) so provides: "Notwithstanding any other provision of this section, a case may not be converted to a case under another chapter of this title unless the debtor may be a debtor under such chapter.". Sarah's job loss and lack of access to a regular and stable source of income (including governmental benefits and/or family support) could be a problem for her.

261. **The correct answer is (A).** Section 1112(a) gives the debtor the right (absent bad faith) to convert a chapter 11 case to a case under chapter 7 provided that one of three limitations does not apply. This situation illustrates one of the three limitations. A debtor does not have the right to convert a case from a chapter 11 case to a chapter 7 case if the chapter 11 case was an involuntary bankruptcy filing. In order to convert, the debtor (in this case, the debtor in possession) must show "cause." The grounds for cause are set forth in Section 1112(b). In this case, the debtor in possession might be able to show cause under Section 1112(b)(4)(A) which refers to the absence of reasonable prospects for reorganization. If the debtor in possession cannot make that showing, it cannot convert the case. So, that is the most important issue for the court to decide. The policy reason for this rule is that it would be unfair and inefficient if the creditors could successfully put CSC into an involuntary chapter 11 case and then have the debtor in possession quickly and easily counter that by a unilateral conversion to chapter 7.

Answer (C) is tempting, but not the best answer. In the course of deciding a cause motion under Section 1112(b)(4)(A) and thus deciding whether there was a reasonable prospect for a rehabilitation, a court might indeed confront the basic policy question of whom is in the best position to decide the company's fate. However, that is not an explicit standard under Section 1112.

Answer (B) is incorrect because whether the creditors filed the involuntary petition in good faith is not relevant to this motion. That issue might have been appropriate for CSC to raise at the time of the filing of the involuntary case (*see* Section 303(i)(2)), but not now.

Answer (D) is incorrect. Whether the debtor in possession brought the conversion motion in good faith could be an issue, but it is not the most important issue at this stage and there does not seem to be much by way of factual support for that theory in the problem.

262. **The correct answer is (A).** Pursuant to Section 1112(b)(3), the court must commence a hearing upon a motion for dismissal (or conversion) for cause no later than 30 days after the filing of the motion. Continuances are possible in specified circumstances (i.e., movant consent and/or compelling circumstances). These time limits are designed to ensure that dismissal and continuance motions do not languish and then become outdated or irrelevant in the face of rapidly changing circumstances. **All of the other answers are incorrect.**

263. **The correct answer is (D).** The absence of an explicit good faith standard in Section 1112(b) does not mean that a chapter 11 bankruptcy case cannot be dismissed if a court determines that the filing was not in good faith. The creditors might have a very good argument that in

this case, Gordon's does not have a present need for relief, but is simply using the Code to subvert a possible legitimate claim. A chapter 11 debtor does not have to be technically insolvent. Nor does it have to be late on its credit obligations. However, some degree of present financial distress and/or a threat to the going concern value of the company is typically required in order to justify bankruptcy relief. Where a debtor is arguably using chapter 11 for a purpose that is outside the legitimate purpose of the bankruptcy laws, the creditors could have a plausible argument that the filing is not in good faith.

Courts sometimes use lack of good faith as cause for relief under Section 1112(b), despite the fact that it is not explicitly listed as a grounds for cause in that section. Other times, courts might use Section 105(a).

Answer (A) is incorrect because Section 1112(b)(4)'s lack of a good faith provision does not mean that creditors cannot use the absence of good faith as possible grounds for a dismissal. Similarly, **Answer (C) is incorrect.** Just because there is no Code section that expressly authorizes a court to dismiss a chapter 11 case on the grounds of lack of good faith does not mean that courts cannot find an implied authorization and that is what they often do.

Answer (B) is incorrect because even solvent companies can file in chapter 11. A chapter 11 filing by debtor that is solvent does not show unequivocally that the debtor has filed in bad faith.

264.   **The correct answer is (A).** Section 349 provides some of the consequences of a dismissal of a bankruptcy case. Pursuant to Section 349(e), the dismissal of a case does not prejudice the debtor with regard to the filing of a subsequent petition, except as provided in Section 109(g). This is why Answer (A) is not an effect of dismissal.

   Answers (B), (C), and (D) are incorrect because the answers describe three events that are a consequence of dismissal.

265.   **The correct answer is (A).** If the employee benefit pension plan is part of the collective bargaining agreement between Acme and the union, then the plan is governed by Section 1113. Section 1113 allows chapter 11 debtors to reject collective bargaining agreements, but it puts certain rules in place for that rejection. This analysis makes **C an incorrect answer.** Additionally, Section 1114 could apply to health insurance benefits for retired employees if Acme promised such benefits outside the context of the collective bargaining agreement. Section 1114 provides special protection to such benefits. The next question demonstrates more about the operation of Section 1114.

   It is important to note that other federal nonbankruptcy law such as ERISA would also likely cover any attempt to modify the employee benefit pension plan. Such law would have to be consulted prior to any move on the part of the debtor in possession to modify the plan.

   Answer (B) is incorrect because the fact that the employee benefit pension plan is not within the industry norm is not what brings the plan into Section 1113. What brings it into the reach of Section 1113 has been explained above.

   Answer (D) is incorrect because it is not entirely clear that Acme's filing is in bad faith. It appears to be having some real financial difficulties and a chapter 11 might give Acme the breathing room it needs to grapple with them. Even if the filing is in bad faith, that is a separate issue from the question of whether it can modify the employee benefit pension plan while it is in bankruptcy.

266. **Answer (C) is correct**, although not totally free from doubt. Section 1114(*l*), as added in 2005, allows a court to reinstate any benefits modified during the 180 days before a chapter 11 filing, if the debtor was insolvent when the modifications were made. There is an equitable exception, however if "the balance of equities clearly favors such modification."

Note that Section1114(*l*) only provides for reinstatement; it does not deal with assumption or rejection. But presumably a more specific section such as Section 1114(*l*) will control over a more general section on assumption, and the debtor will have to deal with the reinstatement rights as part of the assumption process. Only if the balance of equities favors the debtor will the court likely permit assumption.

Answer (A) is incorrect because it does not take into account the reinstatement right put in the Code in 2005 as discussed above.

Answer (B) is incorrect because it ignores the "balancing of the equities" that Section 1114(*l*) specifically recognizes.

Answer (D) is incorrect because Dearheart should be able to assume the contract if it can show a balancing of the equities. **Since (C) is the only answer that recognizes this possibility, it is the correct answer.**

267. Yes. The argument is credible. In fact, it is possible that a court would side with the employees. A look at the plain language of Section 1114 reveals that it applies to "retiree benefits" and that the benefits must be both medical in nature and intended for retirees. The benefits to the five employees include payments for health insurance. Spernco describes them as part of an early retirement package and they are not covered by a collective bargaining agreement. The health insurance premium payments could thus be governed by Section 1114. For more on this, see *In re Arclin U.S. Holding, Inc.*, 416 B.R. 117 (Bankr. D. Del. 2009).

268. **The correct answer is (D).** One element of the definition of "small business debtor" in Section 101(51D) of the Code requires the debtor to have $2,343,300 or less in noncontingent, liquidated secured and unsecured debts. Remember that this amount is adjusted for inflation every three years, so if you are doing this problem after April 1, 2013, then you will have to account for the adjustments. This could change the outcome of the problem. There are other elements contained in the definition (i.e., a person engaged in business and commercial activities, for example). The debt limit excludes debts to affiliates and insiders from the debt threshold. Barber would meet the definition of an "insider" under Section 101(31(B)(ii) (an officer of the debtor if the debtor is a corporation). With the 2 million dollar debt to Barber excluded, CFC could meet the debt limit because it has only 1 million in secured and unsecured debt. The debt is liquidated and noncontingent, so it counts toward the limit. For the above reasons, **Answer (C) is incorrect**.

Answer (A) incorrect because it assumes that the definition of "small business debtor" is linked to the geographical size and reach of the company. This is not a factor under the definition in Section 101(51D).

Answer (B) is incorrect because it assumes that status as a "small business debtor" is a matter of choice. Prior to the 2005 Act, it was a matter of choice. However, the 2005 Act changed that so that all debtors that fit the statutory definition are considered small business debtors.

269.   **The correct answer is (B).** Pursuant to Sections 101(51D) and 1102(a)(1), a case is no longer a small business case if an unsecured creditors' committee is appointed. This state of affairs remains in effect until there is a court order that determines that the committee has not been sufficiently active to be effective and that the debtor satisfies all of the other requirements for being a small business debtor. **All of the other answers are incorrect.**

270.   **The correct answer is (B).** In a small business case, only the debtor may file a plan during the first 180 days of the case under Section 1112(e) (150+30 = 180). Section 1112(e) provides a 300-day time limit for filing a plan and disclosure statement in a small business case. What this means is that BTC has 180 "exclusive days" and an additional 120 "non-exclusive days" to file a plan. During the 120 days, nondebtor parties can file plans that compete with BTC's (although a nondebtor party can file a plan whether BTC does or not). These deadlines can only be extended if the debtor, after notice and hearing, proves to the court by a preponderance of the evidence that it is more likely than not that the court will confirm the plan within a reasonable time. **All of the other answers are incorrect.**

271.   You need to tell him that Section 1112(b)(4)(P) gives a creditor to whom is owned a domestic support obligation grounds to move for dismissal or conversion of a chapter 11 case. This provision applies to domestic support obligations (arising either from an agreement or from a court order) that "first become payable after the date of the filing of the petition." Since the divorce agreement was a post-petition agreement, Rex's alimony obligation to Andrealina (which would be considered a domestic support obligation under Section 101(14A)) would be covered. Failure to pay such an obligation could give Andrealina grounds to ask the bankruptcy court to either dismiss Rex's case or convert it to chapter 7 for cause.

272.   **The correct answer is (A).** Under Section 1141(d)(5), discharge is deferred in a chapter 11 case until the court grants a discharge on completion of all payments under the plan (". . . confirmation of the plan does not discharge any debt provided for in the plan until the court grants a discharge on completion of all payments under the plan."). **All of the other answers are incorrect.**

       Under certain conditions, a court may grant a discharge to an individual chapter 11 debtor who has not competed payments under the plan. *See* Section 1141(d)(5)(B) (which is modeled after Section 1328).

273.   Yes. Pursuant to Section 1115(a)(2), the money Sam earns after August 14 would be considered property of the estate ("In a case in which the debtor is an individual, property of the estate includes, in addition to the property specified in section 541 . . . (2) earnings from services performed by the debtor after the commencement of the case . . ."). This should be compared to chapter 7 where postpetition earnings are not considered property of the estate. This should also be compared to chapter 13 where the rule is similar to the chapter 11 rule. *See* Section 1306.

       Authors' note: You will find many more questions on the topic of how individual chapter 11 cases differ from other types of chapter 11 cases in Chapter 12 of this book (general dischargeability issues for individual debtors in chapter 11), Chapter 17 of this book (specific nondischargeable claims for individual debtors in chapter 11), and in subtopic A of this Chapter (commencement of a chapter 11 case where the debtor is an individual).

274.   **The correct answer is (D).** The best legal strategy among those listed above would be

Answer (D), particularly if United Bank is seeking quick relief from the automatic stay. TopFlight's case would probably qualify as a single asset real estate case under Section 101(51B). Case law supports the position that the stay can be lifted for cause in a single asset real estate case if a court concludes that the bankruptcy filing was not made in good faith. For an example of this approach, see *Laguna Assoc. Ltd. Partnership v. Aetna Casualty & Surety Co.*, 30 F.3d 734 (6th Cir. 1994).

Answer (A) is incorrect because United Bank cannot file a foreclosure action in state court unless and until it gets the automatic stay lifted. It cannot get the automatic stay lifted unless and until it meets one of the grounds listed in Section 362(d).

Answer (B) is incorrect because bankruptcy laws are constitutional pursuant to Article I, Section 8, clause 4 of the United States Constitution and the Constitution's Supremacy clause (*See* Article VI, clause 2). Courts have interpreted the Code in a manner that had led to the conclusion that its application does not unconstitutionally deprive United Bank of its property rights.

Answer (C) is incorrect because there are no facts to indicate that TopFlight obtained the mortgage through fraud.

275. **The correct answer is (C).** In a chapter 11 case involving a single asset debtor, a court can grant relief from the automatic stay 90 days after the order for relief unless the debtor has either filed a plan that has a reasonable possibility of being confirmed within a reasonable time or has commenced making monthly payments to stay current on regular interest. *See* Section 362(d)(3). Forty-five days have already gone by, so TopFlight has only 45 more. The single asset real estate provisions were instituted in 1994 and strengthened in 2005 in order to correct perceived abuses of the Code by single asset real estate debtors, particularly in turbulent real estate markets. **All of the other answers are incorrect.**

276. **The correct answer is (C).** The definition of single asset real estate in Section 101(51B) refers to, among other things, whether "substantial business is being conducted by a debtor other than the business of operating the real property." *See* Section 101(51B). If no such substantial business is being conducted, then that makes it more likely that the debtor qualifies as a single asset debtor. If such substantial business is being conducted, that makes it less likely that the debtor will qualify as a single asset debtor. In this instance, it is fairly clear that Advent has been conducting its regular business (software creation and development) in a substantial fashion while at the same time operating the real property (or hiring an agent to do it).

All of the other answers are incorrect. In particular, **Answer (B) is incorrect** because there is no debt limit in Section 101(51B).

277. **The correct answer is (A).** In order to get the court to conclude that MSI should be a single asset real estate case, the creditors will need to prove that MSI did not conduct substantial business other than operating the real property. MSI will want to argue that many of its activities such as conducting planning and construction of homes, marketing and selling homes, and doing maintenance constitute substantial business activities and that it is thus excluded from Section 101(51B). The best argument from among those listed here would be Answer (A) because it connects all of the activities of MSI to its primary activity: selling real estate.

Answers (B) and (C) are not the best answers because they rely on policy judgments that most bankruptcy judges would conclude are beyond the scope of the judge's authority to impose in light of the specific language of the statutes. Perhaps Sections 101(51B) and 362(d)(3) should have broader reach. However, that would be up to Congress to accomplish in a redraft of the statute.

Answer (D) is incorrect because it is the exact opposite of what the creditors would want to argue. In fact, it would be an attractive argument in favor of a conclusion that favors MSI. The argument would be that since MSI's business model resembles a manufacturing outfit and not a passive investment activity, that MSI's filing should not be treated as a single asset real estate case.

278.   **The correct answer is (C).** It is unclear whether the corporate debtor could put claim 1 and claim 2 in separate classes. More broadly, it is not clear whether claims that are "substantially similar" must be in the same class. The Code requires all claims in a class to be substantially similar, but courts generally do not mandate that all substantially similar claims be placed in the same class. So, the corporate debtor may be able to separately classify otherwise substantially similar claims as long as it can provide a business, economic, or legal justification for separate classification. The justification should be independent of the debtor's need to confirm a plan. Claim 1 and claim 2 share similarities. They are both employment-related claims and they are both unsecured, nonpriority claims. If, for example, one of the claims was considered an administrative expense claim, then they would probably have to be classified separately.

On the other hand, it is possible that the claims differ in terms of their legal rights. Claim 1 consists of severance payment rights that arise out of a contract between the corporate debtor and the affected employees. Claim 2 consists of a pension benefit payment rights that arise out of a separate contract as the facts indicate.

If the corporate debtor can make a persuasive argument for separate classification on business, economic, or legal grounds, then separate classification could be possible. Since Section 1122 does not address the question of whether the debtor who puts claims that are substantially similar in different classes has done anything improper, either Answer (A) or Answer (B) could be correct and that **makes (C) the correct answer.**

Answer (D) is incorrect because the reasonableness of the payments would not have a bearing on the classification issue. It might bear on other issues.

Although not relevant to this question, the easiest point on classification to remember is that priority claims under Section 507(a) are almost always classified separately from either general unsecured claims or secured claims.

279.   **The best answer is (C).** Separate classification can be justified if it is based on the legal nature of the claim. Claims with different legal interests have different business, economic, and practical incentives that may influence them to accept or even prefer separate classification.

All of the other answers are either incorrect or not as good as Answer (C). First, administrative convenience can justify separate classification, but that is usually invoked under Section 1122(b) in the case of a very large number of relatively small claims. Second, the debtor's desire to create an impaired class that will vote in favor of the plan is not, by itself, a persuasive reason for separate classification. There has to be a business, economic, or legal reason apart from the need to confirm a plan. Finally, the debtor's desire for a faster plan confirmation is also not a persuasive reason, at least by itself. Speed of the reorganization process should not trump the principle of equality of treatment of similarly situated creditors.

280. **The correct answer is (B).** "Claims" and "interests" must be classified separately. Eliza is a preferred shareholder which gives her a proprietary (i.e., ownership) interest in Berger. This legal ownership interest is different from a "claim" which is defined in Section 101 of the Code as a "right to payment." Eliza's loan to Berger is a claim. Because the essential nature of interests and claims is fundamentally different and thus give rise to very different legal rights, Eliza's interest and her claim must be separately classified.

Answer (A) **is incorrect** because the identity of the holder of the claim or interest is not the key factor in classification.

Answer (C) **is incorrect** because Eliza's status as a preferred vs. common shareholder is not the key factor. Her legal ownership interest in Berger would need separate classification from her claim regardless of which type of shares she owned.

Answer (D) sounds like an interesting policy argument, but it is not necessary since the basic rule cited above gives Eliza plenty of grounds on which to object to lumping the interest and the claim together.

281. **The correct answer is (A).** Indeed, there is split in the case law on the question of whether the Section 1111(b) deficiency claim of an undersecured creditor can be separately classified from the claims of general unsecured creditors. *Compare Phoenix Mut. Life Ins. Co. v. Greystone III Joint Venture*, 995 F.2d 1274 (5th Cir. 1991) (no separate classification) with *In re Woodbrook Assoc.*, 19 F.3d 312 (7th Cir. 1994) (requiring separate classification).

The argument against separate classification usually boils down to a concern about fairness to the secured creditor, especially in light of the protective policies behind Section 1111(b). There is also a general tendency on the part of these courts to be skeptical of the debtor's motives (i.e., are they doing this for a permissible reason or just to rig the votes?). The argument for separate classification is rooted in the notion that unsecured deficiency claims created by Section 1111(b) are not substantially similar to regular unsecured claims for several different reasons. **All of the other answers are either incorrect or raise extraneous issues.**

282. **The correct answer is (A).** Section 1129(a)(9) mandates as a condition of confirmation that a chapter 11 plan provide for cash payment of Section 507(a)(3) priority claims on the effective date of the plan unless the holder of the claim agrees to less favorable treatment. Thus, a majority of a class having Section 507(a)(3) priority claims cannot restrict the minority to treatment at variance with Section 1129(a)(9). Each claim within the class has the right to full, immediate payment. This explains why Section 1123(a)(1) does not require the designation of this class of claim. **All of the other answers are incorrect.** For more on this, see Section 1123 (a)(1) which excepts Sections 507(a)(2) (involuntary gap claims), 507(a)(3) (administrative expense claims), and 507(a)(8) (certain unsecured tax claims) from class designation under the mandatory plan provisions.

283. **The correct answer is (C).** The Section 507(a)(5) class of claims is impaired because the plan alters the legal and contractual rights of the holders of the claims. Thus, it must be specified pursuant to Section 1123(a)(3) (specification of treatment of impaired classes). The Section 507(a)(7) class of claims is unimpaired because the holders of these claims are not having their rights altered under the plan. It also needs to be specified, but under Section

1123(a)(2) (specification of unimpaired classes). The point of this question is to get you to see that specification of both unimpaired and impaired classes is mandatory in chapter 11. For more on the underlying concepts of impairment and nonimpairment, consult the next subtopic in this chapter. **All of the other answers are incorrect.**

284. **The correct answer is (A).** If the same creditor holds both an allowed secured claim and an unsecured claim and both are impaired, the plan must separately specify the treatment to be provided for each of class of claims under Section 1123(a)(3). A secured claim has different legal rights than an unsecured claim and thus secured claims cannot be placed in the same class with unsecured claims, even if the same creditor holds both claims. This is because if you read Section 1123(a) (1), (2), and (3) carefully, you will see that it refers to "class or classes of claims" and not just to "claims." Remember that since Brad is in chapter 11 and not chapter 13, he may be able strip down the car loan. **All of the other answers are incorrect or raise extraneous issues.**

285. **The correct answer is (B).** The issue of whether and under what circumstances a chapter 11 plan can effectuate transactions that would otherwise be restricted or even banned under federal law has been an issue for some time. It is not entirely clear whether the debtor in possession or Third Bank would win here because the issue is complicated, but Answer (B) is likely to be the debtor in possession's most attractive argument of those mentioned. For a representative sampling of the issues, see *Pacific Gas & Electric v. Cal. ex. rel. Cal. Dept. of Toxic Substances Control*, 350 F.3d 932 (9th Cir. 2003), *cert denied*, 543 U.S. 956 (2004) and *In re Combustion Eng'g, Inc.*, 390 F.3d (3d Cir. 2004).

Answer (A) is incorrect because it misstates the nature of Section 1123 generally and Section 1123(a)(5) in particular. Section 1123 and its provisions are not discretionary or permissive. They are mandatory (". . . a plan shall. . . ."). A chapter 11 debtor must comply with them to the extent they are applicable to the debtor's unique situation.

Answer (C) is incorrect because it is an incorrect statement of the law. The Code does not contain any express provisions that expressly preempt other federal law in single asset real estate cases.

Answer (D) is not incorrect. It is just not the best argument of those mentioned. Section 1123(a)(5)(E) allows for the modification of liens, but Third Bank is arguing that such modification is illegal and improper because such modification would otherwise be restricted under federal law. This means that the debtor in possession has to confront the preemption argument directly. Merely citing Section 1123(a)(5)(E) will not be the best argument. In other words, it is simply a starting point.

286. **The correct answer is (D).** Section 1124(1) provides that a class of claims or interests is impaired unless the plan "leaves unaltered the legal, equitable, and contractual rights to which such claim or interest entitles the holder of such claim or interest." It is thus generally understood that virtually any alteration of a claimant's rights is considered an impairment, even when the claimant's rights are enhanced by a plan. However, this question reveals a fundamental principle that accompanies 1124(1) and that principle is that an alteration of rights *by the Code* does not constitute impairment. Under bankruptcy law, Green River is forced to surrender certain state law rights once Summit files chapter 11, but that is an alteration arising from the Code and judicial decisions interpreting the Code. It is *statutory* impairment, *not* plan impairment. Section 1124(1) covers only plan impairment and Green

River's class of claim is not impaired under the plan.

Answer (A) is incorrect because while it is true that Green River could not sell the collateral when it wanted to, that is a feature of the interaction of Sections 362, 541, and 542 of the Code and accompanying decisional law. It is not a feature of the plan.

Answer (B) is incorrect because it is an erroneous statement.

Answer (C) is a decent policy argument, but it does not work well here. Congress and the courts decided some time ago that secured creditors in chapter 11 must exchange state law collection rights for bankruptcy rights and remedies in facts similar to the ones in this case. For more on this, see *United States v. Whiting Pools, Inc.*, 462 U.S. 198 (1983).

287. **The correct answer is (C).** Since neither the second nor the third mortgage has been changed in any way, neither one of them would be considered impaired. The plan in no way changes the rights of the holder, so no impairment of each class of claim.

Answer (A) is incorrect because the mere fact that the first mortgage is impaired by the plan does not mean that the second and third mortgages are automatically or necessarily impaired. Each class of claimants must be analyzed separately when it comes to determining impairment.

Answer (B) is incorrect because the mere fact that the second mortgage is first in time compared to the third and thus closer to the first does not change the analysis. Again, each class of claimants must be analyzed separately. This also makes **(E) an incorrect answer.**

Answer (D) is incorrect because speculation about what might happen to a class of claimants in the future is not relevant. The issue is whether the class of claimants is impaired *by the plan*.

288. No. When looking to see whether a class of claims or interests is impaired, courts tend to look at whether the plan alters legal, equitable, or contractual rights. The focus is not on whether the class of claims or interests improves its *economic* position. In the question, a positive net worth for the corporate debtor would likely result in an economic benefit for those holding legal ownership interests. However, that does not mean that the classes of interests are impaired under the plan unless their legal, economic, or contractual rights are altered.

289. You will need to tell Spectrum that Section 1125 forbids the solicitation of creditor approval of a plan until the court has approved, after notice and a hearing, the disclosure statement. The court will need to determine that the disclosure statement contains "adequate information" as that term is defined in Section 1125(a)(1).

In the bankruptcy world, "solicitation" means the official process in which the disclosure statement, ballot, and other materials are presented to creditors. It does not include informal negotiations and discussions with respect to the general terms or possible outcomes of the case.

290. Yes. Section 1125(g) allows plan solicitation to occur without a court approved disclosure statement under circumstances that resemble a prepackaged bankruptcy case (i.e., postpetition continuation of solicitation of votes in a chapter 11 case based upon prepetition negotiation and acceptance).

291. **The correct answer is (C).** The key word in the question is "insist." Section 1125 provides that the information provided in a written disclosure statement does not have to follow otherwise applicable state or federal law. So, the DEP cannot insist on a statement of its choosing. The DEP is not entirely voiceless, however, because Section 1125(d) allows it to be heard on the issue of whether the disclosure statement is adequate. **This makes (D) an incorrect answer.**

Answers **(A) and (B) are incorrect** because they both assume the supremacy of nonbankruptcy law where none exists.

292. **The correct answer is (C).** Section 1125(a)(1) clearly states that the duty to provide adequate information does not include information about any other possible or proposed plan. **Answer (D) is not incorrect.** However, it is not the best answer since the statute clearly covers the question. This obviates the need for judicial interpretation. **All of the other answers are incorrect.**

293. No. Only the holder of an allowed claim or interest may vote its claim or interest in chapter 11 under the terms of Section 1126(a). A claim or interest can be "deemed filed" under Section 1111(a), or "actually filed" under Section 502 and not objected to by a party in interest. The consumer claims in this example cannot be "deemed filed" under Section 1111(a) because they are contingent and unliquidated. The consumer warranty claims could not be actually filed unless they had been estimated pursuant to Section 502(c) (estimation for purposes of claims allowance), but the question says such allowance has not happened.

Bankruptcy Rule 3018(a) allows certain disputed claims to be temporarily allowed for the purposes of voting. *See* Bankruptcy Rule 3018(a). This is not the same process, however, as claims estimation for purposes of allowance.

294. **The correct answer is (B).** If a class is not impaired under the plan, Section 1126(g) provides that the class is "conclusively presumed to have accepted the plan," and the solicitation of its acceptance is not required. This means that the class does not vote. The secured creditor might have legitimate concerns about future events, but chapter 11 plan voting is not intended to provide unimpaired creditors with general economic protection outside the terms of the plan or with assurances of perfect democracy. **This explains why answers (A), (D) and (E) are incorrect. Answer (C) is incorrect** because the same rule ("no impairment, no vote") applies to both secured and unsecured creditors.

295. No. Class 4 rejected the plan. For it to have been accepted, there would have to be acceptance by at least two-thirds in amount and more than one-half in number of the allowed claims actually voting on the plan. In this question, class 4 met the number majority (40 > 35), but not the amount majority ($170,000 < $333,333). Remember that Section 1126(c) requires both the amount majority and the number majority and it only includes those claims actually voting.

296. No. Acme's plan does not satisfy the test. Five annual payments of $8,000 is worth less than $40,000 payable immediately as would (hypothetically, anyway) occur in liquidation. The best interests test requires that each dissenting claim holder receive at least as much under the plan as it would have received in a chapter 7 liquidation. This requirement protects dissenting members of a class that has voted to accept the plan.

297.   We focus on holders of claims in applying Section 1129(a)(7) because the statute specifically refers to "each holder of a claim or interest of such class." Since the "best interests test" is intended to protect dissenting members of a class that has voted for the plan, it makes sense for the section to focus on individual members of the class.

298.   **The correct answer is (D).** Certain priority claims are entitled to special treatment of various kinds pursuant to Section 1129(a)(9). Administrative expenses, involuntary gap claims, priority tax claims, and others so listed are included in the full payment category, although not all require full payment, in cash, on the effective date of the plan. *See* Section 1129(a)(9). The point of this question is that drunk driving claims are not so listed and are thus not entitled to special treatment. The exception, of course, is that such claims must be paid in full prior to the payment of any general unsecured claims pursuant to the absolute priority rule.

   Answer (A) is incorrect because this plan would not violate the absolute priority rule since general unsecured creditors will not receive payment.

   Answer (B) is incorrect because the nondischargeability of the claim does not bear on the question of how the claims needs to be treated in order to confirm a plan under Section 1129(a)(9). This claim would be nondischargeable under Section 1141(d)(2) since the debtor is an individual, but that is not legally relevant to its treatment under the plan.

   Answer (C) is a policy argument in favor of requiring special treatment in the form of full payment. Congress has determined, mostly for policy reasons, which payments it thinks deserve such special treatment and which ones do not. Until Congress states otherwise, bankruptcy courts have to apply the priorities as Congress determines them.

299.   **The correct answer is (A).** Before Section 1129(b) can be applied, the plan must be accepted by at least one impaired class. *See* Section 1129(b) and Section 1129(a)(10). The problem for Vandelay Industries is that no impaired class has accepted the plan. So, the debtor has to go back to the drawing board and design a plan that will be accepted by at least one class. This requirement ensures that debtors do not waste valuable time seeking nonconsensual confirmation of plans that have absolutely no creditor support. Fulfillment of all of the requirements of Section 1129(a), including Sections 1129(a)(10), is required before Section 1129(b) can be invoked. **All of the other answers are incorrect for the reasons stated above.**

300.   **The correct answer is (D).** Section 1129(b)(1)'s anti-discrimination provision applies only to *unfair* discrimination. It is important to keep in mind that before a court ever gets to the issue of unfair discrimination, the debtor will have to affirmatively prove the other elements of confirmation. Therefore, the dissenting class has already received at least what it would have received if the case had been a chapter 7 case. Thus, it is assumed that the debtor can treat creditors differently if it needs to so long as the different treatment has a reasonable basis and is necessary for the reorganization.

   On the other hand, differential treatment that arises out of a significantly lower percentage recovery or that imposes significantly greater risk to the dissenting class without a reasonable justification is more problematic and could form the basis for a creditor to block nonconsensual confirmation under Section 1129(b). *See In re Quay Corp. Inc.*, 372 B.R. 378 (Bankr. N.D. Ill. 2007). **All of the other answers are incorrect.**

301. **The correct answer is (D).** Section 1129(b)(2)(A) contains several possible treatments for a secured claim: a note in the amount of the secured claim secured by the same collateral and accompanying payments of it allowed secured claim, a sale of the collateral free of the lien with a transfer of the lien to the sale proceeds, or the "indubitable equivalent" of the claim. If the secured creditor receives any of these (and thus the plan is probably "fair and equitable") and is not being unfairly discriminated against as a class, the secured creditor is getting paid in full under the plan and has no argument against cramdown. But, in order to analyze these possible treatments, one has to know the answers to the facts in (B) and (C). For this reason, **Answer (E) is incorrect.**

There are many complications associated with the facts in Answer (B). Space does not permit us to delve into the valuation and interest rate questions here. Your professor should cover those in a basic bankruptcy course that covers chapter 11. We have provided a number of questions associated with the facts in Answer (C) (i.e., the Section 1111(b) election) in this chapter and in chapter 20.

Answer (A) is incorrect because it only takes one nonassenting class to invoke cramdown. Secured creditors are typically placed in separate classes as is the case in this question. In other words, if the debtor in possession requests nonconsensual confirmation and the basic Section 1129(a) requirements are met, then the debtor in possession has to prove, as to the objecting secured creditor, that the plan is both fair and equitable and not unfairly discriminatory. The debtor in possession cannot do an end run around the secured creditor by attempting to have other secured creditor classes veto the preference of the dissenting secured creditor.

302. The debtor in possession will need to make deferred cash payments, under the chapter 11 plan, with a discounted present value of at least $1,500,000 ("deferred cash payments . . . of at least the value of such holder's interest in the estate's interest in such property") and a face amount of plan payments that totals at least $2,000,000 ("deferred cash payments totaling at least the allowed amount of such claim."). *See* Section 1129(b)(2)(A)(i). Remember that when an eligible secured creditor makes the Section 1111(b) election, its secured claim becomes a secured claim for the full amount of the debt (If you are unclear on this, go back to subtopic D in Chapter 20). Thus, when applying Section 1129(b)(2)(A)(i) in the case of a secured creditor who has made that election, you have to go back to that section to determine whether the treatment is fair and equitable. If you do that carefully, you will see that the debtor in possession must provide payment to this secured creditor under the terms outlined above.

Of course, to determine all of this with specificity it would still be necessary to determine the applicable interest rate for the deferred payments. Your bankruptcy course should cover this question in detail if your course covers chapter 11.

303. **The correct answer is (E).** Under Section 1141(a), a plan is binding upon a very broad list of entities once the plan is confirmed. This would include all of the entities listed above, including interest holders, prepetition creditors who were not scheduled or who did not file a claim, and priority creditors impaired under the plan. It also binds these parties whether or not they have accepted the plan. With a few exceptions, a confirmed chapter 11 plan also operates as a discharge pursuant to Section 1141(d).

304.   No. Pursuant to Section 1141(d)(3), a chapter 11 corporate debtor is eligible for a discharge unless its plan is a liquidating plan and the debtor terminates its business after consummating its plan.

305.   **The correct answer is (B).** Under Section 1127(b), only the plan proponent or the reorganized debtor can modify the plan once it has been confirmed. After confirmation, a proposal to modify a plan must be submitted before the plan has been "substantially consummated" under Section 1101(2). So, there is an opportunity for plan modification in this question if it is determined that circumstances warrant such modification. But, your creditor client has no legal grounds on which to formally request modification before a bankruptcy court. **All of the other answers are incorrect.**

As a result of the 2005 Act, the rule in individual chapter 11 cases is different in certain respects. Under Section 1127(e), modification is allowed after a plan has been substantially consummated. Additionally, parties other than the debtor can request modification, including the trustee, the U.S. Trustee, or the holder of an allowed unsecured claim.

306. Yes. Section 525(a) bars discrimination against persons who have been debtors under the Code, the nonpayment of a debt by such persons that is discharged or dischargeable, or insolvency by such persons whether before or during the case if the discrimination is based solely on one or more of the above factors. It is a broad statute and it is designed to make sure that debtors can get a genuine fresh start, unburdened by the unfair and/or irrational assumptions and prejudices.

However, the reach of Section 525 is not limitless. It does not prohibit discrimination based upon nonpayment of a debt that is not dischargeable. That is what the state is doing here. Also, it does not prevent a governmental unit from asking about prior bankruptcy filings if all applicants are asked about it, if there is a reason why the government needs to know, and if the decision to a deny a license is not made solely on one of the factors listed in Section 525(a).

307. **The correct answer is (C).** Section 525 applies in all bankruptcy chapters. So, it would not matter whether Bob filed chapter 7, 11, or 13. *See* Section 103(a).

Answer (A) is a policy argument that has no support in the Code or in decisional law. Perhaps there should be different postbankruptcy treatment of chapter 13 debtors as compared to chapter 7 debtors (i.e., more protection against discrimination). However, Congress has not indicated its agreement with this notion by amending Section 525.

Answer (B) is incorrect because it is an incorrect statement of the law. Debts for spousal support are not dischargeable in chapter 13 cases.

Answer (D) is a policy argument that has appeal, but it is not the policy judgment that Congress embraced in enacting Section 525. Congress indicated that some amount of discrimination can continue as long as it is uniformly applied and based upon legitimate and reasonable factors.

308. No. Section 525(c) prohibits discrimination in the treatment of applicants for student loans or grants. Prior to the enactment of Section 525(c), student loan administrators had argued that since student loans did not look like "permits" or "licenses," student loan programs were free to discriminate against an applicant solely on the basis of a bankruptcy filing. Congress responded to that argument and similar ones by enacting Section 525(c). Like governmental entities or private employers, the student loan program can consider factors such as future financial responsibility, but it cannot discriminate solely on the basis of the factors prohibited in the statute.

309. Without the lien avoidance, Mary would not be able to use her homestead exemption because upon liquidation of the home by the bankruptcy trustee, the mortgage holder would receive $200,000 and the judgment lien holder would receive $200,000. Mary would receive nothing from such a distribution. With lien avoidance, the distribution goes like this: $200,000 for the

mortgage holder, $100,000 for Mary (the amount of her exemption), and $100,000 for the judicial lien holder. Pursuant to Section 522(f), Mary is able to avoid the judicial lien to the extent that it impairs her exemption, to the extent of $100,000.

A relatively easy way to understand the concept of impairment in Section 522(f) problems is to use the following formula: Take the amount of the exemption, the amount of the judicial lien, and the amount of all other liens on the property and add them together. Here, that amount would be $500,000 ($100,000 + $200,000 + $200,000 = $500,000). Then, subtract from that amount the value of the house. Here, the result of that calculation would be $100,000 ($500,000-$400,000 = $100,000). Thus, the lien impairs the exemption to that extent. You will need to study Section 522(f) carefully to pick up all of its requirements. Also, remember that the part of the judgment lien holder's claim that was avoided does not disappear. It becomes a general unsecured claim to that extent that it was avoided.

310.   No. As a part of the 2005 Act, Congress eliminated the use of Section 522(f)(1) to avoid judicial liens that secure nondischargeable "domestic support obligations." This amplifies the result reached by the United States Supreme Court in 1991 when it decided *Farrey v. Sanderfoot*, 500 U.S. 291 (1991) and other related decisions reached by lower courts. In that case, the Supreme Court held that a debtor whose interest in property was created simultaneously with the creation of a lien, could not use Section 522(f) because the lien had not "fixed" to the property. In light of *Farrey*, many courts hold that if a lien is created simultaneously with the creation of an interest in property, it is not avoidable under Section 522(f) whether it is a judicial lien securing a domestic support obligation or whether it is a judicial lien securing some other kind of obligation.

311.   Go back to the formula we used earlier in applying Section 522(f). First, $15,000 + $28,000 + $50,000 = $93,000. Then, $93,000-$65,000 = $28,000. The judicial lien now impairs the exemption by an amount equal to the amount of the lien ($28,000) and thus the entire judicial lien can be avoided. After the avoidance of the lien, the debtor will have equity in the property that equals the amount of the exemption ($65,000-$50,000 for the mortgage = $15,000).

312.   **The correct answer is (C).** Section 522(f)(1)(B) allows debtors to avoid nonpossessory, nonpurchase-money security interests to the extent such interests impair the debtor's exemption in certain items. The credit union's loan is a purchase-money security interest because the credit union gave Olivia the credit that in fact enabled her to purchase the optical equipment. **All of the other answers are incorrect.**

Section 522(f)(1)(B) deserves careful study by those who work regularly with consumer debtors, but many of its policy goals have been eclipsed by other federal rules and regulations that govern the provision of certain kinds of consumer credit by certain types of lenders.

313.   **The correct answer is (D).** The request for revocation, assuming it is actually filed within the next 60 days, would be timely. Section 1144 allows a party in interest to request revocation at any time before 180 days after the date of the entry of the order of confirmation. After notice and a hearing, the court may revoke confirmation, but only on the grounds that the confirmation was "procured by fraud." *See* Section 1144. Because of strong reliance interests and the need for finality, there are no other permissible grounds. **This**

makes (D) the correct answer. All of the other answers are incorrect.

If the facts were different and the secured creditor could prevail on such a request, the revocation would revoke the discharge of the debtor pursuant to Section 1144(2). This could obviously be a extreme consequence, especially for an individual chapter 11 debtor when it comes to debts that would otherwise be dischargeable.

314.   **The correct answer is (C).** Jergen filed a standard breach of contract action. Such actions generally must be heard by a state court of general jurisdiction, or if by a federal court, by a court staffed with judges with Article III status; that is, judges with life tenure and a guarantee that their compensation will not be reduced during their term of office. As bankruptcy judges do not have life tenure, their terms being only 14 years, and their compensation not being protected while in office, they do not qualify. That is the holding of the plurality opinion in *Northern Pipeline Constr. Co. v. Marathon Pipeline Co.*, 458 U.S. 50 (1982).

One way to look at this is that Congress has the power to create such inferior courts as it wishes, and to staff them with judges with Article III status. Such judges are then members of the judicial branch and able to exercise the full judicial power of the United States found in Art. VI of the Constitution. Congress can also create adjudicatory tribunals with judges that do not have such powers, but then such courts are legislative courts under Article I of the Constitution, and assigning them powers that can only be exercised by the judicial branch violates, among other things, separation of powers. As this analysis demonstrates that the bankruptcy court cannot hear and determine this matter without more, **Answer (D) is incorrect.**

Answer (B) is incorrect, because federal courts have separate jurisdiction to hear and determine matters that are "related to" a bankruptcy case, pursuant to 28 U.S.C. Section 1334(b). "Related to" jurisdiction is very broad. Most courts have adopted the so-called "*Pacor* test." Under this test, the test is whether "the outcome of the proceeding could conceivably have any effect on the estate being administered in bankruptcy." *Pacor, Inc. v. Higgins*, 743 F.2d 984, 994 (3d Cir. 1984). The Supreme Court has held that *Pacor* correctly balances the issues. *Celotex Corp. v. Edwards*, 514 U.S. 300 (1995). As the amount owed by Xeres could possibly affect the distributions in Jergen's case, it is "related to" that case.

On the same logic, **Answer (A) is incorrect**, as federal bankruptcy jurisdiction under 28 U.S.C. Section 1334(b) is separate and independent from diversity jurisdiction under 28 U.S.C. Section 1331. Either statute will sustain federal court jurisdiction, and so the absence of diversity here is irrelevant.

315.   **The correct answer is (A).** This question requires analysis of the jurisdiction and of the venue provisions of title 28. Start first with the jurisdiction provisions. Although this matter is likely only in federal court because of the "related to" jurisdictional hook of Section 1334(b) of title 28, there still remains a question as to whether the matter will be heard in federal district court or in federal bankruptcy court. Although not a "core" matter under Section 157(b) of title 28, that does not end the matter. Section 157(c) allows a bankruptcy court to hear a matter (take evidence, hear testimony, and the like) so long as it submits proposed findings of facts and conclusions of law to the district court, who then hears the matter de novo. But — and this is a large "but" — Section 157(c)(2) allows the bankruptcy

judge to hear *and determine* the matter with the consent of the parties. That means that if consent is present, the bankruptcy court will not only hear the matter, but will have the power to enter a final judgment that the district court can review only on appeal (which means, for example, that instead of having a de novo review of factual findings, the district court will be able to reverse a finding only if it is clearly erroneous, see Bankruptcy Rule 8013).

Consent, in turn, can be given implicitly, or by the failure to object. Bankruptcy Rule 7008(a) requires a complaint to state whether the matter is core and whether the pleader consents to jurisdiction, and Rule 7012(b) imposes a similar requirement on defendants in their answer. Failure to follow these rules and silence in the answer is taken as consent. Accordingly, the motion will not be granted for lack of jurisdiction, so **Answer (B) and Answer (D) are incorrect.**

What about venue? While nonbankruptcy venue rules typically look to the location of the defendant, bankruptcy venue rules do not. Section 1409(a) of title 28 states that venue of all proceedings related to a case is properly venued in the district in which the case is pending. The rationale here is that the extra inconvenience to the defendant is outweighed by the cost savings to the estate. There are exceptions, however. Section 1409(b) states that the bankruptcy venue rule does not apply when there is a consumer debt of less than $17,575 and business debts of less than $11,725 (as of April 1, 2010). As a result, Fatma had the opportunity to object to venue (since the debt is owes is only $10,000). But failure to object to venue is like failing to object to jurisdiction. Once the opportunity to raise it has passed, it may not be raised anew after proceedings have progressed beyond the initial complaint and answer stage. As a result, **Answer (C) and Answer (D) are incorrect.**

That leaves **Answer (A) as the correct answer.**

316.   **The correct answer is (C).** Two of the answers, **(A)** and **(D)** rely on the absence of jurisdiction in the federal bankruptcy court for their truth. But federal bankruptcy courts do have jurisdiction over all bankruptcy claims resolution. The path to that jurisdiction is somewhat complicated. Initially, to cure the problems the Supreme Court found in *Northern Pipeline Constr. Co. v. Marathon Pipeline Co.*, 458 U.S. 50 (1982), Congress rewrote the jurisdictional statute in 1984. The basic grant of jurisdiction for matters to be heard in federal court is found in 28 U.S.C. Section 1334(b). That statute states that "the district courts shall have original but not exclusive jurisdiction of all civil proceedings arising under title 11, or arising in or related to cases under title 11." Here, the action against Jergen clearly is at least related to Jergen's case, and so there is jurisdiction in federal court. The question that remains is whether it is in federal district court or in federal bankruptcy court.

Section 157(a) provides that "[e]ach district court may provide that any or all cases under title 11 and any or all proceedings arising under title 11 or arising in or related to a case under title 11 shall be referred to the bankruptcy judges for the district." Every district court has entered such an order. So the matter will, in the parlance of bankruptcy, be automatically referred to the bankruptcy court.

Can the bankruptcy court hear and determine the matter? The words "hear and determine" imply that the court can not only hear the matter, but also enter a final order that is reviewable by the district court only by appeal. Section 157(b) of title 28 contains the sorting mechanism for those matters which are "core" to the bankruptcy court's jurisdiction as granted by Congress, and thus may be determined by the bankruptcy court. Subparagraph

(B) of Section 157(b)(2) states that core matters include the "allowance or disallowance of claims against the estate," which is exactly the type of dispute Fatma has initiated. As the bankruptcy court would thus have jurisdiction over the matter, **Answers (A) and (D) are incorrect.**

As between Answers (B) and (C), one first has to determine whether Jergen could remove the action to federal court. The answer is yes. Bankruptcy has its own removal statute, 28 U.S.C. Section 1452, under which either a debtor or a litigant can, within certain time limits, remove an action or any claim for relief to the federal district court (to be immediately referred to the bankruptcy court under 28 U.S.C. Section 157(a)). All that is required is that the action or claim be such that the federal court would have jurisdiction under 28 U.S.C. Section 1334 quoted above.

So Jergen can remove the action. Will it? Probably not. The bankruptcy claims resolution process is much simpler than regular debt collection litigation, and simplicity generally translates into inexpensiveness as well. Thus, Jergen will likely successfully interpose the objection that the commencement of the action on the prepetition claim is stayed, and force Fatma to file a proof of claim and submit to the claims resolution process found in Section 501-503 of the Code. This makes **Answer (B) incorrect,** and makes **Answer (C) correct** since it is the far more likely outcome.

317.   **The correct answer is (D).** The history of jury trials in bankruptcy is a tortured one, but the answer to this question is fairly simple. The Supreme Court has held that the filing of a proof of claim, as Fatma has done, constitutes consent to the bankruptcy court's jurisdiction, *Granfinanciera, S.A. v. Nordberg*, 492 U.S. 33 (1989), and a waiver of jury trial rights, *Langenkamp v. Culp*, 498 U.S. 42 (1990). As a result, **Answer (D) is correct.**

Given this waiver analysis, **Answers (A) and (B) are incorrect.** Regardless of whatever jury trial rights Fatma had, it waived them by filing its proof of claim.

Bankruptcy courts do have the right to hold a jury trial, if consent is given by the district court in which the bankruptcy court sits and if all parties expressly agree, 28 U.S.C. Section 157(e). But in practice this is quite rare. Since this statute requires the consent of all parties, Jergen's consent would be necessary to hold a jury trial, and its opposition means that the bankruptcy court will hear the objection without a jury. As a result, **Answer (C) is incorrect.**

What if Fatma does not file a proof of claim? Well, it would preserve its jury trial rights, but at a cost of rendering them virtually worthless. All property of the debtor becomes property of the estate, Section 541(a), and the federal district court (and federal bankruptcy court by automatic reference) has exclusive jurisdiction of such property. 28 U.S.C. Section 1334(e)(1). By not filing the proof of claim, Fatma would not be able to share in any distributions from Jergen's estate, and if a discharge is granted to Jergen under Section 1141, Fatma will never be able to sue Jergen on the debt. So Fatma's choice is to waive a jury trial and share with other creditors, or elect to receive nothing. Most creditors choose the former.

318.   **The correct answer is (A).** The initial question should be whether the removal was appropriate. The bankruptcy removal section, 28 U.S.C. Section 1452(a), states that "[a] party may remove any claim or cause of action in a civil action. . . . to the district court for the district where such civil action is pending, if such district court has jurisdiction of such

claim or cause of action under section 1334 of this title." Here, the removal meets these requirements. The courts are in the same district. The district court (which would immediately and automatically refer the matter to the bankruptcy court) has at least "related to" jurisdiction since the liquidation of the amount Randy owes may affect his bankruptcy case.

Remand, in turn, is governed by Section 1452(b), which states that "[t]he court to which such claim or cause of action is removed may remand such claim or cause of action on any equitable ground." Here, the offer to merely liquidate the claim without any collection activity would persuade most courts to remand. Randy is involved in complex litigation in which one of his claims will be liquidated and the amount fixed. There is no indication that the bankruptcy court is in any better position to do this; indeed, the state court may be in a better position, and may have clearer jurisdiction over other claims that don't directly involve Randy. As a result, most courts would remand the action. This reasoning indicates that **Answer (B) is incorrect**, and that **Answer (C) is incorrect**, as both indicate that the remand motion would be denied.

The next step is to analyze abstention. Abstention is governed by 28 U.S.C. Section 1334(c). That section says that:

> (1) Except with respect to a case under chapter 15 of title 11, nothing in this section prevents a district court in the interest of justice, or in the interest of comity with State courts or respect for State law, from abstaining from hearing a particular proceeding arising under title 11 or arising in or related to a case under title 11.

> (2) Upon timely motion of a party in a proceeding based upon a State law claim or State law cause of action, related to a case under title 11 but not arising under title 11 or arising in a case under title 11, with respect to which an action could not have been commenced in a court of the United States absent jurisdiction under this section, the district court shall abstain from hearing such proceeding if an action is commenced, and can be timely adjudicated, in a State forum of appropriate jurisdiction.

Here, abstention is not applicable. Abstention requires two lawsuits; one in a nonbankruptcy court (usually a state court, but it could be in a federal district court, or a tax court or something similar), and one in federal bankruptcy court. It provides that, as set forth in paragraph (2), if the federal action is based only on "related to" jurisdiction, then the federal court will abstain and defer to the state court in the resolution of that matter if a state court can timely adjudicate the matter.

Here, of course, there is only one action. It was removed to federal court, and as indicated above, set back to state court. Without two actions, there can be no issues of abstention. As a result, **Answer (D) is incorrect**, in that the federal court cannot abstain since there is nothing to abstain from. That means that **Answer (A) is correct**.

319. **The correct answer is (D).** Bob is being hired by the estate representative. As such, his employment is governed by the Bankruptcy Code. Specifically, Section 327(a) requires that he not hold an interest adverse to the estate and that he be a disinterested person. A "disinterested person" is a defined term in Section 101(14). Among other things, it requires that Bob not be a creditor. Is Bob a creditor? Under nonbankruptcy law, he is not. But his payment on the eve of bankruptcy means that he is the recipient of a preference. As such, he is a contingent creditor, and potentially disqualified, at least as was held in one case. *In re*

Pillowtex, Inc., 304 F.3d 246 (3d Cir. 2002). Indeed, under Pillowtex, it is insufficient to indicate a willingness or commitment to return the fee if a preference is found; the fee has to be disgorged and the debt waived.

Unless Bob returns the money and waives the fee, he will be a creditor and thus not a disinterested person able to represent the debtor.

Answer (A) is thus incorrect because the Bankruptcy Code embodies the principal that experience with the debtor takes second place to creditor status; no matter how much knowledge Bob has, he cannot overcome the status of being a creditor. The same logic **precludes Answer (C) from being correct**; Mellow's preferences are not relevant.

Can Bob waive his fee and no longer be a creditor? The answer is yes. Since the disability is linked only to status as a creditor, waiving that status by disgorging the fee and forgiving the debt restores Bob to being a distinterested person, and able to represent the estate. As a consequence, **Answer (D) is correct**, and the unequivocal **Answer (B) is not correct**.

320.   **The correct answer is (D).** Professional fees in bankruptcy are governed by Section 330. This section requires professionals to be formally employed by the estate and that their employment be approved by the court in order to get paid.

In this case, Section 330 does not provide for the employment of counsel by the debtor (as opposed to the debtor in possession) in a chapter 11 case. This has been confirmed by the United States Supreme Court. *See Lamie v. U.S. Trustee*, 540 U.S. 526 (2004). As a result, Lucy will not receive her fees under Section 330 as that section does not authorize payment from the estate for work done for the debtor. **Answer (A) is incorrect.**

Professional fees are administrative expenses, and thus are not paid pro rata with other claims (unless the estate is administratively insolvent). There is no provision in the Bankruptcy Code for postpetition creditors whose claims are not otherwise provided for to seek to be paid with prepetition creditors. **Answer (C) is thus incorrect.**

The choice thus comes down to whether Lucy can get paid for a "substantial contribution." Compensation for substantial contributions is allowed in chapter 11 cases, pursuant to Section 503(b)(3)(D). Most, but not all cases, however, do not allow substantial contribution compensation to professionals whose fees would not be allowed under other sections. Thus, most courts would deny the allowance on the basis that Section 330 doesn't allow the fees, and Section 503(b)(3)(D) cannot be used as a "back door" to get what Section 330 denies. Accordingly, **Answer (B) is incorrect**, and **Answer (D) is correct**.

321.   **The correct answer is (C).** In circuits which have adopted a Bankruptcy Appellate Panel, the normal course of appeal is to the Bankruptcy Appellate Panel. 28 U.S.C. Section 158(a). The only other option is the District Court, making **Answer (B) incorrect**. Appellants who wish to have the District Court hear the appeal instead must affirmatively elect to opt out of the Bankruptcy Appellate Panel. 28 U.S.C. Section 158(c). That election must be done in a separate writing filed concurrently with the filing of the notice of appeal, pursuant to Bankruptcy Rule 8001(e). Appellees have 30 days to make a similar election.

Here, Heavenly did not file any election. As a consequence, **Answer (D) is incorrect.**

The question is then whether the order being appealed from is interlocutory, and if so, whether that would cause the District Court not to hear the matter. While the order is interlocutory, because the court could go back and approve a different plan, *see, e.g., Lievsay v. Western Fin. Sav. Bank*, 118 F.3d 661 (9th Cir. 1997), *cert. denied*, 522 U.S. 1149 (1998); *Flor v. BOT Fin. Corp.* 79 F.3d 281 (2d Cir. 1996), that is not the reason the District Court would not hear the appeal. So **Answer (A) is incorrect.** By process of elimination, and because no election was made, **Answer (C) is the correct answer.**

322.   **The correct answer is (C).** The 2005 Act for the first time made provision for direct appeals to the courts of appeal. 28 U.S.C. Section 158(d). This process involves certification to the court of appeals that the issues presented are sufficiently important to warrant a direct appeal. These include a controlling issue of law for which there is no prior precedent; a issue for which there is conflicting precedent; and whether granting the appeal will materially advance the progress of the case. 28 U.S.C. Section 158(d)(2)(A). With this possibility in place, **Answer (D) is incorrect.**

Section 158(d) also requires a combination of parties and courts to permit certification. Because of this, **Answer (A) is incorrect.**

As between Answer (B) and Answer (C), the issue becomes whether the court of appeals needs to be involved in the process. The statute is clear that the court of appeals has to accept the appeal before the direct appeal can be made, thus making **Answer (C) correct.** Because it is incomplete, and because Answer (C) is better, **Answer (B) is incorrect.**

323.   **The correct answer is (D).** The commencement of a chapter 15 proceeding enables a United States court to aid and assist a foreign insolvency proceeding. In proceeds in two stages: the commencement of the case, and the recognition of the person commencing the chapter 15 case. Commencement is simply the filing of a petition seeking recognition. *See* Section 1501(a). It is filed by someone who claims to be the "foreign representative" of a "foreign proceeding." Both these terms are defined in the Code. A foreign proceeding is a collective judicial or administrative proceeding relating to the insolvency or adjustment of debts of a debtor, whose assets and affairs are subject to control or supervision by a foreign court. *See* Section 101(23). A foreign representative is a person or body appointed in the foreign proceeding as the representative of that proceeding, pursuant to Section 101(24).

Here, the facts establish that Teresa is the foreign representative. The question in chapter 15 cases is whether the foreign proceeding is a foreign main proceeding or a foreign nonmain proceeding. A "foreign main proceeding" is one pending in the county in which the debtor has the "center of its main interests," pursuant to Section 1502(4). In the absence of contrary evidence, a debtor's center of main interests is presumed to be the debtor's "registered office" (usually taken to be its state of incorporation if a corporation) or if the debtor is an individual, the debtor's place of "habitual residence."

Here, Juan is a resident of Mexico, and all other facts indicated that the chapter 15 would be a foreign main proceeding.

The facts also state that Teresa has been recognized by the Arizona bankruptcy court. Section 1520(a)(1) states that upon recognition, "sections 361 and 362 apply with respect to the debtor and the property of the debtor that is within the territorial jurisdiction of the United States." Thus, the recognition of Teresa as a foreign representative essentially gave Juan the same protections as if he had filed a regular case and received the benefit of Section 362. As a result, **Answer (D) is correct.**

Answer (A), Answer (B) and Answer (C) are incorrect. Answer (A) ignores the fact that chapter 15 can override and impose a stay on domestic proceedings. Answer (B) assumes that notice is necessary of the chapter 15 case, and the incorporation of the automatic stay of Section 362 belies this point. Finally, Answer (C) seems to indicate that Frank's specific property has to be brought to the court's attention; while this may be the case for foreign nonmain proceedings, it is not the case here.

324. **The correct answer is (C).** The change in facts here indicate that the Arizona chapter 15 filing is now a nonmain proceeding. The Spanish proceeding is the main proceeding since that is where Juan lives and does most of his business. Under Section 1502(5), a "foreign nonmain proceeding" means a foreign proceeding, like the Mexican ancillary proceedings in the problem, pending in a county in which the debtor has an "establishment." An "establishment," in turn, is a "place of operations where the debtor carries out a nontransitory economic activity." *See* Section 1502(2). Juan's conducting business in Mexico qualifies.

The effects of recognizing a foreign nonmain proceeding are quite different than those of recognizing a foreign main proceeding. Relief requested is discretionary, rather than mandatory, pursuant to Section 1521. A stay of Frank's action is still possible, but Teresa will have to specifically request it. *See* Section 1521(a)(2). This makes **Answer (C) the correct answer.**

Answer (A), Answer (B) and Answer (D) are incorrect. Answer (A) is incorrect because chapter 15 can and does affect nonbankruptcy actions in the United States. **Answer (B) is incorrect** because notification of the recognition is not a prerequisite for a stay, nor does it independently invoke or initiate a stay. **Answer (D) is incorrect** because stay relief is not automatic in a foreign nonmain proceeding.

PRACTICE FINAL EXAM: ANSWERS

Authors' Note: These answers contain references to Code sections and general principles of bankruptcy law and policy. On your essay answers for your bankruptcy exam, you will probably be expected to supplement your answers with citations to specific cases that are covered by your professor and/or by the casebook used in your particular course. Moreover, there may be issues raised by these questions that your professor expects you to discuss, based on his or her particular coverage of the topics.

1. The issue raised by this fact pattern is whether the "use clause" in the lease is enforceable by the lessor when the lessee goes into bankruptcy. The general rule is that if there are no defaults under the lease and the lease is unexpired, Section 365 gives the trustee the power to assume and assign the lease. The facts indicate that there has been no default. Thus, the trustee has the basic authority to assume and assign the lease to the other tenant. The trustee will cite Section 365(a) and the policy goal of maximizing the value of the estate for creditors. In furtherance of the plain meaning of Section 365(a) and this policy goal, the trustee will argue that the debtor should be able to capture lease profits on the assignment. Additionally, the trustee will cite Section 365(e) and (f) which strike down anti-assignment clauses and ipso facto clauses in furtherance of the general policy goal cited above.

    The landlord, on the other hand, will contend that the use clause is enforceable for two reasons. First, it is not an anti-assignment clause, nor is it an ipso facto clause, so it is not covered by Sections 365(e) and (f). The landlord will also argue that the trustee's proposal is in specific violation of the use clause and that the purpose of the use clause is to protect the landlord's legitimate ownership interest in the property and its expectations with regard to the performance of a specific lease covenant. A change from an upscale women's clothing store to a sporting goods store for extreme sports enthusiasts could significantly affect the landlord's ownership interest and its interest in the performance of the lease covenants. Among other facts, it would be useful to know whether and to what extent the landlord has strictly enforced such clauses in its dealings with other tenants, the overall current tenant mix in the commercial building, any significant alterations in the nature of the tenant's occupancy, as well as the financial suitability of the proposed assignee. It is difficult to predict how this case would be resolved because much will depend on how a court weighs the relevant policy concerns as applied to the particular facts.

2. The issue raised by this fact pattern is whether the payments would be considered property of the estate under Section 541(a). The more precise issue is the extent to which expectancy interests can be considered property of the estate. The debtor will contend that she did not have an interest in the funds on the date of bankruptcy because the Crop Appropriations Act had not yet passed Congress. She will contend that her entitlement to receive the payments did not technically arise until after the filing. Her right to the payment was conditional on the date of bankruptcy (i.e., conditional on legislative action) and thus not sufficiently vested.

    The trustee will argue that Mary did have an interest in the funds because the losses occurred before bankruptcy (in 2004). The trustee will thus contend that her entitlement to the funds can be traced to prepetition events. The trustee will assert that her entitlement was sufficiently mature and certain at the date of bankruptcy. She had already suffered the losses and Congress was only ten days away from passing the law. As of the date of bankruptcy, there was nothing else that Mary had to do or any other services or acts that she had to perform subsequent to the petition to be entitled to receive the money. The trustee will also cite the broad language of Section 541 and the generally accepted notion that Congress intended Section 541 to be construed broadly so as to sweep into the bankruptcy estate all interests of value to the estate. The outcome of this case will depend on whether a court believes that Mary's interest in the funds was sufficiently mature and certain on the date of filing to be included in the estate.

3.   The issue is whether the injunction lawsuit would be stayed by the automatic stay in Section 362(a). Section 362(a) automatically stays certain actions against the debtor. However, it only applies to actions arising out of prepetition claims. This claim, it could be argued, arose after the petition because that is when the nuisance began. Moreover, it could be argued that the nuisance lawsuit is not technically an action against property of the estate. It is not like a foreclosure action. It is intended to restrain the debtor from continuing the objectionable activity. This argument is bolstered by the fact that Janie is not in default under the lease. This makes the action look less like an attempt to collect and more like an action designed to enjoin the activity, not collect payment. It is likely that the action would not be stayed under Section 362(a). However, it is possible that the action could be stayed pursuant to Section 105(a).

Note: This question also raises the issues of whether the debtor's use of the premises violates the use clause and whether the use clause is enforceable in bankruptcy. Those issues were discussed in question 1 and the analysis for question 3 would proceed along similar lines.

4.   Section 365(i) and Section 365(j) apply to this fact pattern. Section 365(i) applies when a seller rejects a land sale contract. Under this section, if Michael is in possession when the developer rejects, then Michael may elect to treat the contract as terminated. He can then file a claim against the estate or he can remain in possession and offset his damages against any amounts remaining due to the developer. If Michael is in possession and intends to remain in possession, the trustee must deliver title in accordance with the provisions of the contract. The trustee, however, is relieved from all other obligations to perform under the contract.

The issue then is whether Michael is in possession or not. The Code does not define "possession." No facts indicate Michael is in physical possession. An argument in favor of possession is that he has made two annual payments. With two payments, it could be argued that Michael has a sufficient expectation of ownership that translates into constructive possession at least. On the other hand, it could be argued that the mere existence of contractual rights is not sufficient to constitute possession. He has not, for example, begun to make any improvements on the land in anticipation of building his vacation home (i.e., clearing the area in preparation for building, erecting signs, building fences, etc.).

If Michael is in possession, he can retain the lot and keep making the payments pursuant to the conditions mentioned in paragraph 1. If Michael is not in possession and the contract is rejected, he gets a lien in the amount of the purchase price paid pursuant to Section 365(j).

5.   The order of payment, with supporting Code section, is as follows:

  1. Claim 2, The Mortgage, pursuant to Section 725.

  2. Claim 1, Postpetition lease payments, Claim 3, Postpetition tax claims and insurance claims, Claim 6, Trustee's legal counsel, all pursuant to Section 507(a)(2) and Section 503(b).

  3. Claim 4, Wage claim, pursuant to Section 507(a)(3). The amount of the priority for each instructor is capped at $11, 725 (as of April 1, 2010). Thus, the full amount ($8,000) for each instructor is subject to the priority.

  4. Claims 5 Websolution's claim, pursuant to Section 726(a)(2), Claim 7 Breach of Contract Claim, pursuant to Section 502(g).

Claim 8 is not a claim against the debtor. It is a claim against the director. Since it is not a claim against the debtor, it is not included in the distribution.

6.   The issue is whether the trustee could use Sections 548 and 550 to avoid the transfer of Whiteacre to the buyer. There is little or no evidence to support a case of actual fraud under Section 548(a)(1)(A) because no one involved in the transaction appears to have acted with actual intent to delay or defraud creditors and the debtor used the proceeds of the sale to pay his creditors. The issue, therefore, is whether the trustee could use the constructive fraud provisions of Section 548(a)(1)(B)(i). Constructive fraud would require the trustee to prove that the debtor received "less than a reasonably equivalent value in exchange for" the transfer, that the transfer took place within 2 years before the petition was filed, and that the debtor was insolvent at the time, or became insolvent as a result. The trustee will contend that the Whiteacre was transferred for less than a reasonably equivalent value because the buyer paid significantly less for the property than it was worth ($580,000 was paid for property worth between $620,000 and $640,000). The trustee will have an easy time meeting the timing requirement. The trustee will probably be able to prove insolvency because the facts strongly suggest it, but we would need more facts to determine that for certain. The buyer will try to counter the reasonably equivalent value point by putting forth evidence that the price paid by the buyer was a fair amount of consideration given the restricted market of buyers ("no one was able to raise the cash in ten days"). The trustee will counter that this is the type of situation that Section 548 is designed to cover. That is, a distressed and desperate debtor who transfers property in haste to the possible detriment of creditors as a group.

If the trustee is able to prove that the transfer was constructively fraudulent under the Code, then the trustee could recover the value of the property from the buyer. However, under Section 548(c), the buyer would have a lien on the property to the extent that he took for value and in good faith. He took for value. Whether he took in good faith is open to debate. Buyer #2 is probably protected by Section 550(b)(1) because he is a subsequent transferee who took for value, in good faith, and without knowledge.

7.   The February 7 transfer is a voidable preference under Section 547(b) because it meets all of the elements in Section 547(b)(1)-(b)(5) (i.e., a transfer of an interest of the debtor in property, to a creditor, for or an account of an antecedent debt, probably made while debtor is insolvent, made within the regular preference period of 90 days, with a preferential effect).

However, the transfer might escape through one of the exceptions. Section 547(c)(2) will not apply because the transfer does not appear to have been made in the ordinary course of business (payment followed the e-mail message) or according to ordinary business terms (larger payment than usual). Section 547(c)(4) might apply because of the subsequent advance of $150,000 in the form of unsecured credit on March 8. If this exception applies, then the trustee's recovery would be limited to $10,000.

8.   Section 507(b) applies, under certain specified circumstances, when adequate protection to a secured creditor proves to be inadequate. It grants an administrative expense priority to the secured creditor for those losses. Section 507(b) would apply under the facts presented here (i.e., creditor sought to have the automatic stay terminated, the cost incurred by the creditor was an actual and necessary expense of preserving the estate, and the anticipated decline in the value of the equipment was due to the trustee's continued use of that equipment). The creditor should submit a $320,000 administrative expense claim ($400,000-$80,000 = $320,000). This represents the decrease in the value of the equipment that is attributable to the trustee's use of the equipment minus the amount of adequate protection payments made by the trustee. The creditor will need to be advised that its claim will be paid after certain other claims, including postpetition credit claims under Section 363(c)(1) and administrative expense claims of appointed trustees who step in to wind up a chapter 7 case under Section 726(b).

9.   John should prevail on his motion for summary judgment. He was discharged from all debts that arose before bankruptcy pursuant to Section 524. Since the debt to GreenTree was scheduled, it would not discharged. GreenTree cannot assert nondischargeability under Section 523(a)(2)(B) because, pursuant to Section 523(c), that provision can only be asserted in bankruptcy court. GreenTree had a chance to object, but did not do so. Therefore, the debt was discharged. Section 524 operates as an injunction against the bringing of such an action and John's summary judgment motion should thus be granted.

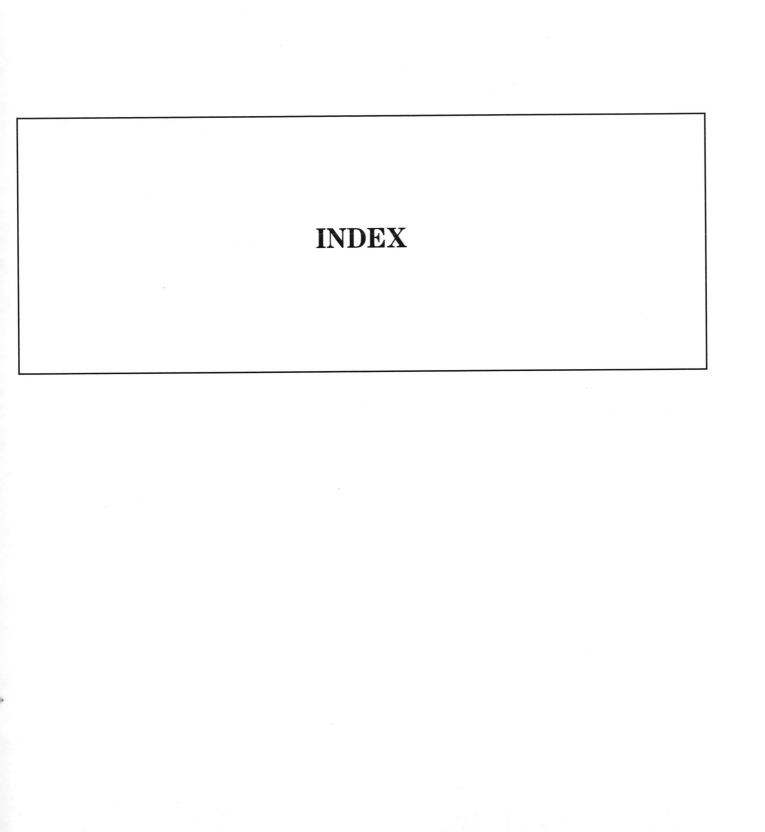

INDEX

INDEX